EFI
Conversions

How to Swap Your Carb for Electronic Fuel Injection

Tony Candela

S-A DESIGN

Car Tech®

CarTech®

CarTech®, Inc.
39966 Grand Avenue
North Branch, MN 55056
Phone: 651-277-1200 or 800-551-4754
Fax: 651-277-1203
www.cartechbooks.com

Edit by Paul Johnson
Layout by Monica Seiberlich

ISBN 978-1-61325-083-9
Item No. SA261

Library of Congress Cataloging-in-Publication Data

Candela, Tony.
  EFI conversions / by Tony Candela.
     pages cm
  ISBN 978-1-61325-083-9
1. Motor vehicles–Motors–Electronic fuel injection systems. 2. Motor vehicles–Motors–Maintenance and repair. I. Title.

TL214.F78C36 2014
629.25,3–dc23

                              2013043955

Written, edited, and designed in the U.S.A.
Printed in China
10 9 8 7 6 5 4 3 2 1

Title Page: This Chevy 383-ci small block was fitted with a Holley HP-series 750-cfm double-pumper, but now it is fitted with the MSD Atomic system. Keith Kanak, the owner, had been considering an EFI conversion to improve fuel economy so this couldn't have worked out better.

Back Cover Photos

Top Left: This throttle body has been designed by MSD to resemble a carburetor and most casual onlookers will assume that's exactly what it is. This is the heart of the MSD Atomic EFI System, which includes the ECU as well as numerous sensors.

Top Right: If you're on a budget, many aftermarket EFI systems allow you to retain your existing ignition components.

Middle Left: A proper-size alternator is critical to the performance of any EFI System.

Middle Right: We install a complete MPFI system on a 455 Olds and illustrate every aspect of the installation. We maximize its performance and unlock the full potential of the system.

Bottom Left: The fuel system on this 1970 Olds Cutlass has performed flawlessly. As we convert the Olds from carburetion to EFI you learn which components you can retain and which you must upgrade.

Bottom Right: Before undertaking a conversion to EFI, it's imperative to get the electrical system sorted out in your project vehicle. This power panel is simple to build and provides an orderly, sensible, and safe way to add aftermarket electronics to your project vehicle.

PGUK
63 Hatton Garden
London EC1N 8LE, England
Phone: 020 7061 1980 • Fax: 020 7242 3725
www.pguk.co.uk

Renniks Publications Ltd.
3/37-39 Green Street
Banksmeadow, NSW 2109, Australia
Phone: 2 9695 7055 • Fax: 2 9695 7355
www.renniks.com

CONTENTS

ABOUT THE AUTHOR

Tony Candela has been in the automotive aftermarket industry for more than 25 years and has held positions in installation, sales, management, manufacturer sales representation, and regional sales management. In his tenure, he has worked for two aftermarket electronics manufacturers, Clifford Electronics and Rockford Fosgate.

In 2009, he founded a sales and marketing company at which he does technical writing, content development, sales, and marketing for numerous companies in the automotive aftermarket. In April of that same year, Candela's first book, *Automotive Wiring and Electrical Systems*, was published. In August of 2011, his follow-up book, *Automotive Electrical Performance Projects*, was published. Each has won awards with the International Automotive Media Awards (IAMA). In 2011, Candela founded an automotive electrical supply company.

Tony has written and given hundreds of seminars on the topics of installation, application, wiring, and basic automotive electronics. He has been a guest speaker at SEMA on two occasions. On the weekends, he can typically be found in his garage working on his vehicles or at any number of car gatherings in the Phoenix area.

ACKNOWLEDGMENTS

This is my third book. Each has been published by CarTech. I'd like to first thank my publisher for giving me the opportunity to pen the titles. Molly, Bob, and Paul, you exemplify how business should be done, and it's a true pleasure to work with a publisher of such caliber. Second, I thank my parents for instilling the value of hard work in me at such a young age and leading by example their entire lives.

I have a close circle of friends and family who influence me daily. I'd like to personally thank Steve Meade, Anthony D'Amore, Frank Beck, Todd Ramsey, Garry Springgay, Bill Basore, Bill Surin, Rob Hummel, Matt Luster, Jim Candela, and Julie Metzler. Each of you has the uncanny ability to challenge me to be my best. Thank you for that!

This book was made possible by the many companies and talented individuals who went out of their way to help. I'd like to thank Beck Racing Engines, Holley, MSD, Auto Meter, Edelbrock, Fuel Air Spark Technology, Mechman, XS Power, Fluke, Painless Performance Products, Aeromotive, and Mitchell1. I'd also like to thank Doug Flynn, Tom Kise, Blane Burnett, Bill Tichenor, and Todd Ryden for making themselves so readily available to me.

Last but not least, I'd like to thank Peter Bodensteiner for taking the chance with an unknown and giving me the opportunity to write the book *Automotive Wiring and Electrical Systems*. This proved to be the springboard for my future.

Jackie – I miss you, buddy.

Let's face it; the idea of converting from carburetion to electronic fuel injection (EFI) is incredibly exciting. In fact, this is one of the most commonly discussed topics among enthusiasts at local gatherings. If you've picked up a car magazine in the past five years, you've undoubtedly seen numerous articles on this topic, nearly as many as the topic of LS conversions. Most people I speak with have numerous questions that the confined space of a magazine article simply cannot address. This book addresses those questions in their entirety.

Some of you may recognize me as the author who writes books on that taboo topic of wiring and electrical systems. I have two such books in print, *Automotive Wiring and Electrical Systems* and *Automotive Electrical Performance Projects*. From time to time, I may refer to bits and pieces of those books where relevant. If you've read my other books, you've likely noticed my "comfortable informality," as one reviewer put it. This book is no different, so have no fear of it reading like the instruction manual for the Retro Encabulator; view it on YouTube.

In addition to being that guy who likes wiring (weird, right?), I'm what most people consider a super-enthusiast. In Chapter 9 of *Automotive Electrical Performance Projects*, I illustrate a conversion from carburetion to EFI on my personal hot rod, a 1972 Oldsmobile Cutlass Holiday Coupe with a 6-71 blown big-block Chevy (sorry, Olds fans). That conversion turned out to be an incredibly simple one, and I've never looked back to carburetion. As it turns out, that project became the inspiration for this book.

Shortly after *Automotive Electrical Performance Projects* was published, I was at a local gathering with my car buddies. We sat in our lawn chairs and discussed EFI conversions at length, including my Olds. I discovered that there was much to learn and discuss regarding the topic. One thing was for sure, every one of them wanted to know as much as they could because they have all considered this upgrade for their own vehicles. A few months passed and my editor called. He and I had a nearly identical conversation and the rest is history.

A book of this nature deals with a lot of high-tech hardware, which is typically replaced or updated with the latest and greatest as the manufacturer makes improvements or introduces new technologies. The aftermarket has come a *long* way in the past few years and advancements in product offerings seem to be coming at a blistering rate nowadays. However, I'm confident that what you learn here is somewhat universal and it applies, generally speaking, to nearly any conversion of any manufacturer's product.

As you've got this book in hand, I assume that you're considering this conversion for your own vehicle. Nothing would make me happier than to know that you undertook it after reading this book. And you know what? It *is* really easy!

Fig. I.1. At the time of this writing, the Holley Terminator EFI system is one of the newest offerings on the market. The 950-cfm throttle body bolts in place of any 4150-style carburetor and its air-entry area is the same design used in the NASCAR Sprint Cup Series. The kit includes the throttle body, ECU, wiring harness, and handheld controller. (Photo Courtesy Holley Performance Products)

THE ELECTRONIC FUEL INJECTION SYSTEM

Let's get the simple stuff out of the way right up front. The job of either a carburetor or fuel injection, whether it's mechanical or electrical, is actually simple, and that's to meter the correct amount of fuel based on the amount of air flowing into the engine. (I address volume versus mass shortly.) I know of many cases in which a correctly tuned carbureted combination made slightly more maximum power than an injected one or vice versa. Obviously maximum power is the goal when racing, and in some applications and combinations, some tuners may choose carburetors over EFI. If you drive your vehicle on the street, EFI offers better overall performance and drivability than carburetors.

Most of us own a modern vehicle with EFI. If you don't own one, you've surely driven one. Forget about horsepower for a second and consider the following attributes of such a vehicle:

- It starts instantly, no matter the temperature.
- After it's started, it keeps running.
- It idles smoothly before and after reaching operating temperature.
- It has immediate throttle response with no bogs at the hit of the throttle.
- It maximizes fuel economy.
- It requires zero input from the operator.

Come on, let's be honest: how many of these attributes does your hot rod or classic currently share? With EFI, you can enjoy them all.

Air Quality

Before talking about EFI specifics, it's important to recognize the role of air quality. As the weather changes, so does the air quality. Here are some factors to consider:

- When barometric pressure increases, the air contracts and its mass increases.
- When barometric pressure decreases, the air expands and its mass decreases.

Fig. 1.1. This 1,000-cfm throttle body from Holley (PN 112-577) has a 4150-style flange and mounts in place of any 4150-style carburetor. Its CNC billet design maximizes airflow and minimizes air turbulence. A throttle body, such as this one, is an integral part of any multipoint fuel injection (MPFI) system. (Photo Courtesy Holley Performance Products)

- When air temperature increases, the air expands and its mass decreases.
- When air temperature decreases, the air contracts and its mass increases.
- As humidity increases, the additional moisture in the air displaces oxygen.

As air quality improves, it is possible to make additional horsepower with an internal combustion engine of any type. This is exactly why your vehicle runs better on a cool spring night than on a hot summer day.

As you drive in elevation, barometric pressure decreases. Even though the volume of air flowing into the engine may be the same at a given speed or RPM, its mass is decreased because it contains less oxygen. Any fuel-metering system, be it carbureted or fuel injected, is bound by the variables of air quality and altitude. Depending on where you live, one or both of these variables is constantly changing.

As you can plainly see, a high barometer on a cool evening with low humidity at sea level is the recipe for good air. Many enthusiasts are in tune with this, and as a result, their engines are in tune as well. What if you're not that guy? Maybe you'd rather drive it and enjoy it than constantly tinker with it? Then EFI is especially for you.

Carburetor Limitations

Most guys who run a carburetor have had it on the car for some time or bought it some time ago. When the carb was installed, they calibrated it or paid a professional to calibrate it for them. Once that was done, they simply left it alone and didn't tune it for changing conditions. Most also

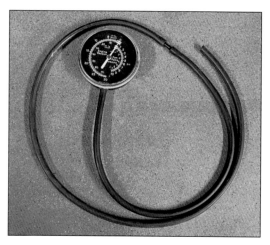

Fig. 1.2. A handheld vacuum gauge like this one is a great tool to have in your toolbox. It allows you to quickly and accurately set the idle mixture screws on your carburetor the first time around. This gauge also has the ability to measure pressure, which is handy to set the fuel pressure. Such gauges are readily available at any automotive parts reseller.

seem somewhat happy with the performance of their combination but they've given no thought to the fact that fuel requirements are constantly changing with air quality, altitude, barometric pressure, etc. Even though the same volume of air is flowing into the engine at a given RPM, it may contain more or less oxygen depending on the conditions.

On the other hand, the diehards take advantage of this and tweak their carburetor(s) often to maximize performance. Remember the jet change in the 1955 Chevy in *Two Lane Blacktop* on the side of the road? Case in point.

Although I don't consider myself a carburetor expert, I kept my Olds in tune when it was carbureted and it ran *really* well that way. It ran so well that numerous friends told me that I was crazy for converting it to EFI. One told me after the conversion, "I don't know why you're saving that stuff. In a month it'll all be for sale." He was referring to the pair of carburetors and the old ignition components that I was intending to keep for a rainy day. Boy, was he right; I think I sold that stuff before the month was up.

I learned many tuning tips and tricks for carburetors from studying the manual supplied with the carburetor and going through the motions with a few basic tools at my side. I also have numerous books on tuning carburetors that I refer to often, as well as a few friends I consider experts who are always able to give practical advice that works. This is definitely a topic that you can never know too much about.

Becoming an expert in tuning carburetors is a science indeed. Not only do you need to understand how each of the individual circuits works, you must understand how they work together because the functions of most circuits overlap. The most accomplished carburetor tuners that I know do the same two things every time:

They select the correct size and type of carburetor(s): mechanical or vacuum secondary. This is a function of many variables, including but not limited to displacement, RPM, camshaft profile, cylinder head airflow capability, transmission type, torque converter stall speed. And they tweak each of the circuits independently and then tweak the circuits as a whole for the best compromise of performance at wide-open throttle (WOT) and drivability. Ideally, the transition between the circuits should be seamless.

I just introduced a *very* important word into the equation. That word is drivability and you hear it often when discussing EFI. Drivability refers to a smoothness of operation when using the throttle (accelerating and decelerating) from idling to WOT to stop, and everything in between.

Compromise is an important part of this equation. Keep in mind that if you spend all Saturday afternoon tuning your carburetor for maximum performance, the tune is going to be slightly off later that night when the temperature drops by 20 degrees and the air is denser as a result. Well, what if you didn't have to compromise? What if you could tune your combination once and forget it? With EFI, you don't have to compromise and you truly can tune it just once. This is exactly why the OEMs made the move to EFI. Fortunately, all of what you may know from tuning carburetors is also applicable to fuel injection.

Air/Fuel Ratio

Regardless of whether an engine is carbureted or fuel injected, the ratio of air entering the engine versus the fuel metered is a critical component. Quite simply, the air/fuel (A/F) ratio of a given engine at a given RPM is stated as pounds of air and fuel. For example, 14:1 means that 1 pound of fuel is metered per 14 pounds of air. A/F ratios are leaner at idle and cruise, and richer when the engine is under load and at WOT.

Carburetors versus EFI

By design, a carburetor meters fuel based on the *volume* of air flowing into the engine. EFI meters fuel based on the *mass* of air flowing into the engine. Thus, EFI is able to make changes to the fuel metering in real time based on the quality of the air entering the engine. In addition, EFI does this automatically, without any input from you. Let me elaborate.

To adjust a carburetor, you change or swap out parts or manually modify it. This means swapping jets or metering rods, air bleeds, power valves, accelerator pumps, pump cams, and other parts. Installing the correct parts helps you achieve the desired A/F ratio at a given RPM and load. If you're using a Holley-style carburetor, you may also make modifications to the metering blocks, such as drilling out the power valve restriction channels, etc.

If you're serious about this, you've got a bevy of such parts on hand as well as a quality wideband A/F meter that you use religiously to evaluate the results of any change. My buddy Bill has three of them (two active at all times) and I've always got to have one in my lap, sounding off readings, when we cruise in his Olds. His carburetor is always *dialed in* and

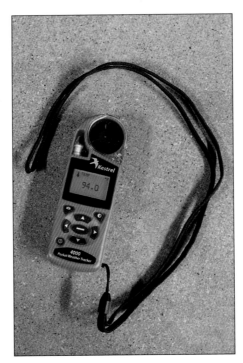

he spends a ton of time tuning it. He never goes out in the car without his handheld weather station and an assortment of jets and air bleeds, and he's not afraid to make a quick jet or air bleed change in a K-Mart parking lot. By the end of this book, I will have converted Bill's Olds to EFI.

Before wideband A/F meters became so affordable and made tuning much easier, owners had to tune the old-school way. They took their cars to the drag strip so they could read the plugs and compare the miles per hour on time slips as they made slow and methodical changes. Holley has excellent video tutorials on how to do this on the street (legally) on their YouTube channel. Either way, you're making mechanical changes to achieve the desired results.

With EFI, it's just the opposite. You program the engine control unit (ECU) to achieve the desired results and it electronically and automatically does the work for you. For example, let's say that your desired A/F ratio at WOT is 12.7:1. With a Holley-style carburetor, you make changes to the power circuit and jetting to obtain this. With EFI, you have a Target A/F Map and you plug in the absolute values you desire based on RPM and manifold absolute pressure (MAP).

Simply stated, you must mechanically change or adjust carburetion to

Fig. 1.3. This Kestrel Pocket Weather Tracker allows you to log temperature, barometric pressure, altitude, relative humidity, heat stress index, dew point, air density, wind speed and gust, etc. A tool like this is indispensable when making changes to a carbureted engine at the drag strip as it provides direction on what changes you should be making.

Target Air/Fuel Ratio

MAP (kPa)	500	700	900	1200	1600	2000	2500	3000	3500	4000	4500	5000	5500	6000	6500	7000
210	11.0	11.0	11.0	11.0	11.0	11.0	11.0	11.0	11.0	11.0	11.0	11.0	11.0	11.0	11.0	11.0
196	11.2	11.2	11.2	11.2	11.2	11.2	11.2	11.2	11.2	11.2	11.2	11.2	11.2	11.2	11.2	11.2
182	11.2	11.2	11.2	11.2	11.2	11.2	11.2	11.2	11.2	11.2	11.2	11.2	11.2	11.2	11.2	11.2
168	11.2	11.2	11.2	11.2	11.2	11.2	11.2	11.2	11.2	11.2	11.2	11.2	11.2	11.2	11.2	11.2
154	11.2	11.2	11.2	11.2	11.2	11.2	11.2	11.2	11.2	11.2	11.2	11.2	11.2	11.2	11.2	11.2
140	12.2	11.8	11.8	11.8	11.8	11.8	11.8	11.8	11.8	11.8	11.8	11.8	11.8	11.8	11.8	12.2
126	12.4	12.0	12.0	12.0	12.0	12.0	12.0	12.0	12.0	12.0	12.0	12.0	12.0	12.0	12.0	12.4
112	12.6	12.1	12.1	12.1	12.1	12.1	12.1	12.1	12.1	12.1	12.1	12.1	12.1	12.1	12.1	12.6
98	13.1	12.5	12.5	12.5	12.5	12.5	12.5	12.5	12.5	12.5	12.5	12.5	12.5	12.5	12.5	13.1
84	13.3	13.7	13.7	13.7	13.7	13.7	13.7	13.7	13.7	13.7	13.7	13.7	13.7	13.7	13.7	13.3
70	13.5	14.2	14.2	14.2	14.2	14.2	14.2	14.2	14.2	14.2	14.2	14.2	14.2	14.2	14.2	13.5
56	13.8	14.7	14.7	14.7	14.7	14.7	14.7	14.7	14.7	14.7	14.7	14.7	14.7	14.7	14.7	13.8
42	14.0	14.7	14.7	14.7	14.7	14.7	14.7	14.7	14.7	14.7	14.7	14.7	14.7	14.7	14.7	14.0
28	14.2	14.7	14.7	14.7	14.7	14.7	14.7	14.7	14.7	14.7	14.7	14.7	14.7	14.7	14.7	14.2
14	14.5	14.7	14.7	14.7	14.7	14.7	14.7	14.7	14.7	14.7	14.7	14.7	14.7	14.7	14.7	14.5
0	14.7	14.7	14.7	14.7	14.7	14.7	14.7	14.7	14.7	14.7	14.7	14.7	14.7	14.7	14.7	14.7

Engine RPM

Fig. 1.4. This is the Target Air/Fuel Ratio table from the tune in my 6-71 blown 1972 Olds Cutlass. There are 256 individual cells in the 16x16 grid. This allows you to achieve much finer tuning for drivability than the most finely tuned carburetor.

achieve the desired results. With EFI, the ECU makes changes electronically, which is based on the desired results plotted in the Target A/F Map.

So, how exactly does EFI do this? It uses feedback from the oxygen sensor in the exhaust, which is typically mounted in the collector of one or both headers. The oxygen sensor provides real-time feedback to the ECU that represents the actual operating A/F ratio of the engine, while the system is in closed-loop mode (see Chapter 3 for more details). Based on this feedback, fuel metering is based on the data that populates the Target A/F Table. For example, let's say that you want a fuel economy–friendly 14.7:1 A/F ratio while you were idling and cruising but desired that ratio to get progressively richer (to a maximum of 12.5:1) at your maximum engine RPM. Done. How cool is that? And it's simple too.

If you're the hands-on type and are familiar with tuning your vehicle in general, you may elect to populate the Target A/F Table yourself. If you're not so familiar, you may elect to begin with a map that was designed for a similar engine configuration to what you have (more on that soon) and tweak it. Depending on the system you choose and the configuration you have, you may also elect to have this done by a qualified tuner on a chassis dyno as I did with my Olds.

Engine Management

So far, I've discussed only fuel metering, mainly because that's the only way I can draw a direct comparison between carburetors and EFI from a functionality standpoint. Many aftermarket conversion systems available today can also influence the engine timing. Systems that can do both are referred to as having "engine management." Herein lies the real power of EFI and the OEMs have been using this since the 1980s.

If your engine is carbureted, you manually perform all ignition timing adjustments to obtain the desired results. To maximize fuel economy and achieve the lowest possible exhaust temperatures (thereby lowering engine operating temperature), more advanced timing is required during part throttle than is required during WOT. With a traditional distributor, this can be easily accomplished by using a vacuum advance.

Now we all know that you can only have so much base timing before it can be difficult to start the engine. For street or street/strip vehicles, you can use both centrifugal and vacuum advance to achieve the total timing desired for drivability and fuel economy as well as optimum performance at WOT. During periods of drivability, total timing is a function of base timing, centrifugal advance, and vacuum advance. At WOT, engine vacuum goes to 0 (ideally), the vacuum advance becomes a non-factor, and total timing is then a function of base timing plus centrifugal advance. Although this sounds difficult, it really isn't. Most manufacturers of quality ignition components provide detailed instructions on how to adjust all of these parameters as well as the rate at which the timing *comes in*.

Now, the above is in no way intended to begin a debate about what is the best way to time a particular engine for a particular application. Rather, it's intended to outline all of the possibilities and the understanding required to unlock the potential a certain combination can offer with a carbureted application for both drivability and WOT performance. If you haven't spent the time to do all of the above with your carbureted vehicle, you've left horsepower and fuel economy on the table.

If you install an EFI system that also includes engine management, timing can be electronically and automatically manipulated based on numerous parameters: RPM, MAP, coolant temperature, engine start-up, and detonation (which I cover in Chapter 3).

Before you plug in the numbers, you need a clear understanding of the exact effect that timing has on your combination. Many enthusiasts have realized the tipping point of their combination. Being greedy with timing and advancing the ignition too far can cause engine damage. Don't be that guy!

By now, it should be clear that tuning your engine for optimum performance is somewhat of an art, especially if you run a carbureted setup. If you have not maximized the A/F ratio and timing, you have work to do to unlock the power and/or fuel economy that your combination may be capable of. The art of tuning for optimum performance is outside of the scope of this book, but I present a few different scenarios for the combinations illustrated in this book.

Keep in mind that no two combinations are the same and when it comes to tuning, the words of my friend and engine builder Frank Beck come to mind, "Give it what it wants."

OEM Conversions

Not that long ago, many of my friends were converting their fuel-injected 1986–1988 Mustang GTs from speed density to mass airflow (MAF). In 1989, Ford changed the 5.0L Mustang to a MAF design, which added a MAF sensor (or meter, as it is sometimes referred to), in front of the throttle body directly aft of the air filter. This provided more-precise fuel metering, which improved both fuel economy and horsepower potential.

In addition, the ECU supplied with MAF systems provided a far greater range of tuning and adjustability. This was ideal for anyone running a supercharger, which at that time was very popular for these cars. This conversion was not an inexpensive one and was incredibly laborious as it required a major portion of the vehicle wiring harness to be replaced.

Other popular conversions have involved transplanting Chevrolet LS, Ford Modular, or late-model Chrysler Hemi engines into older vehicles. All are electronically fuel injected, and each of these conversions offers its own unique set of challenges, especially those systems plucked from donor vehicles equipped with a drive-by-wire interface between the accelerator pedal and throttle.

So, you really have three choices when it comes to an EFI conversion:

- Source the system, harness, and ECU from a donor vehicle and adapt it to your application.
- Source parts of the system from a donor vehicle and pair it with an aftermarket ECU and harness.

Speed Density versus Mass Airflow

The inclusion of a MAF sensor with an EFI system provides more-precise fuel metering. Quite simply, the MAF provides real-time feedback to the computer on the mass flow rate of the air entering the engine.

Speed-density systems rely on the ECU to calculate the mass of the air entering the engine, which is based on RPM, manifold pressure, air temperature, and barometric pressure. Although the ECU may be able to calculate the mass of air extremely accurately, this is still a calculation.

Most aftermarket EFI systems that include a throttle-body assembly based on a 4150-style body lack a MAF meter, so they are considered speed-density systems. On the other hand, some aftermarket systems permit the use of a MAF before the throttle body. In other cases, some systems have a MAF built into the throttle body.

Both speed-density and MAF systems can be incredibly effective when tuned properly. ■

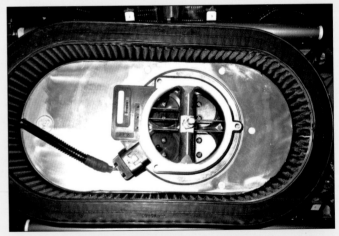

This is an aftermarket MAF meter designed to fit directly over a 4150-style throttle-body assembly on a 427-ci Ford. Pro-M Racing offers this complete kit for Ford FE engines and the MAF is included. (Photo Courtesy Pro-M Racing)

Fig. 1.5. This harness from Painless Performance Products allows you to easily transplant a 2005–2006 LS2 into your project vehicle. The harness includes provisions to also plug in the pedal assembly from the donor vehicle so that the drive-by-wire functionality is retained. (Photo Courtesy Painless Performance)

- Install a complete aftermarket EFI conversion system.

Although the focus of this book is the third option, let's talk briefly about the second option: pulling an LS2 out of a wrecked 2006 GTO and installing it in your 1965 GTO, for example. Just a few years ago, this was an incredibly tough proposition because of the drive-by-wire system. But today, thanks to advancements in the aftermarket, this is not so daunting. Companies such as Painless Performance offer plug-and-play wiring harnesses to make such a swap far simpler.

Electronic Fuel Injection Components

Any EFI system, OEM or aftermarket, relies on multiple components to perform the fuel metering. Those components include the following:

- Engine Control Unit (ECU)
- Fuel Injectors
- Throttle Body (TB)
- Throttle Position Sensor (TPS)
- Idle Air Control Valve (IAC)
- Mass Airflow (MAF) Sensor, standard for OEM
- Intake Air Temperature (IAT) Sensor
- Barometric Pressure Sensor
- Coolant Temperature Sensor (CTS)
- Oxygen Sensor

- Manifold Absolute Pressure (MAP) Sensor
- Knock Sensor, standard for OEM, optional on aftermarket systems
- Wiring Harness

Engine Control Unit

This is the heart of any electronic fuel injection system. It takes input from the various sensors so that it meters fuel based on parameters programmed into it. No different than a personal computer, an ECU employs a powerful microprocessor to ensure that fuel metering is immediate, smooth, and responsive. Some ECUs can also perform engine management, in which case they may be referred to as engine control modules (ECMs). In other cases, the ECU can also manage the control of an automatic transmission, such as the Holley Dominator, for example, in which case they can be referred to as a powertrain control module (PCM). For simplicity, in this book, I stick to ECU.

Fuel Injectors

In my opinion, fuel injectors are one of the neatest inventions of modern times, and elemental in increasing performance and fuel economy. Their job is to introduce a finely atomized mist of fuel into the engine based on direction from the ECU.

The ECU uses two methods to manage injector output:

- By turning individual injectors on or off depending on requirements (see "Aftermarket

Systems" on page 14 for more details).
- By varying the output of each of the injectors depending on requirements; it does this via pulse width modulation (see sidebar "Pulse Width Modulation" on page 13 for more details).

Depending on the system, it may have as few as four injectors, or as many as sixteen. Fuel injectors are rated based on pounds per hour (lbs/hr), or how many pounds of fuel they can flow in one hour.

Throttle Body

The throttle body (TB) is an integral part of any EFI system, and just like the throttle blades of a carburetor, it regulates the air flowing into the engine. TBs can have a single throttle blade, dual throttle blades, or a pair of dual throttle blades.

Throttle Position Sensor

When the throttle is opened, the throttle position sensor (TPS) tells the ECU what percentage the throttle blade is open. The TPS is very accurate and provides real-time feedback of the position of the throttle blade to the ECU.

Mass Airflow Sensor

The job of the MAF sensor is to provide the ECU real-time feedback as to the quality of the air entering the engine. As discussed in sidebar "Speed Density versus Mass Airflow" (on page 10), it measures the mass flow rate of the air entering the engine.

Fig. 1.6. This complete MPFI kit from FAST, designed for small-block Chevys, supports engines up to 1,000 hp. Note that it includes an intake manifold complete with injector bungs in the runners, fuel injectors, fuel rails, fittings, a distributor with cam sensor, fuel pump, regulator, fuel filters, and all sensors. A kit like this really does take the guesswork out of the equation. The system includes the following: engine control unit (1), fuel injectors (2), throttle body (3), throttle position sensor (4), idle air control valve (5), intake air temperature sensor (6), coolant temperature sensor (7), oxygen sensor (8), manifold absolute pressure sensor (9), and wiring harness (10). (Photo Courtesy FAST)

Fig. 1.7. This is the Holley HP EFI system on my Olds Cutlass. This kit differs from the FAST kit, as it has the injectors located above the throttle bodies themselves and not in the intake runners. It works well for blown applications as the fuel cools the charge as it passes through the blower. All the components are installed on the engine. The reference numbers correspond to components in the above photo and caption.

Pulse Width Modulation

ECUs utilize pulse width modulation (PWM) to manage the output of the fuel injectors by controlling their duty cycle. Duty cycle is a measure of ON time and is expressed as a percent, 100 percent being fully ON.

By utilizing PWM, the ECU is able to vary the output of the fuel injector based on requirements by the engine at a given RPM and load. ∎

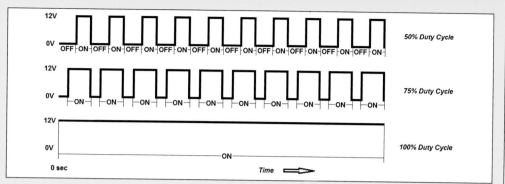

PWM is simply a method of rapidly switching a DC voltage on and off. The rate at which this is done each second is defined as the switching frequency. PWM is used to manage the output of fuel injectors, speed of fuel pumps, etc.

Idle Air Control Valve

The idle air control (IAC) valve has a simple job: it allows air to bypass the throttle blade, so the engine can idle when the throttle blade is closed. The IAC valve is actuated electronically by the ECU based on parameters set forth in the tune and can thereby control the idle RPM of the engine regardless of whether the vehicle is idling in neutral or in gear.

Intake Air Temperature Sensor

The intake air temperature (IAT) sensor senses the temperature of the air entering the engine and provides that data to the ECU. In non-boosted applications, it's often the ambient air temperature. In boosted applications, the ambient air is compressed and thereby heated in the process. Therefore, this sensor is often located aft of the blower or turbo in an effort to provide the most accurate data to the ECU.

Barometric Pressure Sensor

Even though this may not be a separate component, some aftermarket ECUs have an internal barometric pressure (BP) sensor to monitor the barometric pressure.

Coolant Temperature Sensor

The coolant temperature sensor (CTS) is located in a water passage in the intake manifold or cylinder head. Its job is to provide the ECU with the actual operating temperature of the engine. Operating temperature is an important criterion as any ECU with engine management can adjust engine timing, fuel enrichment, and IAC settings based on it.

Oxygen Sensor

The oxygen sensor(s) provides real-time feedback of the actual operating A/F ratio of the engine to the ECU. The ECU meters fuel according to this feedback, based of course on the parameters set forth in the Target A/F Ratio Table. The oxygen sensor(s) is typically located in the collector(s) of the header(s).

Manifold Absolute Pressure Sensor

The MAP sensor provides real-time feedback of the pressure in the intake manifold to the ECU. This is a bit different from what we're used to seeing on a vacuum or boost gauge, and it is measured in kiloPascals (kPa).

For the sake of this discussion, consider that 1 bar (or atmosphere) equals 14.7 psi (at sea level), which equals 101.325 kPa.

At sea level, air exerts 14.7 psi of force on everything, including an internal combustion engine. A naturally aspirated engine has 14.7 psi of force exerted on it and therefore it requires only a 1 bar MAP sensor. A 2 bar MAP sensor is required for boosted applications not exceeding 14.7 psi of boost, a 3 bar MAP sensor is required for boosted applications not exceeding 29.4 psi of boost, etc.

Knock Sensor

This sensor is designed to detect detonation. As we all know, detonation is the killer of even the best of parts and it is to be prevented at all costs in high-performance engines. Pre-ignition causes detonation and it results in combustion occurring too soon while the piston is on the compression stroke. This causes tremendous force to be exerted on the pistons, rods, crankshaft, etc. The net result is ultimately parts failure. When the knock sensor detects detonation, the ECU can quickly retard timing to eliminate it well before you could detect it by ear and lift off the throttle.

Not all of the applications are knock-sensor friendly, especially those with Roots-blown combinations or those using gear drives. The harmonics of the belt in a toothed pulley or that of the timing gears meshing can trigger a knock sensor, causing an undesired retard in timing.

Wiring Harness

Don't be intimidated by the wiring harness. Although it may look daunting, most of the connections are plug-and-play between the ECU and the various sensors. Only a handful of hard connections to the vehicle are required.

The key to a properly functioning EFI system is the sum of the parts. Like anything else, some of the sensors, specifically the IAC, MAF, and oxygen sensors, require periodic maintenance. Once you've learned your way around the software of an EFI system, it's easy to pinpoint a potential problem.

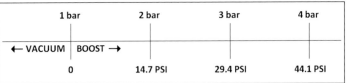

	1 bar	2 bar	3 bar	4 bar
← VACUUM	BOOST →			
	0	14.7 PSI	29.4 PSI	44.1 PSI

Fig. 1.8. This illustrates the relationship between boost and the actual pressure in the cylinder. It's easy to forget that at one atmosphere (1 bar), 14.7 psi, exists in the cylinder at sea level without any boost.

Fig. 1.9. These are the OEM knock sensors found in the valley of an LS engine from a 2002 Chevrolet Corvette. (Photo Courtesy Keith Aguirre)

Aftermarket Systems

The main different types of aftermarket systems currently available are: TBI, MPFI/MPI, application-specific, stack, and special-application.

In addition, you can pick and choose components from various manufacturers to assemble an EFI system custom tailored to your specific needs.

Throttle-Body Injection Systems

As the name implies, these systems are built around a throttle body. This category includes many of the systems advertised today as "easy to install" and self-tuning. A TBI system

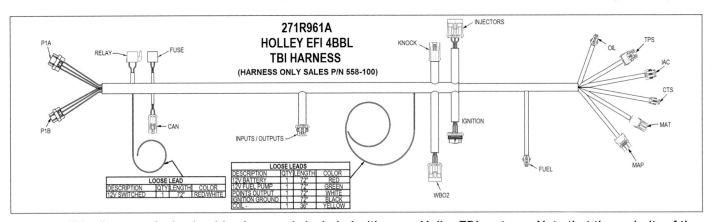

Fig. 1.10. This diagram of a basic wiring harness is included with some Holley TBI systems. Note that the majority of the harness is pre-terminated with plugs specific to the components they mate with. There are only a handful of connections to make to your vehicle's wiring. Holley refers to these as "Loose Leads" in this diagram. (Illustration Courtesy Holley Performance Products)

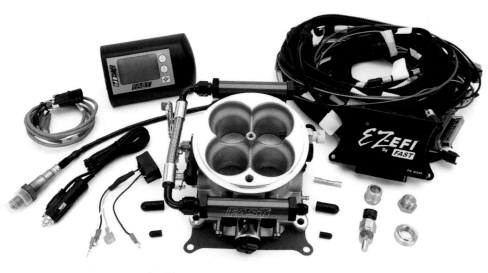

Fig. 1.11. This TBI system offered by FAST is based on a 4150-style mounting flange so it's compatible with a wide range of applications. The fuel injectors are built into the throttle body, which greatly simplifies the installation. This complete system is in the EZ-EFI series and supports engines up to 650 hp. A dual-throttle-body upgrade is available for engines making 1,200 hp or more. (Photo Courtesy FAST)

is any system that locates the fuel injectors within the throttle-body (TB) assembly. These are typically built on a 4150-style base, which is identical to that of a Holley-style 4-barrel carburetor. The system shown on my Olds (Figure 1.7) is a TBI system.

The injectors typically are mounted above the throttle blades and can be oriented vertically or horizontally with respect to the blades. On a TBI system for a V-8 engine, it is common to have four injectors: one above each of the primary and secondary throttle blades. Depending on the system, the ECU may only activate the secondary injectors once the TPS reaches a certain percentage. In addition, depending on the system, the injectors may alternate from side to side to keep the mixture evenly distributed in the intake manifold.

Fuel distribution is similar to that of a carbureted engine, so it is entirely possible to have uneven A/F

ratios from one cylinder to another, especially in Roots-blown applications. Roots blowers tend to push the fuel forward in the intake manifold under boost.

Multi-Point Fuel Injection Systems

These systems (MPFI or MPI) have the injectors located in the runners of the intake manifold itself. This offers better control of the fuel distribution. In addition, some systems allow you to adjust each injector individually to maximize the A/F ratio for each cylinder. The FAST system illustrated in Figure 1.6 is an

MPFI system. MPFI systems have different ways of managing the firing of the fuel injectors. They can be batch fired or sequentially fired.

Batch Firing: Here, the ECU fires an entire batch of injectors simultaneously. For example, GM engines have an odd batch (cylinders 1, 3, 5, 7) and an even batch (cylinders 2, 4, 6, 8). AMCs and most Chryslers use this arrangement as well. The ECU fires *all* of the odd or even batch of injectors based on what cylinder is next in line on the intake stroke.

Sequential Firing: Here, the injectors are individually triggered according to the firing order of the engine and position of the camshaft. This system is more precise because the ECU can fire a specific injector just before the respective intake valve opens. This requires a cam sensor so that the ECU knows the precise location of the camshaft when the engine is running. A Hall effect sensor in the distributor easily determines camshaft position, as shown in the distributors in Figure 1.6 and Figure 1.14. MSD, Mallory, Fast, and others also offer a handful of distributors with this sensor built in.

Application-Specific Systems

Some manufacturers offer complete systems that are designed from the ground up for a specific application. These systems are typically MPFI based and include an intake manifold

Fig. 1.12. An MPFI system has a great benefit, and that is its low profile. Notice how nicely these fuel rails tuck between the throttle body and valve covers on this 434-ci small-block Chevy. Special attention was paid to overall height, including the selection of this low-profile throttle body, so that this package easily fits under the hood of a classic Corvette. This engine was built and tuned by Beck Racing Engines.

Fig. 1.13. Here, a 434-ci small-block engine is installed in a 1963 split-window Corvette. The project was well planned and engine position was considered so it cleared the hood. The casual observer wouldn't recognize they were looking at a 600+hp engine with a modern fuel injection setup. Only the fuel rails give that away. (Photo Courtesy JE Pro Streets)

with fuel injector provisions. The advantage to choosing such a system is that all of the components have been designed to work together.

Just a few years ago, such systems were limited to Chevrolet small- and big-block applications. Now, Edelbrock, Pro-M Racing, and other manufacturers have expanded their offerings to include application-specific kits for AMC, Chrysler, Ford, and Pontiac. Pro-M Racing also offers application-specific kits for Buick, Cadillac, Oldsmobile, and believe it or not, even Studebaker.

Stack Systems

Look no further if you love the look of vintage velocity stacks but don't want the hassle of tuning a mechanical fuel injection system. Several manufacturers, including Enderle, Kinsler, Inglese, and many others, offer "stack" systems, which give you the great look of velocity stacks

Fig. 1.14. This Edelbrock Pro-Flo 2 EFI system is available for Pontiac 326- to 455-ci V-8s. This complete MPFI system includes a single-plane intake manifold with injectors located in the intake runners, fuel rails, throttle body, Mallory distributor with cam sensor, programmable ECU, and handheld calibration module. Two versions of this kit are offered, depending on maximum horsepower, as well as similar kits for AMC, small- and big-block Chevy, AMC/Jeep, small- and big-block Chrysler, and small- and big-block Ford. (Photo Courtesy Edelbrock)

Fig. 1.15. Most enthusiasts agree that nothing tops the looks of velocity stacks. This 540-ci big-block Chevy is sporting a complete Hilborn EFI system. It has the classic stack look with all of the benefits of modern electronic fuel injection. This engine was built and tuned by Beck Racing Engines.

Fig. 1.16. This 383-ci small-block Chevy is equipped with a Hilborn EFI system with short stacks and air cleaners. Yes, with EFI, you really can have it all. This engine was built and tuned by Beck Racing Engines.

Fig. 1.17. If you're looking for eye candy, this eight-injector EFI hat from BDS fits the bill. Sitting atop this 572-ci big-block Chevy with a setback 14-71 BDS blower, this combo makes more than 1,580 hp on C16. Not only does it look awesome, it functions exactly like those you see used in the Top Fuel classes. Each of the red throttle blades can support up to 600 hp. This engine was built and tuned by Beck Racing Engines.

with the convenience of modern electronic fuel injection.

These systems typically have one "stack" for each cylinder and are much simpler to tune than the mechanical variety. In addition, they're totally suited for street use.

Special-Application Systems

When it comes to eye candy, not much tops a functioning injector hat sitting atop an old-school Roots blower. Blower Drive Service (BDS) and Enderle offer such systems. Both provide jaw-dropping looks and the performance of modern electronic fuel injection.

In some cases, an off-the-shelf system may not be compatible with your application. Or maybe you'd like to combine one manufacturer's throttle body with another's engine management system and use a specific size and quantity of injectors. It's not as uncommon as you may think and it's easier than ever to mix-and-match components from several manufacturers to accomplish this. If you build a unique combination, you should speak directly to the manufacturers of the parts to ensure that they work well with one another.

Option Considerations

If you own a vehicle with a small-block Chevy and you're doing a basic naturally aspirated conver-

sion, your options are mind boggling. If you own any other vehicle, you also have a lot of options thanks to TBI conversion kits. Regardless of what kind of vehicle you own, here are the things that you need to consider before shopping for a system.

Maximum Horsepower

What's the peak horsepower of your combination? Once you've installed the EFI system, are you considering also maximizing other parts of your combination to increase horsepower? If so, how much maximum horsepower does that yield, ideally?

Power Adders

Do you use nitrous oxide, a supercharger, or turbocharger on your combination presently? If not, is this something that you want to consider down the road? (See Chapter 3 for more details.)

Budget

As they always say, the devil is in the details. Sure, there may be a group buy in your favorite forum on the system you've had your eye on. But have you considered that you may not be able to use any of your existing fuel system and ignition components? You're better off asking those questions up front so that you know just how much you'll outlay for all of the components required for the conversion (see Chapter 2 for more details).

Installation

Are you doing the installation or are you having it done by a professional? Even if you undertake the installation yourself, you may have to farm out part of the work; having a vent and return provision added to your stock fuel tank, for example.

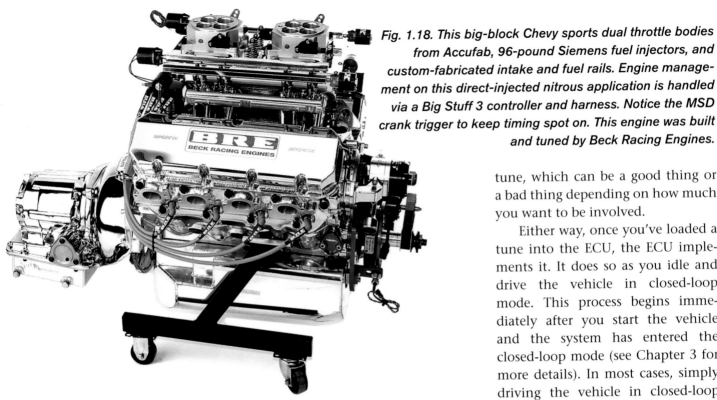

Fig. 1.18. This big-block Chevy sports dual throttle bodies from Accufab, 96-pound Siemens fuel injectors, and custom-fabricated intake and fuel rails. Engine management on this direct-injected nitrous application is handled via a Big Stuff 3 controller and harness. Notice the MSD crank trigger to keep timing spot on. This engine was built and tuned by Beck Racing Engines.

Tuning

Are you doing the tuning yourself or are you farming it out to a professional? If you are doing the tuning, you will certainly benefit from a system with self learning.

Self-Learning Basics

Most aftermarket EFI systems have the ability to self learn. People remark, "I just drove it and it learned my combination." Is this true? Yes, but how is that possible? The system uses feedback from the oxygen sensor to implement the tune loaded into the ECU. This is referred to as operating the system in closed-loop mode.

The two types of self-learning systems are those with a handheld controller and those without. Both operate in much the same way.

Handheld Controller

Systems that include a handheld controller require you to input some basic data about your combination into the ECU via a series of questions or available choices. After you've done so, a base tune is created in the ECU from the data you've input. These types of systems are designed to be easily configured and to get the vehicle running smoothly in short order. However, this kind of interface limits your tuning options to those that are only available via the handheld controller.

Laptop Computer

Most more-flexible systems require a laptop computer to talk to the ECU. At a minimum, you load a pre-existing tune that approximates your combination into the ECU via the laptop. You can also build a tune from scratch or modify a pre-existing tune to suit your particular combination. Such systems include numerous files in the software, and it's up to you to choose one that closely approximates your combination. Laptop-based systems offer much greater user control over the tune, which can be a good thing or a bad thing depending on how much you want to be involved.

Either way, once you've loaded a tune into the ECU, the ECU implements it. It does so as you idle and drive the vehicle in closed-loop mode. This process begins immediately after you start the vehicle and the system has entered the closed-loop mode (see Chapter 3 for more details). In most cases, simply driving the vehicle in closed-loop mode for 5 to 10 miles gets your tune really close. Hard to believe? You'll be a believer once you agree to take the plunge.

User Interface

Each aftermarket EFI system has a unique user interface, but it's simply not possible to illustrate them all. For that reason, I use examples of the user interfaces of the systems installed in Chapter 5 (MSD Atomic EFI Handheld Controller) and Chapter 6 (Holley EFI V2 Software) throughout the book. This allows you to become intimately familiar with two examples rather than trying to cover all the popular user interfaces. The MSD Atomic controller and Holley EFI V2 software are representative of their respective product categories.

The user interface is your portal to adjusting the parameters of the system. I strongly encourage you to look closely at it on the manufacturer's website when considering which system is right for you.

CHOOSING THE RIGHT SYSTEM

Now that you're convinced that converting to EFI is right for you, the legwork begins.

Converting to EFI isn't quite as simple as purchasing a system, unpacking it, and bolting it on. Furthermore, no system that I'm aware of is designed to work in all applications. Fortunately, the process of narrowing the field of available products to determine which system or systems are best suited to your needs is a pretty easy one. This chapter provides all the information you need to easily choose a system for your vehicle as well as any additional parts to ensure your installation goes smoothly and gives you years of reliable service.

I'm one of those guys who prefers to do a job once and then enjoy the fruits of my labor. And that means I install it right the first time so I can drive and enjoy my vehicles versus spending a bunch of time trouble-shooting an installation that wasn't done correctly on the front end.

Before you can choose which system is right for your application, it's vital to consider the following: parts combination compatibility, fuel system requirements, ignition system requirements, and electrical system requirements.

Parts Combination Compatibility

Most aftermarket EFI kits are designed for naturally aspirated engines making less than 650 hp. The size of the injectors included in the kit (typically four), the airflow capability of the throttle body itself, the fuel pressure, fuel pump, etc. determine how much horsepower the engine can produce. These kits represent 90 percent of the market. That being said, some products are compatible with much-higher horse-power, naturally aspirated combinations as well as those kits that are fully compatible with power adders.

650+ HP Applications

If your naturally aspirated combination makes in excess of 650 fly-wheel horsepower, you should be looking at an MPFI system, a TBI

Fig. 2.1. The FAST EZ-EFI 2.0 system is the company's latest offering at the time of this writing. The 4150 throttle body has eight injectors and supports up to 1,200 hp. The base system includes all of the components shown here, including the color touch screen handheld/dash-mount controller. This system performs fuel metering and offers electronic timing control when you add the company's EFI-style distributor and crank trigger. (Photo Courtesy FAST)

Fig. 2.2. This .030-over 327-ci small-block Chevy sports a pair of FAST EZ EFI throttle bodies on an Offenhauser Cross Ram manifold. A setup like this provides that classic look with the performance of modern fuel injection! (Photo Courtesy Ed Taylor)

system that allows you to run dual throttle bodies, or a stack system. At the time of this writing, both FAST and Holley offer TBI systems that allow you to run a slave throttle body.

In addition, FAST offers a TBI system that uses a single throttle body with eight injectors that is capable of 1,200 hp.

Power Adders

If you're using or intend to use a power adder (nitrous oxide, superchargers, or turbochargers), you should shop for an EFI system that was designed from the ground up to be compatible with your power adder of choice. For example, the Holley HP-EFI and Dominator EFI systems

are designed to work with all power adders and have lots of features that are readily accessible in the tuning software. Either platform is ideal for nitrous or water/methanol users, and both have four stages of progressive control available.

I've used a Holley HP-EFI system with my 6-71 blown big-block Chevy for three years now and I couldn't be happier (see Chapter 4 for more details).

Camshaft Compatibility

One of the limitations of speed-density EFI systems is that they typically require a good vacuum signal at idle, such as 10 inches of manifold volume or more. Some manufacturers specify camshaft profile limitations (e.g., duration at .050 inch must be less than 250 degrees). If your camshaft profile falls outside of their recommendations, you should pick up the phone and contact their tech support department for recommendations before proceeding. Don't be shocked if they recommend a different camshaft profile.

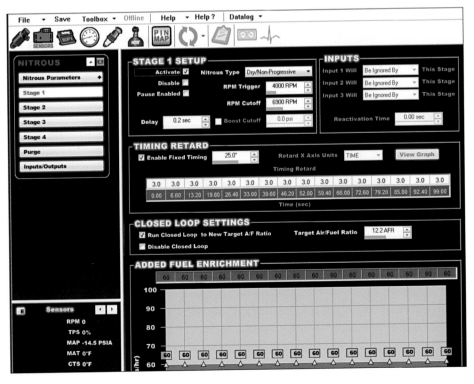

Fig. 2.3. Holley HP and Dominator EFI systems are fully compatible with nitrous and water/methanol systems. If you're a hard-core nitrous user, the software allows you to configure the ECU for up to four stages of nitrous, each of which can be wet or dry and even progressively controlled if you desire.

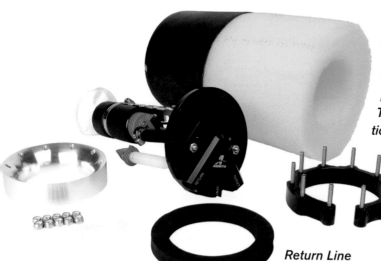

Fig. 2.4. This Phantom 340 Stealth Fuel System from Aeromotive allows you to add an EFI-specific fuel pump inside your factory tank. The kit includes the 340 Stealth fuel pump, baffle, pre-filter, and all parts required to install it. The kit supports naturally aspirated EFI engine combinations making up to 850 hp or forced-induction EFI combinations up to 700 hp. (Photo Courtesy Aeromotive)

Fuel System Requirements

Each of the following should be considered in an effort to ensure your fuel system works efficiently and reliably.

Fuel Pressure

If you didn't already know, EFI systems operate at a much higher fuel pressure than do carburetors. A typical carbureted system requires between 5 and 7 psi of fuel pressure. EFI systems require a higher operating fuel pressure (typically from 20 to 80 psi). This necessitates the installation of an EFI-style electric fuel pump, which can be installed in the tank or externally. If your vehicle is still equipped with the stock fuel line, it may also be necessary to upgrade it to meet the fuel demands of the system. Keep in mind, some systems are not compatible with hard lines.

Fuel Filters

Equally important are filters for the fuel system: one before the pump itself (pre-filter) and a much finer one before the injectors (post-filter). Some systems include one or both filters; others rely on you to supply them.

Return Line

Many aftermarket EFI systems also require a return line to the tank, which requires that the tank also have a vent. Don't let the installation of a return line discourage you from considering a particular system. Most factory tanks have a vent, but its size may be a limiting factor. Some EFI systems, such as the MSD Atomic system, can be installed with or without a return line. However, MSD encourages the use of a return line (see page 76 for installation details). It is imperative with a returnless-style system that the fuel pump be located in the tank to keep it from overheating.

In addition, you really shouldn't expect to supply fuel to your brand-new EFI system from a 40-year-old tank that is full of sediment and rust. Also, realize that such a tank was designed for a low-pressure carbureted fuel system, not a high-pressure fuel injected system. If you elect to use the stock fuel tank, you're going to have to remove it to add the provisions for the return line so this is the perfect time to flush it out. If you are running a stock-style tank, you have a few options. You can flush it and add provisions for a vent and return line, or you can install one of the readily available in-tank fuel pump kits.

Additionally, a return-style system requires the use of a return-style regulator. Many companies offer them. The main difference between a return-style and a traditional regulator is that a return-style regulator is designed to install at the *end* of the fuel system and is the point of origin for the return line.

Fuel Tank

Another option is to replace the tank altogether with one that has been specifically designed for an EFI system. If you elect to go that route, several companies offer fuel tank kits that have a fuel pump, filter, and sending unit located within the tank and all the provisions to easily install it.

Removing the stock fuel tank and replacing it with an EFI-specific tank is really not as expensive as you may think, and it offers several benefits:

- You start with an absolutely fresh tank with zero rust or sediment
- The internal fuel pump is cooled by the fuel it is submerged in
- The pickup has been located in such a way that it won't be uncovered during hard acceleration or cornering, as is possible with a stock pickup

Keep in mind that fuel injection systems don't have a fuel reservoir, such as the bowls of a carburetor, in which fuel is stored. Aside from the relatively small amount of fuel in the

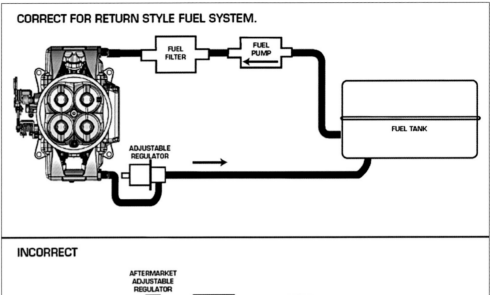

CORRECT FOR RETURN STYLE FUEL SYSTEM.

INCORRECT

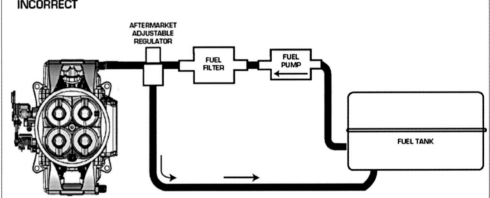

Fig. 2.5. This Holley EFI regulator is designed for return-style EFI fuel systems, on which the regulator is located after the throttle body/fuel rails and before the return line (see Figure 2.6 for clarification). (Photo Courtesy Holley Performance Products)

Fig. 2.6. Plumbing a return-style EFI fuel system differs from a return-style system for a carburetor, specifically in the location of the regulator. Thus, EFI systems utilize return-style regulators. (Illustration Courtesy MSD Performance)

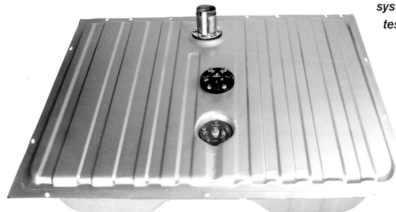

Fig. 2.7. This Stealth Fuel Tank for 1964–1968 Ford Mustangs from Aeromotive allows you to remove the factory tank and install one that is completely EFI specific. The kit includes a 340 Stealth fuel pump, pre-filter, internal baffling, sending unit, flanged filler-neck adapter, universal rubber-filler neck, and three ports for the outlet, return, and vent. (Photo Courtesy Aeromotive)

fuel lines and the fuel rails, no fuel is stored other than in the fuel tank. If you spend time autocrossing, road racing, or in high-g cornering situations, you absolutely should consider a fuel tank specifically designed for EFI as fuel slosh can uncover the pickup in a stock tank.

If you elect to use the stock tank, you should consider keeping it more than half full at all times to prevent fuel starvation from the pickup being uncovered. Edelbrock has an ingenious solution that allows you to retain the stock fuel tank. Their Universal EFI Sump Fuel Kit is designed

to work in conjunction with your stock tank to provide predictable performance with an EFI system of up to 60 psi in fuel pressure.

Fuel Type

The type of fuel you intend to run influences the type of fuel lines, pump, and regulator you should run. For example, if you're presently running E85 in your carbureted setup, you know that this fuel is caustic and corrosive to traditional fuel system components. I recommend that you determine this early in the process so you can narrow down your choices.

If your E85 combination produces in excess of 450 hp, some kits may not be compatible simply because of the additional fuel volume requirements of E85 as compared to traditional gasoline. In some cases, the fuel requirements are beyond the capability of the included fuel injectors. In other cases, the components themselves may not be designed to work reliably with E85 (see Chapter 6 for more details).

All components of a fuel delivery system should be chosen to complement one another: feed line, delivery line, return line, regulator, filters, etc. Some kits include some of these

components; others include none. Because fuel system components can be one of the biggest expenses in an EFI conversion, it's best to understand the exact requirements of a particular system before selecting it for your application.

Fortunately, I've got some fuel system gurus at my fingertips and they've proven to be an incredibly valuable resource. The more time I spend designing and building fuel systems the more I find hints and tricks for getting the job done correctly (and avoiding problems). When designing a fuel system for your vehicle, your goals should be performance, reliability, and safety.

Fuel Lines

The fuel system should be designed so that it is capable of supplying all the fuel your engine requires. Choosing the correct fuel pump is the easy part, as most companies provide compatible maximum

horsepower levels. Once you choose the pump, it's also easy to select the pre-filter, post-filter, and regulator to go with the pump because most manufacturers recommend components that are compatible with a particular pump.

The difficult part is deciding what size and type of fuel lines to use with all the new parts. If you're installing a throttle-body-style EFI system, the system's manufacturer typically specifies a given diameter of fuel line to supply the throttle body, but not much more. And, depending on who you ask, you may get varying answers. In my experience, I have found the following to be true:

Fuel Line Size to Throttle Body: Use what the manufacturer of the throttle body specifies. This should be in agreement with the manufacturer of the fuel pump. (Keep in mind that the post-filter is in-line here.)

Fuel Line Size from Throttle Body to Regulator: Use what the throttle body manufacturer specifies. This should be in agreement with the manufacturer of the regulator. Use a minimum of -6 line for returns.

Fuel Line Size from Regulator to Tank: Use what the manufacturer of the throttle body specifies. This should be the same size as the size of the fuel line from the throttle body to the regulator. Use a minimum of -6 line for returns.

Size of Line from Tank to Pump: Use one size up from the size of the fuel line to throttle body. Keep in mind that the pre-filter is in-line here.

Size of Line for Vent: Use the same size as that of the return line. For example, if you install a throttle-body EFI system that calls for -6 feed line to the throttle body, the line specifications are as follows:

Fig. 2.8. This clever EFI Sump Kit from Edelbrock allows you to retain the stock fuel tank and mechanical fuel pump. The kit installs under the hood and the fuel pump and regulator are mounted within the sump assembly. The kit includes pre- and post-filters, fuel line, fittings, and all of the hardware required to install it. Edelbrock offers kits designed to deliver a constant 49 or 60 psi. (Photo Courtesy Edelbrock)

Line	Size	Inside Diameter (inch)
Tank to Pre-Filter	-8	1/2
Pre-Filter to Pump	-8	1/2
Pump to Post-Filter	-6	3/8
Post-Filter to Throttle Body	-6	3/8
Throttle Body to Regulator	-6	3/8
Regulator to Tank (return)	-6	3/8
Tank Vent	-6	3/8

Fig. 2.9. This Aeroquip push-lock hose has a tough core that is very resistant to collapsing. It is also compatible with E85 fuel.

The type of line you use is a function of the fuel you run as well as personal preference. Push-lock line is probably the most common choice for fuel systems because it's inexpensive and easy to install. That being said, if you choose a push-lock line that does not have a non-collapsible design with a tough core, it absolutely *cannot* be used for the inlet of a high-volume pump. High-volume fuel pumps are in many cases capable of creating a high vacuum on the inlet. This can collapse any line that does not have a non-collapsible design, creating a restriction and possible pump failure.

Pump Location

Mount the fuel pump in a location where it can run cool. Heat is a fuel pump's worst enemy and you want your electric fuel pump to live a long and healthy life. If you choose to locate the pump externally, choose a location that has good airflow and is preferably not within close proximity to the exhaust.

Or, you can do what the OEMs do, which is to locate the pump in the tank. The obvious advantage to this is submerging the pump in the

fuel keeps it cooler than locating it externally. If you elect to locate the pump in the tank, it (and the wiring to it) should be designed specifically for an in-tank application. As with any vehicle with an in-tank electric fuel pump, you should avoid running the gas below 1/4 tank so that the pump is always submerged in the fuel, especially in the summer.

Ask any engine builder where you should install an external electric fuel pump, and they will tell you the same thing: locate the pump rearward of the fuel tank and below the lowest point of the tank. This is because electric fuel pumps are better pushers than pullers. By locating the pump below the lowest point of the tank, gravity feeds fuel to the pump, no matter the level in the tank. Locating the pump rearward of the tank ensures that the pump is never starved of fuel during hard acceleration, which is also sound thinking. In many cases, however, this is simply undesirable as it places the pump well below the rear bumper of the vehicle and in plain sight.

Regardless of whether or not you locate an external pump rearward of the tank, it absolutely needs to be mounted as low as possible with respect to the fuel tank. It goes without saying that you can't locate it in such a fashion that it or the fuel lines can be damaged from debris on the road. In some cases, you can find a place along (or even within) the frame rail to locate the pump that

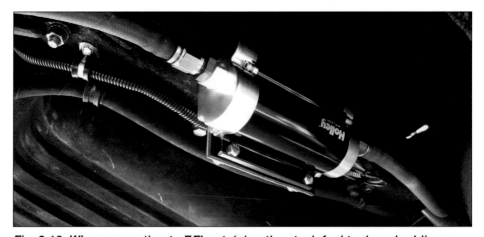

Fig. 2.10. When converting to EFI, retaining the stock fuel tank and adding an external fuel pump is the least expensive way to upgrade your fuel system. The pump in this 1970 Olds (featured in Chapter 6) is located along the frame rail on the passenger's side of the fuel tank as low as possible. The factory tank in this Olds has been upgraded with a sump.

Fig. 2.11. The fuel pump and pre-filter are installed in this 1964 Chevelle (featured in Chapter 5). These components are located in front of the stock fuel tank and as low as possible. We used the stock pickup assembly in the tank in this installation. If this pickup has a sock, it should be removed as it can be a restriction and isn't necessary with the pre-filter.

keeps it protected and places it below the lowest point of the fuel tank. If you are simply unable to locate the pump below the lowest point of the fuel tank, you need to keep the level of fuel in the tank above the inlet of the pump or you risk damaging the pump.

Pickup for External Pumps

Any competent engine builder will also tell you to use a sump to supply an external electric fuel pump. Again, this is not always possible and you may choose to rely on a pickup within the tank. This is fine, as the principle of a siphon allows fuel to remain in the fuel line all the way to the pump, once it has been filled by the pump during the initial power up of the pump, that is. If you elect to run a pickup, keeping the level of the fuel in the tank above the inlet of the pump is that much more critical.

Return Fuel

Placement of the return line within the tank is often overlooked. I'm talking about where the fuel is returned within the fuel tank and

whether that's above or below the level of the fuel within the tank. Any fuel system with a return line returns all unused fuel to the tank. It is preferable to return the fuel below the fuel level in the tank and not above it. If fuel is returned above the level of the fuel within the tank, this can cause aeration (the addition of air to the fuel) which can cause the pump to cavitate.

High-Horsepower Fuel Pumps

So, you've got a nasty combination that makes serious horsepower. This means that you're also running a high-flow electric or mechanical fuel pump. As you convert to EFI, you may need to replace that fuel pump with a high-flow electric fuel pump capable of much higher operating pressure. Big electric fuel pumps require big current, so it's critical to wire it per the manufacturer's explicit instructions and even more important that your charging system can adequately power it. If you're also converting to a return-style system at the same time, you've got a new concern: heating the fuel.

Most of the big high-volume electric fuel pumps on the market (including those for carbureted applications) are really more suited for short-term operation at the drag strip than they are for long-term operation on the street. When you use such a fuel pump in a return-style fuel system for a street application, you're moving a great deal of fuel to the front of the vehicle and fuel that's not burned is returned to the tank. As the fuel is circulated it is also heated. Operating a high-volume pump for long periods of time isn't the best idea as it can result in pump failure. Managing the pump speed based on fuel demand is a far better idea, but how? Pulse width modulation (PWM). That's how.

PWM allows the pump speed to vary based on the actual fuel demands of the engine. A PWM fuel pump controller manages the pump speed by varying the duty cycle in the same way that the ECU manages the output of a fuel injector. This is

Fig. 2.12. This fuel pump controller from Weldon offers PWM technology to manage the speed of electric fuel pumps. A controller such as this allows you to use even the biggest fuel pumps without fear of premature pump failure. In addition, such a controller minimizes fuel heating of any return-style fuel system, critical in street-driven applications.

Fig. 2.13. The Prodigy series of fuel pumps from Fuelab utilize built-in PWM technology. When used with the matching Fuelab PWM regulator, pump speed is managed based on actual fuel requirements of the engine. The two are interconnected by a single wire. Prodigy fuel pumps can also be interfaced to the PWM output of a compatible ECU to manage pump speed. (Photo Courtesy Fuelab)

Fig. 2.15. The Holley 12-810 Fuel Pump Safety Pressure Switch can be used to shut off any electric fuel pump when oil pressure drops below 5 psi; never a bad idea. (Photo Courtesy Holley Performance Products)

typically done by tracking engine RPM. A few companies offer PWM solutions for high-volume electric fuel pumps, including Fuelab, Weldon, and Aeromotive. (See Chapter 4 for details on installing an Aeromotive Fuel Pump Speed Controller, a PWM controller compatible with any electric fuel pump.)

Fuelab offers high-volume fuel pumps with built-in PWM control. In fact, these can be interfaced directly with their mating electronic regulator so that fuel pressure can be managed in real time based on actual fuel requirements.

One of the benefits of installing such a controller (or pump with a built-in controller) is that the pump noise is greatly reduced. Anyone who has ever used an electric fuel pump knows full well that they're super noisy. I don't know about you, but I'd rather listen to the blower whine and exhaust tone at the stoplight than the annoying buzz from the fuel pump.

In my time at cruises and car shows, I've heard plenty of stories about high-volume fuel pump failures. I'm convinced that 99 percent of these failures are a function of incorrect installation. If your installation requires a high-volume EFI pump, you're well advised not to cut corners in its installation. Otherwise, when it fails, you know exactly who to blame.

Pump Safety

Consider that an electronic fuel pump can move a lot of fuel. What would happen if you were to become involved in an accident and the fuel system became compromised? Obviously, turning the ignition off would be your first move, which would instantly disable the fuel pump. But sometimes our brains don't work like that in such a situation. Holley recommends the use of a simple pressure shutoff switch (PN 12-810) that can automatically disable the fuel pump if fuel pressure drops to below 5 psi. It can be wired to disconnect the trigger lead between the ECU and fuel pump relay or controller.

OEMs often use an inertia switch that disconnects power to the fuel pump in the event of a sudden impact. They're readily available and one could easily be wired to work with an aftermarket fuel system.

My dad taught me as a kid that any job worth doing is a job worth doing correctly. The fuel system is the heart of an EFI system so you mustn't take any shortcuts. If you do, you will certainly have problems and you risk damaging the fuel pump and possibly your engine. Why take that chance?

Ignition System Requirements

As discussed in Chapter 1, some aftermarket EFI systems also offer the ability to manage the engine timing (engine management). In my opinion, this is absolutely the way to go. The MSD Atomic system and other more expensive systems offer this

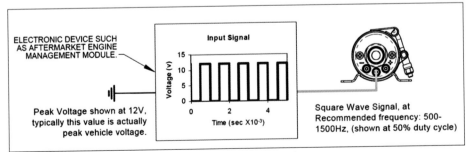

Fig. 2.14. Interfacing the PWM signal to the Fuelab Prodigy fuel pump is simple. (Illustration Courtesy Fuelab)

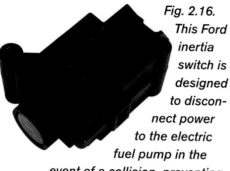

Fig. 2.16. This Ford inertia switch is designed to discon-nect power to the electric fuel pump in the event of a collision, preventing the fuel pump from pumping fuel. If the fuel pump continues to operate, a bad situation can turn into a really bad situation. The red button allows it to be reset in the event it has been tripped. Ford used these for years and they can be found in your local salvage yard (located just in front of the driver-side taillight assembly of Fox-Body Mustangs) on the cheap and easily interface it with your aftermarket fuel system.

Fig. 2.17. When converting to an EFI system that offers the ability to manage the timing, you need to choose ignition components that are compatible with the system to allow it to do so. I used these MSD components when converting the big-block Chevy in my Olds to EFI. An HEI-style distributor was required as I used the distributor to trigger the ECU as well (see Chapter 5 and Chapter 6 for more details).

feature. Managing fuel delivery and engine timing separately is an anti-quated idea, albeit a more afford-able one. Managing fuel delivery and engine timing simultaneously and electronically provides so much more tuning potential, which allows you to more easily achieve better drivability and performance.

Regardless of which path you choose, it's vital to understand the manufacturer's recommendation for lighting the fire in the cylinders. Some kits allow you to utilize some or all of your existing ignition com-ponents. Other kits require that you upgrade some or all of them. Even others, such as the Edelbrock Pro-Flo EFI kits, include a distributor as part of the equation. However, most kits require that you supply these com-ponents separately.

If you elect to go with a system that provides engine management, however, you need to eliminate all

Fig. 2.18. A crank trigger is an inexpensive way to get rock-solid timing. MSD offers kits for numerous applications. Shown here is their part (PN 8633) for small-block Chryslers (see Chapter 6 for more details). (Photo Courtesy MSD Performance)

outside influences on timing, such as centrifugal advance, vacuum advance, boost retard, nitrous retard, dash-mounted timing controls, etc. The ECU electronically manages the timing automatically based on all of these variables. If your distributor has centrifugal or vacuum advance, it may be as simple as locking these out. Also, if you're like most performance enthusiasts who use a stand-alone capacitive discharge (CD) ignition box for a hotter spark, you absolutely want to ensure that you select a kit that allows you to retain it.

In addition, this may be an excellent time to consider the triggering of the ignition system itself, either independently or via the ECU. Most common is the traditional method of allowing the distributor to manage this. However, it would be remiss of me not to mention that this is the time to consider a crank trigger. Several companies offer complete kits that are compatible with most EFI systems.

Running a crank trigger allows you to sidestep any slop in the timing chain and/or cam gear on the distributor. If you've fought a timing problem for whatever reason with your carbureted combination, you will fight it with the EFI system as well. Why not eliminate it altogether? The owner of the Olds Cutlass featured in Chapter 6 fought this problem for years. Converting to a crank trigger solved this problem once and for all.

Electrical System Requirements

If electrical isn't your strength, consider picking up a copy of my other books, *Automotive Wiring and Electrical Systems* and *Automotive Electrical Performance Projects* to supple-

ment this discussion. Look at it like this: The electrical system is the only system in the vehicle that can influence the performance of the others. If you have electrical problems that you've been "gonna get around to fixing," get to them before undertaking an EFI upgrade. You will avoid all the heartache associated with choosing to address this "if it becomes an issue." Trust me; it will.

I read many of the enthusiast automotive magazines, and all too often, readers have written to them when experiencing problems with their aftermarket EFI conversion. In many cases, the tech editor identified problems that were caused by electrical system inadequacies. It's amazing to me how many perfectly good fuel pumps are burned up by inadequate wiring and excessive voltage drop especially when you consider how clear the included manuals are in regards to their electrical requirements.

If you take nothing else from this chapter, recognize that an EFI system is a major investment. If you starve its components of the current they require to operate optimally, you run the risk of damaging the components themselves or even damaging your engine. At a minimum, you have one heck of a time getting the system to operate properly, let alone getting it to work optimally.

Choosing the wrong alternator is the number-one mistake enthusiasts make again and again. If you're making the conversion to EFI, you may also have to upgrade your alternator and possibly its wiring. You can easily (and definitely should) make this determination with your vehicle while it is in running state with the carburetor. I can't stress enough how important this is.

Depending on the system you choose, the ECU can require between 10 and 40 amps of current to do its job. In addition, the electric fuel pump can require between 10 and 30 amps of current. On the low side, this is a 20-amp increase in current requirements over a carbureted application with a mechanical fuel pump. Now, let me quantify that further. On the low side, this is a 20-amp increase in the current required of your alternator at idle (800 engine rpm).

Establish Size of Alternator

Here's the correct way to learn what size alternator you require after the upgrade:

1. Determine the maximum amount of current the system requires at 14.4 volts.
2. Determine the maximum amount of current the fuel pump requires at 14.4 volts.
3. Determine the maximum amount of current the ignition components require at 14.4 volts.
4. Determine how much current your existing vehicle accessories require at idle with the engine at operating temperature. (This process is outlined below.)
5. Add the above amounts together.

The ECU, fuel pump, and ignition components all require less current at idle than at 6,000 rpm, but that's okay. By using these worst-case-scenario numbers, you have a bit of a buffer, which prevents your alternator from working at 100 percent of its capacity at idle. The net result is a reduction in heat created by the alternator at idle, so it has a nice long life.

Why Connect to the Battery?

The instructions included with all aftermarket EFI systems I've seen direct you to connect both the main power and ground leads to the battery directly. Why is this? The answer is simple. Not only is the battery a convenient place to source power for a high-current accessory, such as an ECU, it's also the cleanest place in the vehicle to do so.

A battery has a tremendous amount of capacitance, and as a result, it is the single best filter in the vehicle's electrical system. One of its functions is to filter the "ripple" created by the alternator as it converts mechanical energy into AC voltage, which is internally rectified into DC voltage. Any measureable AC voltage that is present at the output stud of the alternator is referred to as ripple. In addition, inductive accessories, such as motors and pumps, create all kinds of "noise" on their power leads as they are turned on and off.

By connecting the power and ground leads of the ECU directly to the battery, you are taking full advantage of the battery's filtering capabilities, which minimizes the amount of ripple or other noise that is picked up by the ECU, which can affect its ability to do its job correctly.

Finally, always fuse *all* power leads that connect to the battery positive terminal directly within 18 inches of the battery. The fuse protects the cable in the event of a short, which could cause a fire. Most ECUs have a fuse on the harness near the ECU itself. In the case of MSD ignition boxes, they are fused internally. However, you still must fuse such devices at the battery. I typically fuse MSD 6-series ignition boxes with a 25A ATC fuse if it has 10-gauge wire and a 20A ATC fuse if it has 12-gauge wire. Fuse the ECU with the same size-fuse included on the harness. ■

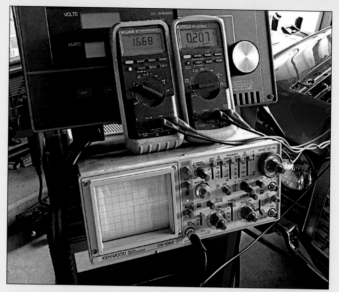

Ripple is defined as any AC voltage still present at the output of the alternator. On my Olds, I measured .207 volts AC with 16.68 volts DC of output (see Chapter 4 for the 14-volt conversion and you'll understand the 16-volt's). That translates to 1.2 percent of ripple and this can be seen on the scope, although it wasn't possible to capture this with the camera as the eye sees it in real time.

Don't sweat numbers 1, 2, and 3, because most manufacturers supply this information on their website in the specifications for the kits. For example, MSD specifies that their 6 series ignition boxes require 1 amp per 1,000 rpm. If you are unable to locate these numbers, I recommend that you contact their technical support department.

Determine Accessory Current Requirements

As I mentioned, it is to your advantage to make this determination with the vehicle in its presently running condition, carburetor and all. This provides a baseline to determine whether you need to upgrade your alternator as part of the conversion. To make this determination, you need access to these tools: a digital multimeter (DMM) to measure voltage at the battery (connect its probes directly to the battery terminals) and a second DMM and DC current clamp (or a stand-alone DC current clamp) to measure the output current of the alternator (install the current clamp around all wires connected to the charge stud).

Here is the basic procedure to get the readings:

1 Record the resting voltage of the battery with the engine not running.

2 Start the engine and bring the vehicle to operating temperature.

3 Turn on all of the accessories, including high-beam headlights, A/C, electric cooling fan(s), audio system at a common listening level, etc.

4 After the engine has reached operating temperature, record the voltage at the battery.

5 Record the output current of the alternator.

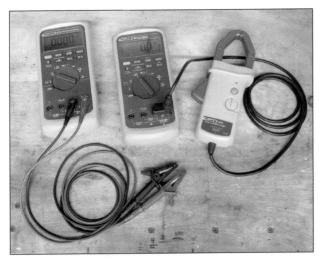

Fig. 2.19. Good-quality DMMs are vital to analyzing the performance from your charging system. Fluke 80-series meters have excellent data-acquisition capabilities as well. I've been using Fluke meters and accessories for nearly 25 years and have had excellent luck with them. (Photo Courtesy MSD Performance)

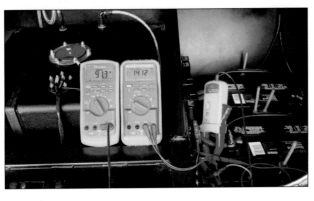

Fig. 2.20. You can quickly and easily determine the health of your charging system with two DMMs and a Hall effect DC ammeter accessory, such as the Fluke i410.

Think of this as a *state of health* for your charging system as my friend Todd Ramsey refers to it. If you don't have the above tools at your disposal, a qualified shop can perform this for you. This data is invaluable if you desire to have your new EFI system work as intended.

Now, keep in mind that a 12-volt battery is *really* a 12.6-volt battery because it has six 2.1-volt cells in series (2.1 x 6 = 12.6). As such, it should rest at a minimum of 12.6 volts with the engine not running and it requires a minimum of 13.4 volts when the vehicle is running to allow a charge from the alternator to flow into it.

A 12-volt battery resting below 12.6 volts is not fully charged. And, if during the running measurements (as outlined above), you recorded the voltage to be below 13.4 volts, your existing alternator isn't big enough for your vehicle in its present state, let alone adding the requirements of an EFI system. I run into this all the time, most commonly because of the addition of electric fans and fuel pumps.

Finally, it's important to know just how much current your alternator is capable of putting out at idle, defined as 800 engine rpm and 2,400 rpm, and at cruise, defined as 2,000 engine rpm and 6,000 alternator rpm. Your alternator should be fitted with a pulley that allows it to spin at three times the crankshaft speed for these measurements taken at operating temperature to be meaningful. To determine this, you have three choices.

One, ask the manufacturer of the alternator. This is actually the least accurate method as operating temperature is typically not factored in and some companies tend to exaggerate their output ratings by not taking this into account. Some do take that into account; you just have to ask.

Two, remove the alternator from the vehicle and take it to your local alternator shop to have this measured. This is far more accurate but operating temperature may still not be factored in during testing. Loading the alternator for a period of time to get it to an operating temperature approximating that of being in use in your vehicle and then measuring its output is the most accurate way to determine these figures.

Three, have a shop make these measurements with the alternator in the vehicle. This requires a charging system analyzer with a built-in carbon pile load. This is a very accurate way to determine this as operating temperature is factored in, but it's critical that engine RPM is kept as close to the specified RPM for each measurement as possible during the load testing, and this can be tricky.

If you'd like to learn more about exactly how your charging system really works, I have a great video on my YouTube channel called, "Charging Systems 101: How does your alternator and battery really work?"

Let's consider the MSD Atomic system as an example. On the manufacturer's website I found the following in their FAQ section:

Q: How much current is the total system capable of drawing?

A: If both fans are on, the fuel pump is at full capacity, the IAC is moving, the injectors are at their maximum, and the input voltage is around 10V (it can draw as much as 30 amps). Normal operation is approximately 14 to 18 amps.

Fig. 2.21. Snap-on AVR charging system analyzers are without peer. Shown here is my trusty MT3750. It has an internal 500-amp carbon pile load that can be used to load any alternator to check for in-vehicle performance. It's an invaluable tool that many well-equipped auto service centers have.

Calculating Alternator Output at Idle

Existing Current Requirements at Idle	64 amps
MSD Atomic EFI System	30 amps maximum
Electric Fuel Pump	included in the kit
CD Ignition System	1 amp per 1,000 rpm = 6 amps
Total	100 amps at idle

Fig. 2.22. Anytime you upgrade to an alternator with higher output, you should also upgrade the wiring. This includes the charge lead and the return path. CE Auto Electric Supply offers complete kits in 4 AWG (up to 150 amps), 2 AWG (up to 225 amps), and 1/0 AWG (up to 300 amps). The kits use full AWG-specification finely stranded and tinned copper cable, are easy to install, include all hardware required, and have complete full-color step-by-step instructions.

First, a correctly operating charging system should *never* be "around 10 volts," so you can see MSD has engineered this system to work to as low as 10 volts, assuming ahead of time that many enthusiasts' charging systems are woefully inadequate.

Second, the "both fans are on" reference does not take into account the actual current requirements of the fans themselves, just the drivers for the fan in the ECU. (Refer to "Calculating Alternator Output at Idle," left.)

If you purchased a 100A alternator, you're off to a bad start because depending on how it's designed, it may have far less output at idle than you really need. In addition, how much output does it really make at operating temp? About 15 percent less output at operating temperature is common, so I always recommend a 20-percent buffer.

This may mean that the maximum output rating of the alternator is 150 amps, which is well above the maximum current required. If you take into consideration a 15-percent loss in output at operating temperature, it gives you about 102 amps of maximum output at operating temperature at idle and 128 amps of maximum output at cruise. That's perfect.

Such an alternator requires a minimum of 4 AWG cable between its output stud and the battery, assuming the battery is under the hood and within 10 feet of the alternator. Cable size increases if the distance between the alternator and battery is greater, such as in vehicles with rear-mounted batteries.

Finally, the size of the charge lead is only half of the equation as the return path of the alternator needs to be similarly upgraded.

Properly Planning an EFI Installation

I was recently sent a referral from local engine builder Beck Racing Engines. Owner Frank Beck had sold a customer a 468 big-block Chevy and a FAST EZ-EFI system. This engine was installed into a gorgeous 1969 COPO Camaro clone. On the dyno, the engine made more than 630 hp. In the vehicle, it ran and performed terribly. So bad, in fact, that the owner was pretty frustrated with it.

I was called to see if the electrical system was up to snuff. The owner brought it by, and as he pulled it into the drive, I noted that the headlight on the passenger's side was not working. He said that he had trouble with his HID headlights and they worked intermittently at best. (This was a hint of things I would soon find.) Then he gave me the scoop on what was in the Camaro: a brand-new American Autowire Classic Update wiring harness, MSD Digital 6AL Pro-Billet distributor, tach adapter (so that he could use the stock tach in the cluster), March drive system (serpentine style), and an Aeromotive fuel system with 11140 Stealth EFI fuel pump (in the tank).

I noticed a few general problems with the underhood electrical wiring, such as poor grounding, lack of proper grounding, and possible undersized charge lead. Considering the poor connections and workmanship in general, I felt it best to perform the "state of health" measurements. The results were not good:

- Resting voltage of the battery with the engine not running: 12.28 volts

- Voltage at the battery at idle, at operating temperature, all accessories on: 12.80 volts
- Output current of the alternator at idle, at operating temperature, all accessories on: 95 amps

I explained to the owner that 12.80 volts were well short of the voltage required to keep the battery charged and operate the accessories, hence the low resting voltage of the battery when the engine wasn't running. He said that he just replaced the battery and couldn't figure out why his other one wouldn't stay charged. I also explained to him that 95 amps was too much for the existing charge lead to support, as it was 10 AWG. As the charge lead was too small, I was unable to make a determination as to whether the alternator was up to the task, so that had to wait for later. He took me for a quick ride, which confirmed that the vehicle ran terribly. He left me the keys: time to dig in.

First, I measured the parasitic draw on the battery at 25 mA (milliamperes) with the vehicle and all accessories off, which is well within reason. I typically measure parasitic draw before I start on a project like this, especially because the owner mentioned that the battery had already been replaced.

Frank always says, "The more you look, the more you find," and that was certainly the case with this Camaro. A quick inspection of the fuel system showed that the regulator was installed in a good location (although it wouldn't pass tech at the local drag strip because it's on the firewall), the feed and return lines

were of the appropriate size, and the tank was vented. I researched the fuel pump and determined it was adequate to supply the horsepower this combination makes.

The ignition system didn't fare so well because the ignition box was shoved behind the heater ductwork on the interior side of the firewall and nearly impossible to access. It and the tach adapter were mounted with velcro and both had pulled loose. This left the box and tach adapter hanging on by their wiring only, which is absolutely unacceptable in any vehicle, let alone one with 630 hp under the hood.

I was unable to access the ECU for the EFI because it was mounted above the glove compartment and short wired.

Charging System Repairs

On the surface, I had assumed that I'd be making the following repairs and upgrades, mainly to get the charging system performing correctly, as well as address the ignition system shortcomings: upgrade the wiring and return path for the alternator; properly ground the engine, ignition system, and chassis; and relocate the ignition box and correctly mount the tach adapter.

In addition, it was obvious that the headlight and engine harnesses (part of the brand-new American Autowire harness) needed some work (correct routing, terminations, etc.) because there were numerous splices and the work was generally sloppy. But the more I dug in, the more I found. And wow! This Camaro was a mess.

Fig. 2.23. This 1969 COPO Camaro clone is sweet! Too bad the electrical system was an afterthought, which is all too common. Not only was it not up to the task of basic vehicle functionality, the aftermarket EFI system was simply unable to work correctly as the vehicle was wired.

In addition, most of the harness for the EFI system was located between the firewall and the passenger-side cylinder head. The small length of harness inside the vehicle was virtually impossible to unplug from the ECU, even after I had removed the glove compartment. As a result, a large portion of the main EFI harness was relocated to correct this.

After a quick phone call to the owner to let him know approximately how long it would take to make these repairs, I was underway.

Fig. 2.24. This is some of the poor work that I uncovered as I repaired the electrical system in the Camaro. Correctly routing cables through this grommet after the fact proved to be quite difficult, but I was able to do so and salvage the grommet.

Fig. 2.25 As delivered, the ECU was located above the glove box. It was short wired so near the firewall I wasn't even able to photograph it. The bulk of the ECU harness, which I pulled out, was found tucked behind the passenger-side cylinder head. I will use this length to find a more accessible place to mount and access the ECU.

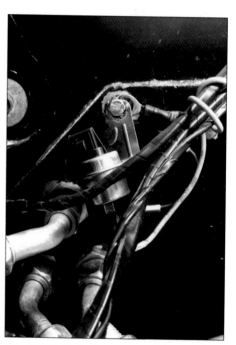

Fig. 2.26. Note the ground lugs behind the mounting bracket, which is mounted to the block-off plate for the aftermarket A/C system, which is sealed to the firewall with caulk. Not only is this a poor ground location, the lugs were so loose that you could spin them around by hand. As if that weren't bad enough, the ECU and MSD Digital 6AL were grounded via the same lug. The ECU and ignition box require separate grounds to operate properly.

Major Repairs Performed

- Remove and relocate the MSD ignition box, including repairing and re-routing the main harness, replacing the magnetic trigger harness to the distributor (the original was shortened), and repairing and extending the main power and ground leads.

- Relocate a large portion of the main EFI harness, including re-routing the harness to the oxygen sensor (passing it through the floor by the firewall), repairing and extending the harness to the fuel pump relay (this was cut unnecessarily short), and repairing and extending the power and ground leads directly to the battery, as directed in the instructions.

- Correctly wire the fuel pump, which involved installing a correct-size waterproof relay (I only use waterproof relays for underhood applications), running the correct-size wire to the fuel pump (I removed a 14-gauge unprotected wire and installed 10-gauge in split-loom tubing per the manufacturer's recommendation), and correctly grounding the fuel pump, also with 10-gauge, as this was done prior with 18 AWG (the last two steps included dropping the fuel tank which was full).

- Correctly wire the cooling fans (same as the fuel pump).

- Wire the alternator with the correct-size cable and upgrade its return path.

- Correctly ground the engine, ignition system, and chassis.

- Build new battery cables specific to this application.

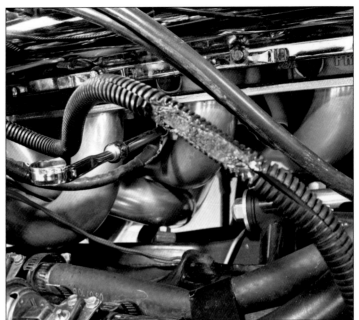

Fig. 2.27. The oxygen-sensor harness wasn't tied up properly and was damaged by the headers. Luckily, the wiring inside the harness wasn't yet damaged. I re-routed this harness through a different location in the firewall to keep it out of harm's way.

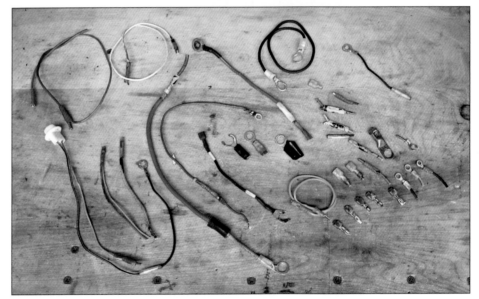

Fig. 2.28. Repairing the underhood wiring in this Camaro was a big job. I couldn't find a single example of a proper termination and the incorrect tools were used throughout. Even though the owner sprang for a brand-new American Autowire harness, the installer cut corners every chance he could to install it. The box of "extra parts" the owner supplied to me contained almost enough parts to do the job correctly.

- Add an auxiliary fuse panel to facilitate the ECU, ignition box, and fuel pump and fan relays.

- Repair, re-route, and correctly terminate the engine and headlight harnesses.

All but the last repair had a direct impact on the operation of the EFI system and fuel delivery. I kept as much of the electrical harnesses and components hidden from view to the casual onlooker as possible.

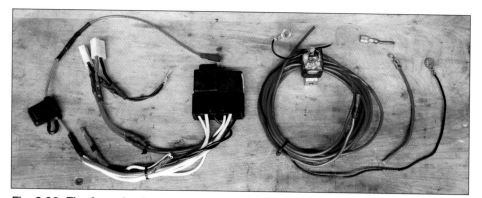

Fig. 2.29. The fan relay is on the left. Note the pair of mismatched relays in pre-assembled 14 AWG (too small!) sockets, a plethora of butt connectors, and the 18 AWG (way too small!) ground leads for the fans. The fuel pump relay wiring is on the right. Note the green corrosion on the relay; it was mounted upside down and got wet. Also note the 14 AWG wiring to the pump and 18-gauge pump ground. Man, oh man, this is among the worst jobs I've ever seen.

Fig. 2.30. Here is the fuel pump relay. It ultimately took out the fuel pump driver in the ECU, so the installer hardwired it to work when the key was in the ignition position. We sent the ECU back to FAST and had the driver repaired.

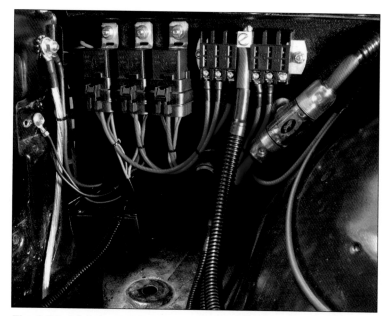

Fig. 2.32. I fabricated a 4-AWG charge lead to replace the 10-AWG charge lead, which was woefully inadequate. This custom cable had the correct end for the alternator. I also mounted an ANL-style fuse holder nearby (at the lower left) to act as a fusible link for the charge lead.

Fig. 2.31. I fabricated a power center of ABS plastic to fit inside the passenger-side fender (see also Figure 4.8 on page 61). The power center contains waterproof relays for the fans and fuel pump (wired with 10-AWG TXL), an ATC fuse panel, the fuse holder for the audio system, and a junction stud to connect the power feed for the wiring harness. Note the upgraded grounding to the core support. Clean, orderly, and serviceable.

Fig. 2.33. I made another ABS mounting bracket for the MSD Digital 6AL ignition Box, which is bolted to the driver-side fender.

Fig 2.34. The box bolts up inside the inner fender and out of sight as the owner wanted but the plug is easily accessed and removed if needed.

Fig. 2.35. It took some time to be able to use the existing hacked-up grommet and get it installed in the firewall connector with all of the harnesses passing safely through it.

Fig. 2.36. I mounted a small fuse panel behind the brake booster. This supplies switched power to the ignition box, tach adapter, and the switched side of the coil for the fuel pump relay.

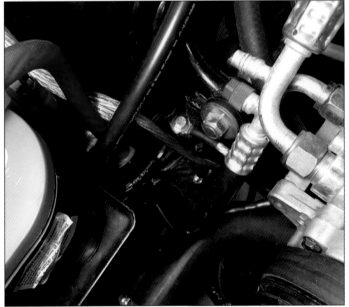

Fig. 2.37. The owner wanted to keep as much of the power and ground cabling from the battery as out of sight as possible. I located a power distribution block below and along the frame rail to connect the battery, alternator, junction stud, and auxiliary fuse panel. I drilled and tapped holes for number-6 sheet-metal screws to attach it to the frame rail. Also note the ground location on the frame rail by the control arm. This location is the point of commonality for the battery ground, alternator ground, and core support ground. The battery is also grounded to the block to provide a solid return path for the starter.

Fig. 2.38. As the owner requested, the battery cables are nice and simple. I added the boots for a finished look. The boots are easily slid down the cables should he need to jump-start the vehicle for any reason.

Three Major Problems

- The fuel pump output of the ECU had been damaged in the original installation (its output was tied directly to ground) so I temporarily wired around it to get the fuel pump working with the key in the IGN/RUN position.

- The oxygen sensor was located in the exhaust downstream of the collector/exhaust junction and there was a noticeable exhaust leak at the collector gasket. This major problem must be repaired before any WOT driving can be attempted as such a leak could allow unmetered air to enter and cause the oxygen sensor to provide incorrect feedback to the ECU.

Fig. 2.39. This is the engine compartment after fixing all the wiring and electrical issues. The interior of this Camaro needs the same amount of attention. After my work was done, we were able to get this Camaro running correctly in very short order.

- The power and ground leads for the FAST ECU were tied together with the power and ground leads of the MSD Digital 6AL. This alone is a no-no as a CD ignition box is a noisy beast by the nature of its design and purpose. To make matters worse, the power leads were tied to the battery terminal on the starter, and the ground leads shoved under the switch mounting bracket on the block-off panel for the aftermarket A/C on the firewall: a terrible place to ground anything, let alone the ECU.

Repair Results

After the repairs were made, it was time for more measurements:

- Resting voltage of the battery with the engine not running: 12.4 volts
- Voltage at the battery at idle, at operating temp, all accessories on: 13.85 to 14.00 volts
- Output current of the alternator at idle, at operating temp, all accessories on: 63 amps

The Parasitic draw remained unchanged at 25 mA. I put the battery on a charger before re-installing it. After the surface charge is depleted, it rests at only 12.4 volts, which is an indication that it has been compromised already. This battery may have to be replaced in the near future.

Notice the dramatic change in operating voltage with the engine running, with more than enough to charge the battery and operate all accessories. I was surprised to see that the output current of the alternator decreased as much as it did.

In this case, I believe this is a direct result of the charge lead being so inadequately sized. The fact is that the alternator is a one-wire design, and it senses voltage off its charge stud. I'd be willing to bet the alternator was at full capacity trying to overcome a problem it would never be able to.

Project Wrap-Up

After I made the repairs outlined above, Frank came by and we did an hour or so of idle/off idle/tip-in learning via the FAST handheld controller. When the owner came by to pick up the car, he and I took it for a drive and it was *way* different. It broke the tires loose on even the hint of throttle application. The engine also had a sinister tone, which was far more representative of its horsepower.

The Camaro now required a lot of drive time or chassis dyno time so that the ECU could get itself back to where it was on the engine dyno in a controlled environment.

It became apparent that the ECU had been working overtime trying to correct things that didn't need to be corrected. This was most likely a direct result of the fuel pump wiring, which inhibited it from performing optimally. As I mentioned before, the oxygen sensor also needed to be relocated before any WOT tuning could be done.

The owner left happy, and first thing the following day shipped the ECU back to FAST to have its fuel pump output repaired. Once that is back in, it'll be time for some tuning on the engine dyno. After that, it's back to me to get the rest of the wiring harness installed correctly . . . Oh, my goodness . . .

I think it's worth pointing out that this Camaro exemplifies some of the conversations that tech support departments have with customers every day. The electrical problems I uncovered in this Camaro were serious enough to cause premature failure of the alternator, fuel pump, battery (the first one failed, the second was well on its way), ECU, and possibly even damage the engine. In addition, given how the electric fans were originally wired, engine overheating was a real concern in the hot Phoenix summer.

I found no fault with the FAST system, the MSD components, the Aeromotive components, the March alternator, or even the HID headlights. The only fault was the way these components were installed.

The owner took the Camaro to have it fine-tuned and has been driving and enjoying it for some time. The alternator failed after only a few months of service and had to be replaced. We replaced it with a BILLET-TECH 170-amp unit from Mechman, which is similar to the unit we installed on the 1970 Olds Cutlass in Chapter 6 (see Figure 6.9 on page 101). I still see no reason to blame the alternator itself, as it was improperly installed and in service that way for far too long. This undoubtedly shortened its life.

It is so important to follow the manufacturer's instructions explicitly. You really should read the included manuals from cover to cover before beginning any installation. The manuals provided by FAST, MSD, and others include comprehensive installation instructions written, in some cases, by the engineers that design the products. If you follow them, you will achieve the performance the product is capable of.

CHAPTER 3

EFI T*uning* B*asics*

Tuning can be an intimidating topic and the verbiage tossed around difficult to comprehend. So, let's get you familiar with it. You may ask, "Why should I learn any more than I need to know if I am converting to EFI anyway?" Quite simply, this is one of those topics that you simply can't know enough about. Since most EFI systems put the power to tune in the palm of your hand, you really should know what you're doing before pressing buttons. And guess what? It really isn't that hard.

This chapter gives you a good understanding of the basics and introduces you to some of the vocabulary that accompanies engine tuning. For an in-depth study on EFI tuning, pick up a copy of *Engine Management: Advanced Tuning* by Greg Banish.

Air/Fuel Ratio

Stoichiometry is the chemistry that defines the relationship between the air and fuel in an engine. Metering the correct mass of fuel based on the mass of the air entering a given engine is the primary job of any EFI system. Numerous factors determine the correct air/fuel (A/F) ratio,

Stoichiometry of Fuels			
Fuel Type	Richer	Stoic	Leaner
Gasoline	< 14.7:1	14.7:1	> 14.7:1
Ethanol	< 9:1	9:1	> 9:1
E85	< 9.87:1	9.87:1	> 9.87:1
Methanol	< 6.47:1	6.47:1	> 6.47:1
Propane	< 15.67:1	15.67:1	> 15.67:1

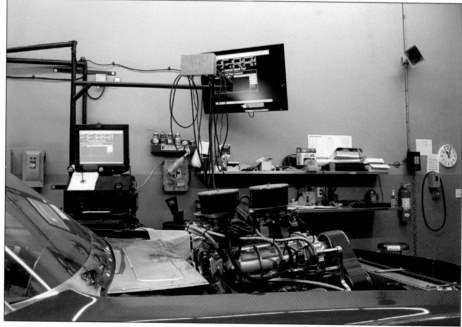

Fig. 3.1. Tuning the more advanced EFI systems with a laptop is actually quite simple. You'll be pleasantly surprised at just how much control you have at your fingertips and how quickly you can make changes in an effort to fine-tune your combination. In my Olds, the laptop has had a lot of seat time. It goes without saying that you should only look at the screen or make changes when you're stopped.

including fuel type, engine load, and engine efficiency.

Fuel Type

Different types of fuels have different ideal A/F ratios. An ideal A/F ratio with a given fuel means that the exact mass of air is flowing into the engine to burn 100 percent of the fuel in the combustion chamber. This is often referred to as stoichiometric or stoic.

Engine Load

As you drive around, the engine has various loads placed on it. Some are easy, some are more difficult and changes in MAP accurately reflect this. As MAP increases (measured in inches of mercury or kPa), a richer mixture is needed. The opposite is true as MAP decreases.

Any true performance car should have a vacuum gauge visible from the driver's seat so that you can gain an understanding of how your particular engine responds to loads placed on it as you drive around.

Engine Efficiency

For naturally aspirated engines, maximum efficiency is achieved at

3 to 5 percent leaner than stoic, and maximum power is achieved at 10 to 15 percent richer than stoic. Precisely where is specific to the engine combination and the types of loads it is subjected to.

Lambda

For a given fuel, the relationship to a given A/F ratio with respect to its stoic ratio is defined as *Lambda* and can be expressed by the Greek letter λ. For example, consider the chart below.

So, Lambda is just a simple way of comparing actual A/F ratio with a given fuel's stoichiometric value. This can be really handy when using a wideband A/F meter to determine the actual A/F ratio and then using that data to make changes in the Target Air/Fuel Ratio Table in the software (see Chapter 6 for more details).

Interestingly enough, the British refer to oxygen sensors as Lambda probes.

Ignition Timing

Igniting the A/F mixture in each of the cylinders is the job of the ignition system. In a four-stroke

engine (intake, compression, power, exhaust), ignition occurs after the intake stroke and during the compression stroke before the piston reaches top dead center (TDC). As the mixture burns, force is exerted on the piston, forcing it down in the cylinder (the power stroke), rotating the crankshaft, and creating torque in the process.

Ignition timing is a measure of degrees before top dead center (BTDC) at which the spark event occurs. For example, 34 degrees of timing means that the spark event occurs in the first cylinder in the firing order at 34 degrees BTDC.

Let's be a little more specific and include valve events so that you get the complete picture of the beauty of the internal combustion engine. Valve timing is a function of the camshaft, which makes one complete revolution for every two revolutions of the crankshaft. The specifics of the camshaft determine when the intake and exhaust valves open and close with respect to the location of the piston in the cylinder.

Intake Stroke: Intake Valve Open

The piston moves downward in the cylinder with the intake valve open. As the piston moves downward in the cylinder, the pressure in the cylinder is lower than the pressure in the intake manifold. This causes the A/F mixture in the manifold to enter the cylinder.

Compression Stroke: Intake and Exhaust Valves Closed

After reaching bottom dead center (BDC), the piston then travels upward in the cylinder compressing the A/F mixture in the process. At some point before the piston reaches TDC, the spark plug ignites the mixture.

Fuel	Stoichiometric A/F Ratio (:1)	Actual A/F Ratio (:1)	Lambda (λ)
Gasoline	14.70	15.88	1.08
		14.99	1.02
		14.70	1.00
		13.52	.92
		12.79	.87
		12.05	.82
E85	9.87	10.66	1.08
		10.07	1.02
		9.87	1.00
		9.08	.92
		8.59	.87
		8.09	.82

The spark must be timed so that the piston is forced downward by the pressure created by the burning mixture. If the spark occurs too soon, incredible pressure is exerted on the top of the piston because it hasn't finished the compression stroke; the burning mixture is working to force it in the opposite direction. This causes detonation (which sounds like marbles in a tin can) and is a recipe for the death of any internal combustion engine. If the spark occurs too late, power is lost.

Power Stroke: Intake and Exhaust Valves Closed

After the mixture has been ignited, it begins to burn. As the burn spreads in the cylinder, the cylinder pressure rises quickly and forces the piston downward in the cylinder. When the piston is forced down in the cylinder, it rotates the crankshaft, producing torque.

Exhaust Stroke: Exhaust Valve Open

After the piston reaches BDC on the power stroke, it returns to TDC on the exhaust stroke with the exhaust valve open. As the piston moves upward in the cylinder, it forces the spent gases from combustion out the exhaust valve and into the exhaust system.

Repeat. What a thing of beauty!

Timing Variables

Exactly when the mixture is ignited *while* the piston is on the compression stroke is a function with many variables, including octane rating of the fuel, combustion chamber volume and design, piston type, cylinder head specifics, compression, load on the engine, and economy versus performance.

Let's discuss only octane rating, load on the engine, and economy versus performance and leave the others to the engine builders.

Octane Rating: Different fuels have different octane ratings. Lower-octane fuels are easier to ignite than higher-octane fuels. This goes against conventional wisdom, doesn't

Base Fuel Table

All ECUs have a Base Fuel Table, even if it isn't user accessible. The Base Fuel Table stores all of the data regarding the actual fuel required to achieve the values set in the Target Air/Fuel Ratio Table. The Base Fuel Table is the primary means of determining how much fuel is injected into the engine at a given RPM at a given MAP. The numerical values in the cells of the fuel table equate to pounds of fuel per hour (lbs/hr). ∎

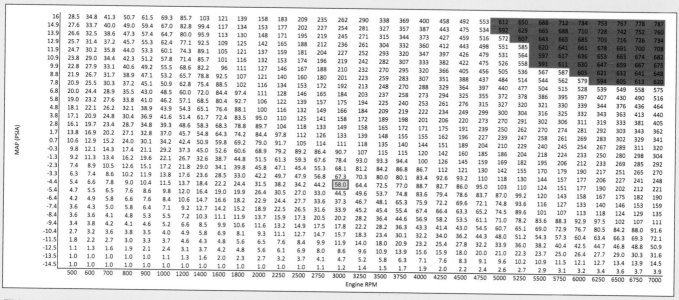

MAP (PSIA)	500	600	700	800	900	1000	1200	1400	1600	1800	2000	2250	2500	2750	3000	3250	3500	3750	4000	4250	4500	4750	5000	5250	5500	5750	6000	6250	6500	6750	7000
16	28.5	34.8	41.3	50.7	61.5	69.3	85.7	103	121	139	158	183	209	235	262	290	338	369	400	458	492	553	612	650	688	712	734	753	767	778	787
14.9	27.6	33.7	40.0	49.0	59.4	67.0	82.8	99.4	117	134	153	177	202	227	254	281	327	357	387	443	475	534	592	629	665	688	710	728	742	752	760
13.9	26.6	32.5	38.6	47.3	57.4	64.7	80.0	95.9	113	130	148	171	195	219	245	271	315	344	373	427	459	516	572	607	643	665	685	703	716	726	734
12.9	25.7	31.4	37.2	45.7	55.3	62.4	77.1	92.5	109	125	142	165	188	212	236	261	304	332	360	412	443	498	551	585	620	641	661	678	691	700	708
11.9	24.7	30.2	35.8	44.0	53.3	60.1	74.3	89.1	105	121	137	159	181	204	227	252	293	320	347	397	426	479	531	564	597	617	636	653	665	674	682
10.9	23.8	29.0	34.4	42.3	51.2	57.8	71.4	85.7	101	116	132	153	174	196	219	242	282	307	333	382	422	475	526	558	591	611	630	647	659	667	675
9.9	22.8	27.9	33.1	40.6	49.2	55.5	68.6	82.2	96	111	127	146	167	188	210	232	270	295	320	366	405	456	505	536	567	587	605	621	632	641	648
8.8	21.9	26.7	31.7	38.9	47.1	53.2	65.7	78.8	92.5	107	121	140	160	180	201	223	259	283	307	351	388	437	484	514	544	562	579	594	605	613	620
7.8	20.9	25.5	30.3	37.2	45.1	50.9	62.8	75.4	88.5	102	116	134	153	172	192	213	248	270	288	329	364	397	440	477	504	515	528	539	549	558	575
6.8	20.0	24.4	28.9	35.5	43.0	48.5	60.0	72.0	84.4	97.4	111	128	146	165	184	203	237	258	273	294	325	355	372	378	386	395	397	407	430	490	516
5.8	19.0	23.2	27.6	33.8	41.0	46.2	57.1	68.5	80.4	92.7	106	122	139	157	175	194	225	240	253	261	276	315	327	320	321	330	339	344	376	436	464
4.8	18.1	22.1	26.2	32.1	38.9	43.9	54.3	65.1	76.4	88.1	100	116	132	149	166	184	209	219	222	234	249	299	300	304	316	325	332	343	363	413	440
3.8	17.1	20.9	24.8	30.4	36.9	41.6	51.4	61.7	72.4	83.5	95.0	110	125	141	158	172	189	198	201	206	220	273	270	291	302	306	311	319	333	381	405
2.8	16.1	19.7	23.4	28.7	34.8	39.3	48.6	58.3	68.3	78.8	89.7	104	118	133	149	158	165	172	171	175	191	239	250	262	270	274	281	292	303	343	362
1.7	13.8	16.9	20.2	27.1	32.8	37.0	45.7	54.8	64.3	74.2	84.4	97.8	112	126	133	139	148	155	155	162	196	227	239	247	258	261	269	283	302	329	341
0.7	10.6	12.9	15.2	24.0	30.1	34.2	42.4	50.9	59.8	69.2	79.0	91.7	105	114	111	118	135	140	144	151	189	204	210	229	240	245	254	267	289	311	320
-0.3	9.8	12.1	14.3	17.4	21.1	29.2	37.3	45.0	52.6	60.6	68.9	79.2	89.2	86.4	90.7	107	115	115	120	142	160	185	186	204	218	224	233	250	280	298	304
-1.3	9.2	11.3	13.4	16.2	19.6	22.1	26.7	32.6	38.7	44.8	51.5	61.3	59.3	67.6	78.4	93.0	93.3	94.4	100	126	145	159	169	182	195	206	212	233	269	285	292
-2.3	7.4	8.9	10.5	12.6	15.1	17.2	21.8	29.0	34.1	39.8	45.8	47.1	45.4	55.3	68.1	81.2	84.2	86.8	86.7	112	121	130	142	155	170	179	190	217	251	265	270
-3.3	6.3	7.4	8.6	10.2	11.9	13.8	17.6	23.6	28.5	33.0	42.2	47.9	56.8	67.3	70.3	80.0	80.1	83.4	92.6	93.2	110	118	130	144	157	177	190	206	227	241	248
-4.4	5.4	6.6	7.8	9.0	10.4	11.5	13.7	18.4	22.2	24.4	31.5	38.2	34.2	44.2	58.0	64.4	72.5	77.0	88.7	82.7	86.0	95.0	103	110	124	151	177	190	202	212	221
-5.4	4.7	5.5	6.5	7.6	8.6	9.8	12.0	16.4	19.0	19.9	26.4	30.5	27.0	33.0	44.5	49.6	53.7	74.8	83.6	79.4	78.6	83.7	87.0	99.2	120	143	158	167	175	182	190
-6.4	4.2	4.9	5.8	6.6	7.6	8.4	10.6	14.7	16.6	18.2	22.9	24.4	27.7	33.6	37.3	46.7	48.1	65.3	75.9	72.2	69.6	72.1	74.8	93.6	116	127	133	140	146	153	159
-7.4	3.6	4.3	5.0	5.8	6.4	7.1	9.2	12.7	14.2	15.2	18.9	22.5	26.5	31.6	33.9	45.2	45.4	55.4	67.4	66.4	63.3	65.2	74.5	89.6	101	107	113	118	124	129	135
-8.4	3.6	3.6	4.1	4.8	5.3	5.5	7.2	10.3	11.1	11.9	13.7	15.9	17.3	20.5	20.2	28.2	36.4	44.6	56.9	58.2	53.5	61.1	71.0	78.2	83.6	88.3	92.9	97.5	102	107	111
-9.4	3.4	3.8	4.2	4.1	4.6	5.2	6.6	8.5	9.9	10.6	11.6	13.2	14.9	17.5	17.8	22.2	28.2	36.3	43.3	41.4	43.0	54.5	50.7	65.1	69.0	72.9	76.7	80.5	84.2	88.0	91.6
-10.4	2.7	3.2	3.6	3.8	3.5	4.0	4.9	5.8	6.9	8.1	9.3	11.1	12.7	14.7	15.7	18.3	23.4	30.1	32.2	34.0	36.2	44.3	48.0	51.2	54.3	57.3	60.4	63.4	66.3	69.3	72.1
-11.5	1.8	2.2	2.7	3.0	3.3	3.7	4.6	4.3	4.8	5.6	6.5	7.6	8.4	9.9	11.9	14.0	18.0	20.9	23.2	25.4	27.8	32.3	33.9	36.0	38.2	40.4	42.5	44.7	46.8	48.8	50.9
-12.5	1.1	1.3	1.6	1.9	2.1	2.4	3.1	3.7	4.2	4.8	5.6	6.1	6.9	8.0	8.6	9.6	10.9	13.9	15.6	15.9	18.0	20.0	21.0	22.3	23.7	25.0	26.4	27.7	29.0	30.3	31.6
-13.5	1.0	1.0	1.0	1.0	1.0	1.0	1.3	1.6	2.0	2.3	2.7	3.2	3.7	4.1	4.7	5.2	5.8	6.3	7.1	7.6	8.3	9.1	9.6	10.2	10.9	11.5	12.1	12.7	13.4	13.9	14.5
-14.5	1.0	1.0	1.0	1.0	1.0	1.0	1.0	1.0	1.0	1.0	1.0	1.0	1.0	1.1	1.2	1.4	1.5	1.7	1.9	2.0	2.2	2.4	2.6	2.7	2.9	3.1	3.2	3.4	3.6	3.7	3.9

Engine RPM

This is the Base Fuel Table from the tune in my Olds. The values in each cell equate to the amount of fuel in pounds per hour (lbs/hr) the engine requires, based on RPM versus MAP. The red cells at the upper right indicate an area that falls outside the area the fuel injectors can safely cover. It's something to keep in mind should I ever elect to take it down the track.

it? For example, premium gas in the state of Arizona has an octane rating of 91 while E85 has an octane rating of between 100 and 110 depending on who you ask. Kind of easy to see why E85 has gained so much attention by hot rodders now, huh?

Fuels with lower octane ratings, such as regular gas, require less ignition timing to complete the burn while fuels with higher octane ratings, such as premium gas, require more ignition timing to complete the burn. If you pay the extra money for premium fuel, your engine should have additional timing in it to take advantage of the extra horsepower that can be gained from using it.

Load on the Engine: As the load on the engine increases, less timing is required to ignite the mixture. This is due to the increased pressure in the cylinder.

Economy versus Performance: The best engine tuners are able to create a timing curve for a particular application that allows the engine to burn the maximum percentage of the mixture with respect to RPM and MAP. The greater the percentage of the mixture that is burned, the greater the efficiency of the engine. This is a function of the A/F ratio, RPM, and the load on the engine. The beauty of any EFI system that performs fuel metering and ignition timing is that you can quickly modify the A/F ratio and timing with respect to each other in an effort to quickly achieve the highest efficiency.

Operating Mode and Sensors

All but the most basic ECUs can operate in one of two modes: closed loop or open loop. While in closed loop, the ECU can also be set to learn. Let's discuss these each in detail.

Closed Loop

When the ECU is operating in closed loop, it uses the feedback provided from the oxygen sensor(s) to make changes to the Base Fuel Table to achieve the values in the Target Air/Fuel Ratio Table (hereafter referred to as the A/F targets). Changes are either adding or removing fuel and factored as percentages.

Closed-Loop Learning

The Learn function is a powerful tool when the ECU is operating in closed loop. Quite simply, when Learn is enabled in laptop-tunable ECUs, the percentage differences are stored in the Learn Table (typically a read-only table). As the vehicle is

Target Air/Fuel Ratio Table

All ECUs also have a Target Air/Fuel Ratio Table. This table stores the targets for the A/F mixture at a given RPM at a given MAP. Some ECUs permit user control over the entire table, others permit only setup by the user (i.e., set the Target Air/Fuel Ratios for idle, cruise, and WOT and the ECU does the rest). ∎

MAP (PSIA)	500	700	900	1200	1600	2000	2500	3000	3500	4000	4500	5000	5500	6000	6500	7000
16	11.0	11.0	11.0	11.0	11.0	11.0	11.0	11.0	11.0	11.0	11.0	11.0	11.0	11.0	11.0	11.0
13.9	11.2	11.2	11.2	11.2	11.2	11.2	11.2	11.2	11.2	11.2	11.2	11.2	11.2	11.2	11.2	11.2
11.9	11.2	11.2	11.2	11.2	11.2	11.2	11.2	11.2	11.2	11.2	11.2	11.2	11.2	11.2	11.2	11.2
9.9	11.2	11.2	11.2	11.2	11.2	11.2	11.2	11.2	11.2	11.2	11.2	11.2	11.2	11.2	11.2	11.2
7.8	11.2	11.2	11.2	11.2	11.2	11.2	11.2	11.2	11.2	11.2	11.2	11.2	11.2	11.2	11.2	11.2
5.8	12.2	11.8	11.8	11.8	11.8	11.8	11.8	11.8	11.8	11.8	11.8	11.8	11.8	11.8	11.8	12.2
3.8	12.4	12.0	12.0	12.0	12.0	12.0	12.0	12.0	12.0	12.0	12.0	12.0	12.0	12.0	12.0	12.4
1.7	12.6	12.1	12.1	12.1	12.1	12.1	12.1	12.1	12.1	12.1	12.1	12.1	12.1	12.1	12.1	12.6
-0.3	13.1	12.5	12.5	12.5	12.5	12.5	12.5	12.5	12.5	12.5	12.5	12.5	12.5	12.5	12.5	13.1
-2.3	13.3	13.7	13.7	13.7	13.7	13.7	13.7	13.7	13.7	13.7	13.7	13.7	13.7	13.7	13.7	13.3
-4.4	13.5	14.2	14.2	14.2	14.2	14.2	14.2	14.2	14.2	14.2	14.2	14.2	14.2	14.2	14.2	13.5
-6.4	13.8	14.7	14.7	14.7	14.7	14.7	14.7	14.7	14.7	14.7	14.7	14.7	14.7	14.7	14.7	13.8
-8.4	14.0	14.7	14.7	14.7	14.7	14.7	14.7	14.7	14.7	14.7	14.7	14.7	14.7	14.7	14.7	14.0
-10.4	14.2	14.7	14.7	14.7	14.7	14.7	14.7	14.7	14.7	14.7	14.7	14.7	14.7	14.7	14.7	14.2
-12.5	14.5	14.7	14.7	14.7	14.7	14.7	14.7	14.7	14.7	14.7	14.7	14.7	14.7	14.7	14.7	14.5
-14.5	14.7	14.7	14.7	14.7	14.7	14.7	14.7	14.7	14.7	14.7	14.7	14.7	14.7	14.7	14.7	14.7

Engine RPM

This Target Air/Fuel Ratio Table is from the tune in my Olds. This table drives the values stored in the Learn Table based on the values stored in the Base Fuel Table.

Learn Table

The Learn Table is a record of changes made to the Base Fuel Table to achieve the values set in the Target Air/Fuel Ratio Table as the system self-tunes. The Learn Table is a user-viewable table in most laptop-tunable ECUs, but not something that can be viewed with entry-level EFI systems. ∎

MAP (PSIA) / Engine RPM

MAP (PSIA)	500	600	700	800	900	1000	1200	1400	1600	1800	2000	2250	2500	2750	3000	3250	3500	3750	4000	4250	4500	4750	5000	5250	5500	5750	6000	6250	6500	6750	7000
16	0.0	0.0	0.0	0.0	0.0	0.0	0.0	0.0	0.0	0.0	0.0	0.0	0.0	0.0	0.0	0.0	0.0	0.0	0.0	0.0	0.0	0.0	0.0	0.0	0.0	0.0	0.0	0.0	0.0	0.0	0.0
14.9	0.0	0.0	0.0	0.0	0.0	0.0	0.0	0.0	0.0	0.0	0.0	0.0	0.0	0.0	0.0	0.0	0.0	0.0	0.0	0.0	0.0	0.0	0.0	0.0	0.0	0.0	0.0	0.0	0.0	0.0	0.0
13.9	0.0	0.0	0.0	0.0	0.0	0.0	0.0	0.0	0.0	0.0	0.0	0.0	0.0	0.0	0.0	0.0	0.0	0.0	0.0	0.0	0.0	0.0	0.0	0.0	0.0	0.0	0.0	0.0	0.0	0.0	0.0
12.9	0.0	0.0	0.0	0.0	0.0	0.0	0.0	0.0	0.0	0.0	0.0	0.0	0.0	0.0	0.0	0.0	0.0	0.0	0.0	0.0	0.0	0.0	0.0	0.0	0.0	0.0	0.0	0.0	0.0	0.0	0.0
11.9	0.0	0.0	0.0	0.0	0.0	0.0	0.0	0.0	0.0	0.0	0.0	0.0	0.0	0.0	0.0	0.0	0.0	0.0	0.0	0.0	0.0	0.0	0.0	0.0	0.0	0.0	0.0	0.0	0.0	0.0	0.0
10.9	0.0	0.0	0.0	0.0	0.0	0.0	0.0	0.0	0.0	0.0	0.0	0.0	0.0	0.0	0.0	0.0	0.0	0.0	0.0	0.0	0.0	0.0	0.0	0.0	0.0	0.0	0.0	0.0	0.0	0.0	0.0
9.9	0.0	0.0	0.0	0.0	0.0	0.0	0.0	0.0	0.0	0.0	0.0	0.0	0.0	0.0	0.0	0.0	0.0	0.0	0.0	0.0	0.0	0.0	0.0	0.0	0.0	0.0	0.0	0.0	0.0	0.0	0.0
8.8	0.0	0.0	0.0	0.0	0.0	0.0	0.0	0.0	0.0	0.0	0.0	0.0	0.0	0.0	0.0	0.0	0.0	0.0	0.0	0.0	0.0	0.0	0.0	0.0	0.0	0.0	0.0	0.0	0.0	0.0	0.0
7.8	0.0	0.0	0.0	0.0	0.0	0.0	0.0	0.0	0.0	0.0	0.0	0.0	0.0	0.0	0.0	0.0	0.0	0.0	0.0	0.0	0.0	0.0	0.0	0.0	0.0	0.0	0.0	0.0	0.0	0.0	0.0
6.8	0.0	0.0	0.0	0.0	0.0	0.0	0.0	0.0	0.0	0.0	0.0	0.0	0.0	0.0	0.0	0.0	0.0	0.0	0.0	0.0	0.0	0.0	0.0	0.0	0.0	0.0	0.0	0.0	0.0	0.0	0.0
5.8	0.0	0.0	0.0	0.0	0.0	0.0	0.0	0.0	0.0	0.0	0.0	0.0	0.0	0.0	0.0	0.0	0.0	0.0	0.0	0.0	0.0	0.0	0.0	-0.8	-0.9	-1.0	-1.0	-1.0	-0.2	0.0	0.0
4.8	0.0	0.0	0.0	0.0	0.0	0.0	0.0	0.0	0.0	0.0	0.0	0.0	0.0	0.0	0.0	0.0	0.0	0.0	0.0	0.0	0.0	0.0	0.0	-1.2	-3.8	-4.0	-3.9	-2.3	-0.1	0.0	0.0
3.8	0.0	0.0	0.0	0.0	0.0	0.0	0.0	0.0	0.0	0.0	0.0	0.0	0.0	0.0	0.0	0.0	0.0	0.0	0.0	0.0	-0.1	-0.3	-0.3	-1.1	-4.7	-5.7	-5.1	-1.8	-0.1	0.0	0.0
2.8	0.0	0.0	0.0	0.0	0.0	0.0	0.0	0.0	0.0	0.0	0.0	0.0	0.0	0.0	0.0	0.0	0.0	0.0	-0.1	-0.2	-0.5	-0.2	0.1	-1.2	-3.7	-3.9	-3.7	-1.3	0.1	0.0	0.0
1.7	0.0	0.0	0.0	0.0	0.0	0.0	0.0	0.0	0.0	0.0	0.0	0.0	0.0	0.0	0.0	0.0	0.0	0.0	0.1	0.1	-0.9	-0.6	-0.8	-0.9	-1.6	-1.5	-1.1	-0.6	-0.3	0.0	0.0
0.7	-0.3	-0.3	-0.3	0.0	0.0	0.0	0.0	0.0	0.0	0.0	0.0	0.0	0.0	0.1	0.1	0.1	0.4	0.4	-0.2	0.2	-0.7	-1.2	-2.4	-2.0	-1.5	-0.4	-0.1	0.0	0.0	0.0	0.0
-0.3	-0.5	-0.5	-0.5	-0.6	-0.9	-0.6	-0.3	-0.1	0.0	0.1	0.1	0.2	0.2	0.1	0.1	0.0	0.2	1.1	1.3	0.3	-0.8	-1.6	-1.2	-2.2	-2.8	-2.4	-1.6	-0.6	-0.1	0.0	0.0
-1.3	-2.1	-2.0	-1.9	-2.0	-2.1	-1.1	-1.4	-1.2	0.0	0.8	1.3	1.5	1.4	1.2	0.4	-0.8	-0.8	1.1	3.4	4.1	0.6	-1.0	-3.6	-4.1	-3.2	-2.3	-1.5	-0.6	-0.1	0.0	0.0
-2.3	-1.9	-0.3	-0.1	-0.1	-0.2	-0.5	-1.2	0.1	2.0	3.7	4.8	5.2	5.4	5.2	4.1	0.4	-0.7	-0.3	0.4	0.3	0.4	-1.0	-4.0	-4.5	-2.4	-0.8	-0.5	-0.3	-0.1	0.0	0.0
-3.3	-1.9	-0.3	0.4	0.4	0.4	0.2	-0.2	-0.4	-0.6	-0.3	2.4	5.1	5.3	4.8	4.0	2.7	0.5	-0.6	-2.3	-3.7	-2.8	-2.7	-4.4	-4.9	-1.8	-0.2	0.0	0.0	0.0	0.0	0.0
-4.4	-2.0	-0.2	0.4	0.5	0.5	0.3	0.0	-0.2	-0.3	1.7	5.8	9.3	10.5	10.7	**11.1**	7.7	5.1	-0.3	-5.3	-7.1	-4.6	-4.9	-5.8	-5.0	-1.4	0.0	0.0	0.0	0.0	0.0	0.0
-5.4	-2.3	-0.5	0.4	0.4	0.4	0.3	0.1	-0.2	-0.3	1.6	9.1	9.6	9.7	10.9	9.9	8.3	4.8	0.5	-3.2	-6.2	-6.2	-6.3	-6.3	-4.5	-1.0	0.0	0.0	0.0	0.0	0.0	0.0
-6.4	-1.6	-1.0	-0.3	0.1	0.2	0.2	0.1	-0.2	-0.3	1.6	9.0	8.3	9.8	10.7	6.5	8.1	4.3	1.9	-2.5	-9.5	-8.0	-8.2	-6.7	-2.9	-0.5	0.0	0.0	0.0	0.0	0.0	0.0
-7.4	-0.6	3.6	0.2	-0.6	-0.4	-0.3	-0.3	-0.3	-0.5	1.4	8.8	9.3	9.7	10.3	9.6	7.8	5.1	2.2	-2.8	-11.9	-11.8	-8.1	-3.3	-0.7	0.0	0.0	0.0	0.0	0.0	0.0	0.0
-8.4	0.0	0.0	1.7	1.1	-0.1	-1.0	-1.0	-1.0	-0.6	1.7	2.2	4.5	5.9	6.2	6.8	7.6	5.6	2.0	-5.0	-14.1	-11.9	-3.3	-0.8	-0.1	0.0	0.0	0.0	0.0	0.0	0.0	0.0
-9.4	0.0	0.0	0.0	1.4	1.3	1.0	1.0	1.0	0.9	-1.0	-0.9	-0.9	-0.9	-0.5	11.2	21.7	13.4	2.0	-9.1	-15.7	-7.8	-1.0	-0.2	0.0	0.0	0.0	0.0	0.0	0.0	0.0	0.0
-10.4	0.0	0.0	0.0	0.0	0.5	0.7	4.0	4.5	4.1	4.0	4.2	4.8	6.2	9.1	16.6	13.9	12.3	2.9	-11.2	-16.3	-3.8	-0.2	0.0	0.0	0.0	0.0	0.0	0.0	0.0	0.0	0.0
-11.5	0.0	0.0	0.0	0.0	0.0	0.0	0.0	-0.1	1.0	2.5	2.8	7.3	8.7	2.8	-5.3	-6.3	-9.4	-10.3	-13.3	-9.5	-0.9	0.0	0.0	0.0	0.0	0.0	0.0	0.0	0.0	0.0	0.0
-12.5	0.0	0.0	0.0	0.0	0.0	0.0	0.0	0.0	0.0	0.0	0.0	0.3	0.0	0.0	-0.5	-2.1	-2.5	-2.1	-2.1	-1.7	0.0	0.0	0.0	0.0	0.0	0.0	0.0	0.0	0.0	0.0	0.0
-13.5	0.0	0.0	0.0	0.0	0.0	0.0	0.0	0.0	0.0	0.0	0.0	0.0	0.0	0.0	0.0	0.0	0.0	0.0	0.0	0.0	0.0	0.0	0.0	0.0	0.0	0.0	0.0	0.0	0.0	0.0	0.0
-14.5	0.0	0.0	0.0	0.0	0.0	0.0	0.0	0.0	0.0	0.0	0.0	0.0	0.0	0.0	0.0	0.0	0.0	0.0	0.0	0.0	0.0	0.0	0.0	0.0	0.0	0.0	0.0	0.0	0.0	0.0	0.0

This is the Learn Table from the tune in my Olds. The values here represent the percentage of deviation required to the values stored in the Base Fuel Table to achieve the A/F targets in the Target Air/Fuel Ratio Table. For example, at 3,000 rpm and −4.4 PSIA of MAP, the engine requires 11.1 percent more fuel than the value in the Base Fuel Table (58.0 lbs/hr) to achieve the Target Air/Fuel Ratio (14.2:1). Note the corresponding highlighted cell in the Learn Table, Target Air/Fuel Ratio Table, and Base Fuel Table.

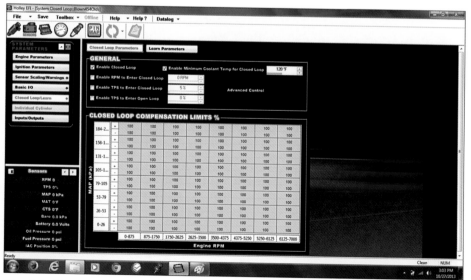

Fig. 3.2. The Holley HP and Dominator ECUs allow you to fine tune when the system operates in Closed Loop, allowing feedback from the oxygen sensor(s) to the ECU to adjust the air/fuel mixture in real time to achieve the targets stored in the Air/Fuel Ratio Table.

driven, the Learn Table is continually mapped, remapped, and percentages continually refined in an effort to achieve the A/F targets in all cells of the Target Air/Fuel Ratio Table. The value in the Base Fuel Table *and* the value in the Learn Table are factored in by the ECU to arrive at the correct amount of fuel.

For example, consider the following at a given RPM and MAP:

Base Fuel Table Value: 74.5 lbs/hour
Learn Table: + 6.2%
Net Fuel Value: 74.5 + (74.5 x 6.2%) = 79.12 lbs/hour

Learning can be intentionally slower at low RPM and intentionally faster at high RPM. This allows the data collected in the Learn Table to be a better reflection of the changes that need to be made to the Base Fuel Table to achieve the A/F targets.

Ideally, the actual A/F ratio as measured by the oxygen sensor(s) ends up within a few percent of the A/F targets. In addition, the Learn percentage in most laptop-tunable ECUs can be user adjusted from OFF to 100 percent. At 100 percent, the ECU can make large changes to the value of any cell in the Base Fuel Table in an effort to achieve the A/F target. When the Learn mode is OFF, the percentage difference between the value in the Base Fuel Table and the A/F targets is not plotted in the Learn Table. Depending on the application, it may be desirable to disable the Learn mode based on RPM, throttle position, etc.

Obviously, none of this is possible with a carburetor.

Open Loop

When the ECU is operating in open loop, it is not looking at the feedback provided by the oxygen sensor(s) to correct the values in the Base Fuel Table to achieve the A/F targets. So, when would you ever want to do that? Anytime that you want the ECU to ignore the feedback from the oxygen sensor(s), such as when using a low-RPM rev limiter such as for a transbrake or line lock. As the ignition intentionally misfires the cylinders to keep the engine within a certain RPM, you don't want the ECU leaning the mixture because of the unburned fuel in the exhaust.

In addition, you may want to fine-tune specific areas of a tune in open loop. For example, engine and chassis tuners may elect to tune in open loop and rely on external wide-

band A/F meters in an effort to avoid the ECU making automatic changes. This allows them to make changes to the tune as they see fit to achieve their goals.

Depending on the software, you may have a lot of control over the closed loop, open loop, and Learn parameters. This provides all kinds of tuning flexibility.

Sensor Feedback

Regardless of whether the system is operating in closed or open loop, the ECU has the ability to adjust the tune based on feedback from other sensors. Most aftermarket systems can be set up to do this automatically.

CTS: When first starting the engine, a richer mixture is required to keep the engine idling smoothly. The ECU can be programmed to enrich the mixture and then slowly lean the mixture as the engine warms up to operating temperature. It does so via the feedback from the CTS. This is similar to the function of the choke of a carburetor.

As the engine temperature rises above the ideal operating temperature, it is beneficial to reduce the ignition timing to stave off detonation. This is also done via feedback from the CTS, although this feature is only available on systems with engine management.

IAT: As the temperature of the ambient air decreases, the air becomes denser as it has a greater mass of oxygen. As the temperature of the ambient air increases, the air becomes less dense as it has a lower mass of oxygen. The ECU tracks the IAT and can automatically enrich or lean the mixture based on temperature changes.

BP: Some aftermarket ECUs have a barometric pressure sensor to mon-

itor barometric pressure. The ECU tracks the barometer and can automatically enrich or lean the mixture accordingly.

TPS: The ECU monitors the position of the throttle constantly. When the throttle is quickly depressed, the ECU knows to enrich the mixture to prevent a lean bog. This is similar to the function of the accelerator pump on a carburetor.

In addition, the ECU tracks the throttle position in an effort to manage the IAC. The IAC is the key to achieving a smooth idle. As you know, when the throttle blades of a throttle body are fully closed, as they are at idle and when releasing the throttle, the IAC manages the airflow into the engine. Some ECUs do all of this automatically in the background with no influence from the user. Others allow the user to fine-tune the IAC via the software.

Drivability Tuning

Depending on the particular system, you have access to some parameters that allows you to influence the overall drivability of the vehicle. Basic EFI systems that perform fuel metering only typically allow you to fine-tune the Acceleration Enrichment (AE) to eliminate bogs on throttle transition. Laptop-tunable EFI systems, and those with engine management, allow you to fine-tune a number of parameters, including (but not necessarily limited to) the relationship of timing and A/F ratio and the operation of the IAC.

Acceleration Enrichment

Acceleration enrichment allows you to tune out bogs as a result of throttle transitions or changes in

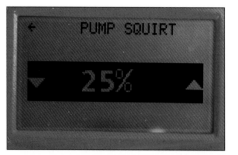

Fig. 3.3. The MSD Atomic EFI system has a Pump Squirt feature similar in function to the accelerator pump of a carburetor. This and the Power Valve Enrich feature, similar in function to the power valve of a carburetor, allow you to quickly and easily dial the acceleration enrichment of the system via the handheld controller while driving the vehicle.

Fig. 3.4. The Holley HP and Dominator ECUs offer very fine tuning of the AE, based on several variables. Here is correction based on the position of the TPS. Values are percentages.

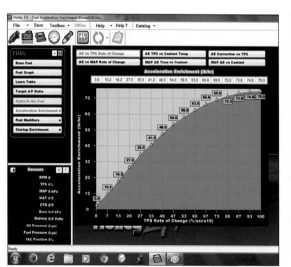

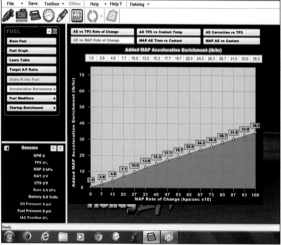

Fig. 3.5. (Left) AE versus TPS rate of change. This and the AE vs TPS position are instrumental in achieving smooth transitions as you open and close the throttle.

Fig. 3.6. (Right) AE versus MAP. I used this to eliminate a bog when shifting 1-2 and 2-3 in my Olds at low speeds with the same throttle position. You could watch the vacuum/boost gauge jump from 12 to 6 inches of vacuum when upshifting. Tweaking this solved the problem entirely.

manifold pressure. The MSD Atomic EFI system we install in Chapter 5 has two such user adjustments: Pump Squirt and Power Valve Enrich. The Pump Squirt feature functions very similarly to the accelerator pump of a carburetor, adding fuel as the throttle position changes. The Power Valve Enrich feature allows you to add fuel as the load on the engine increases, which is monitored via the MAP sensor (this can vary widely

via camshaft profile as well). Engine load is not always a function of the position of the throttle. For example, you may be cruising down the highway at 70 mph at a given throttle position. As the grade increases, the load on the engine also increases even though throttle position hasn't changed.

These simple adjustments allow you to calibrate the Atomic EFI system while you're driving the vehi-

cle, but it's safer and better for the passenger to make the adjustments. The net result is that you can quickly achieve the smoothest drivability with a few presses of the buttons on the handheld controller.

Most laptop-tunable EFI systems allow far greater control over the AE. The Holley HP and Dominator EFI systems we install in Chapter 6 allows you to finely calibrate it as follows:

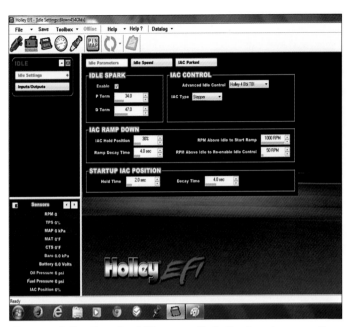

Fig. 3.7. Adjusting the IAC correctly is the key to smooth transitions off idle and returning to idle.

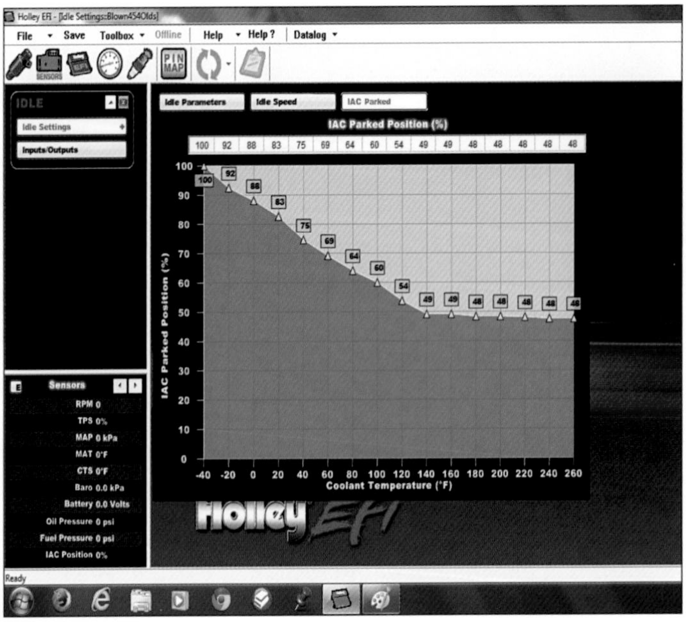

Fig. 3.8. The IAC Parked Position settings allow you to fine-tune the IAC while the engine is cranking.

- AE vs TPS Rate of Change
- AE vs MAP Rate of Change
- AE vs Coolant Temperature
- MAP AE Time vs Coolant Temperature
- AE Correction vs TPS
- MAP AE vs Coolant Temperature

It takes a bit of knowledge and practice to perfectly dial in the acceleration enrichment for these systems. This is definitely an area at which an experienced tuner can be worth their weight in gold.

Ignition Timing to A/F Ratio

Any EFI system with engine management allows you to adjust ignition timing in relation to A/F ratio. In the idle and drivability areas, you realize the best fuel economy with the correct engine timing with respect to the A/F Ratio at a given RPM. This can take a bit of trial and error to achieve. If the engine surges at any RPM in the drivability area, this can be an indication that the

relationship between timing and A/F ratio is the culprit (see Chapter 5 for more details).

Fine-Tuning the IAC

Achieving the correct relationship between the IAC and the throttle-blade adjustment is the key to a smooth idle. Once you've set the throttle-blade position, the ECU manages the IAC position so the correct mass of air enters the engine at idle based on atmospheric conditions. Laptop-tunable EFI systems allow you to fine-tune the IAC to achieve the smoothest idle, smoothest transition from idle, and smoothest transition back to idle.

If you're a first-time tuner, you'll find it comforting to know that any changes you make that do not have the desired results are quickly and easily reversed. I sometimes take a picture of the settings with my smart-phone before making changes. That way, I can easily get back to the original settings if what I thought would work, didn't.

Tuning Tools of the Trade

Any serious carb tuner has a bevy of specific carb-tuning tools as well as a bunch of parts that can be swapped within the carburetor in the tuning process. The good news here is that EFI systems don't require any tuning *parts,* so to speak, but if you intend to do your own tuning and you want to achieve the best drivability and performance, you really should consider investing in the following tools.

Wideband A/F Meter

The cost of a quality wideband A/F meter has come down to a point where any enthusiast can now afford one. They are offered in single-channel (one oxygen sensor input) and dual-channel (two oxygen sensor inputs) units. Some have the ability to connect several more oxygen sensors for the nth degree in tuning. At a minimum, you want a single-channel unit with the ability to also track RPM.

Nicer units also afford you the opportunity to input any 0-5V sensor

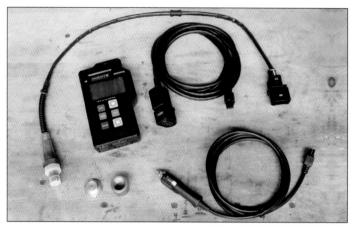

Fig. 3.9. The Innovate LM-2 wideband A/F meter is an incredibly powerful and inexpensive tool. The single-channel Basic Kit (shown) has full datalogging capabilities. A quality wideband A/F meter allows you to quickly pinpoint drivability problems and dial them out. Incidentally, this tool is equally as valuable for carbureted applications.

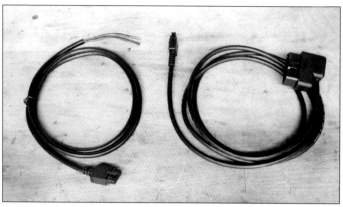

Fig. 3.10. The analog IN/OUT cable (left) allows you to monitor RPM, output the wideband signal to an external device, as well as connect any 0-5 VDC accessory that you may want to datalog, and this includes TPS, MAP, MAF, etc. The OBD-II cable for the LM-2 (right) allows you to use the LM-2 to monitor or datalog via the OBD-II port of any late-model vehicle.

Fig. 3.11. Moroso offers oxygen weld rings and plugs for oxygen sensors. I obtained these locally and your local speed shop may stock them as well.

(TPS, IAT, CTS, MAP, etc.) by interfacing an included or optional harness with those sensors. Another nice feature is the ability of the meter to make a datalog of all inputs connected to it.

Oxygen Sensor Weld Rings

No matter what EFI system you ultimately settle on, it's just good planning to have the exhaust shop install oxygen sensor weld rings (oxygen bungs) in both sides of the exhaust at the same time, even if the system you've got your eye on has only a single oxygen sensor. The standard thread size is 18 mm. Most wideband A/F meters, wideband A/F gauges, and EFI systems include these, but you can also purchase them separately from numerous companies.

If you're looking at an EFI system with dual wideband oxygen sensors, you need to have a minimum of three weld rings installed to give you some options down the road. You'll thank me later.

Datalogger

Many laptop-programmable ECUs have internal datalogging

Fig. 3.12. The LM-2 also allows you to display data in the form of gauges, both during run and when viewing a datalog as shown here. As you can see, the A/F ratio among five different oxygen sensors is nearly identical at WOT.

capabilities. If you're looking at one of the entry-level EFI systems, this is typically not available. Datalogging allows you to collect data in real time while you're driving the vehicle in an effort to maximize the tune. This can

be super handy to diagnose a drivability issue or optimize the tune to realize the peak performance of your engine.

If the ECU offers it, make sure that you become familiar with how

to use it. If the EFI system you're considering doesn't offer datalogging, many quality wideband A/F meters do offer this, so you can kill two birds with one stone.

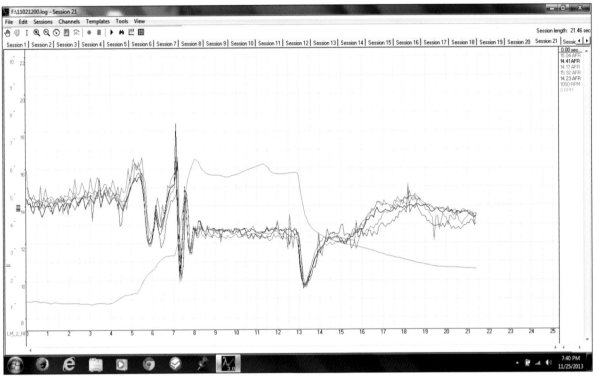

Fig. 3.13. The datalogger function of the Innovate LM-2 is an incredibly powerful tool. This is a datalog taken from the Olds featured in Chapter 6 and Chapter 7. WOT takes place beginning at about 7 seconds and lasts about 6 seconds, as illustrated by the orange line, which represents RPM.

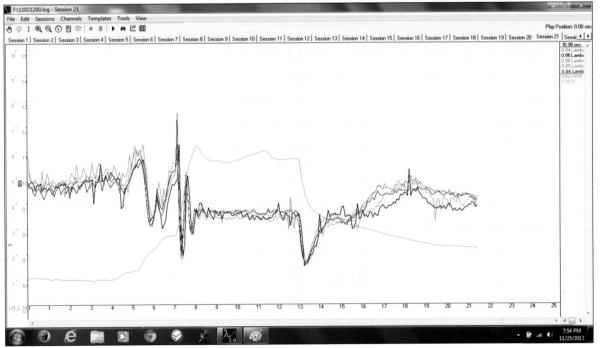

Fig. 3.14. You can easily select one of any of the parameters datalogged for a closer view. Here, the blue line displays the recorded A/F readings of the oxygen sensor in the number-7 primary of the headers.

Digital Multimeter

If you've read either of my automotive electrical books, you know how much of a stickler I am for a good DMM. A quality DMM with a MIN/MAX scale can be used to quickly diagnose charging system problems, fuel delivery problems, etc. Most of my car buddies are amazed at the data I can ascertain with one of my trusty Fluke meters. They watch in awe . . . it's not that hard; really it isn't! I use the Fluke 87 and 88 meters, but at minimum you should consider a 115.

Power Adders

Thus far, I have focused on naturally aspirated combinations. But what if you're a power adder kind of enthusiast? I certainly am. Regardless of the power adder that you run, this is where the power of engine management proves to be incredibly valuable. Allowing the ECU to manage the timing lets you unlock 100 percent of the performance your power adder is capable of and do so safely.

No matter what kind of power adder you are (or will be) running, you need to consider the octane requirements of the fuel in relation to the horsepower gain from the power adder. In addition, you need to select plugs with a complementary heat range to maximize the performance of your combination. Both can take a bit of testing to determine.

As discussed in Chapter 1, if you use a power adder with your new EFI system, it's important to purchase an EFI system that's designed to work properly with it. Make certain that a particular manufacturer's system works well with your power adder and contact them if necessary to verify this. Just because some guy

on the Internet has been using a Brand-X EFI system with twin turbos doesn't mean that you can too and not have problems in getting the vehicle tuned properly. Sure, it may be fine at WOT, but it may not be fine cruising around town . . . or vice versa. The most common power adders include nitrous oxide, boosted applications (such as centrifugal superchargers, Roots superchargers, twin-screw superchargers, and turbochargers), and water/methanol injection.

Nitrous Oxide

This is the easiest of the power adders to manage. It's also one of the only power adders that you can add to a high-compression naturally aspirated engine.

Shots less than 100 hp typically require only a few degrees less timing to prevent detonation. This is typically very simple to achieve but the ECU needs to have engine management to be compatible. In some cases, you can run a dry system (nitrous only) and the ECU can be set up to enrich the A/F mixture automatically. In other cases, you

must run a wet system (nitrous and fuel), which adds the fuel manually to enrich the mixture.

There are two ways of interfacing a nitrous system to the ECU. The simplest method is connecting the ECU to an existing nitrous system so that the ECU knows when it is in use. This interface typically involves connecting the WOT switch that

Fig. 3.15. If you're a nitrous fan, you can certainly appreciate the workmanship of this custom-built dual-throttle-body Hogan Manifold and Nitrous Pro Flow fogger system. A Holley Dominator ECU manages engine ignition timing, A/F ratio, and a single-stage wet fogger system. (Photo Courtesy David Segunda/Wilson Manifolds)

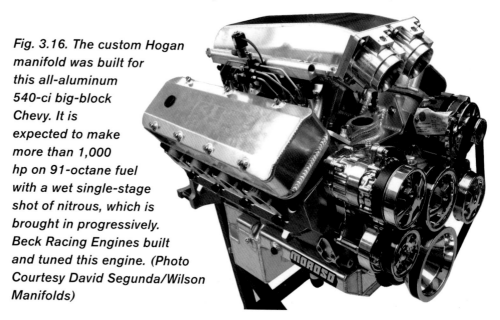

Fig. 3.16. The custom Hogan manifold was built for this all-aluminum 540-ci big-block Chevy. It is expected to make more than 1,000 hp on 91-octane fuel with a wet single-stage shot of nitrous, which is brought in progressively. Beck Racing Engines built and tuned this engine. (Photo Courtesy David Segunda/Wilson Manifolds)

activates the nitrous to an input of the ECU. When the WOT switch is activated, the ECU reduces the timing accordingly.

If you're a more hard-core nitrous user, you may elect to design a nitrous system that the ECU can manage. ECUs, such as the Holley Dominator (see Chapter 6 and Chapter 7 for more details), offer far more control.

They can do the following:

- Interface a master ON/OFF arm switch for the nitrous
- Progressively control the nitrous solenoids via PWM
- Control multiple stages of nitrous
- Automatically retard the timing
- Automatically enrich the A/F mixture
- Govern activation by certain criteria (e.g., disabled when using a trans-brake)

When the arm switch is activated, all of the nitrous management is automatic. Also, the additional fuel required with the nitrous can be metered via the injectors, eliminating the expense and complexity of installing a wet nitrous system. Gone are the days of complex installations with multiple controllers and interfaces that must be set up and tuned separately (see Chapter 7 for more details).

Boosted Applications

Superchargers and turbochargers of any kind require an EFI system with engine management and boost compatibility. Regardless of which type of boosted application you run, you can safely and easily manage the timing when you're in the boost. When using pump gas, it is necessary to reduce the engine timing proportionally to the amount of boost produced by the engine. It is also a good idea to remove timing as the charge temperature in the manifold increases. Both keep detonation at bay and allow your engine to live a long and healthy life. These are simple operations for the ECU to manage.

The obvious parts change is the MAP sensor, as the standard 1 bar sensor is for naturally aspirated combinations only. Here's a guideline, depending on which sensor you have:

- 2 bar: up to 14.7 psi of boost
- 3 bar: up to 29.4 psi of boost
- 4 bar: up to 44.1 psi of boost
- 5 bar: up to 58.8 psi of boost

Centrifugal Superchargers: The supercharger is before the throttle body and blows through the throttle body. MAP is constant at all RPM and engine loads between the blower and the intake manifold. Timing and mixture enrichment are managed automatically via the timing and fuel tables.

Roots-Type Applications: There are two types of Roots-blown applications. Modern vehicles using

MAP (PSIA)	500	700	900	1200	1600	2000	2500	3000	3500	4000	4500	5000	5500	6000	6500	7000
16.0	7.0	10.0	12.0	13.0	15.0	16.0	22.0	22.0	22.0	22.0	22.0	22.0	22.0	22.0	22.0	22.0
13.9	8.0	12.0	14.0	15.0	15.0	25.0	23.0	23.2	23.3	23.5	23.5	23.5	23.5	23.5	23.5	23.5
11.9	9.0	13.0	16.0	16.0	16.0	25.0	24.0	24.3	24.6	25.0	25.0	25.0	25.0	25.0	25.0	25.0
9.9	10.0	14.0	17.0	17.0	17.0	25.0	25.0	25.5	26.0	25.5	25.5	25.5	25.5	25.5	25.5	25.5
7.8	11.0	15.0	18.0	18.0	18.0	25.0	26.0	26.6	27.3	27.0	27.0	27.0	27.0	27.0	27.0	27.0
5.8	12.0	16.0	19.0	19.0	19.0	25.0	26.9	27.8	28.6	28.5	28.5	28.5	28.5	28.5	28.5	28.5
3.8	13.0	17.0	20.0	20.0	20.0	25.0	27.9	29.0	29.9	30.0	30.0	30.0	30.0	30.0	30.0	30.0
1.7	14.0	18.0	21.0	22.0	22.0	25.0	28.9	30.1	31.3	31.5	31.5	31.5	31.5	31.5	31.5	31.5
-0.3	15.0	19.0	22.0	25.0	25.0	25.0	29.9	31.3	32.6	34.0	34.0	34.0	34.0	34.0	34.0	34.0
-2.3	16.0	20.0	24.0	25.0	25.0	26.0	31.6	32.8	33.8	35.0	35.0	35.0	35.0	35.0	35.0	35.0
-4.4	16.0	21.0	24.0	25.0	27.0	29.0	33.3	34.2	35.1	36.0	36.0	36.0	36.0	36.0	36.0	36.0
-6.4	16.0	21.0	24.0	25.0	25.0	30.0	35.0	35.7	36.3	37.0	37.0	37.0	37.0	37.0	37.0	37.0
-8.4	16.0	22.0	25.0	25.0	25.0	30.0	36.6	37.1	37.5	38.0	38.0	38.0	38.0	38.0	38.0	38.0
-10.4	18.0	24.0	27.0	28.0	28.0	32.0	38.3	38.5	38.8	39.0	39.0	39.0	39.0	39.0	39.0	39.0
-12.5	18.0	24.0	27.0	28.0	30.0	34.0	40.0	40.0	40.0	40.0	40.0	40.0	40.0	40.0	40.0	40.0
-14.5	18.0	23.0	27.0	28.0	32.0	36.0	40.0	40.0	40.0	40.0	40.0	40.0	40.0	40.0	40.0	40.0

Engine RPM

Fig. 3.17. This is the Base Spark Table from the tune in my 6-71 blown Olds. Notice that the engine has plenty of timing in it in the drivability areas and progressively less timing as the boost comes in. This allows me to safely run 91-octane fuel, the best available at the pump in Arizona.

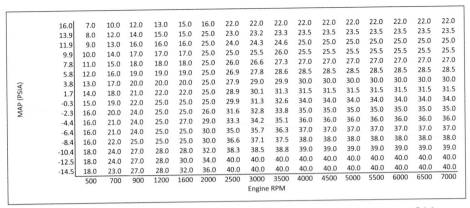

Fig. 3.18. This small-block 434-ci Chevy is fitted with an ATI ProCharger centrifugal supercharger and Accufab 1,215-cfm throttle body. A Big Stuff 3 system performs engine management. This supercharged small-block makes more than 900 hp on 91-octane fuel. Beck Racing Engines built and tuned this engine.

Fig. 3.19. This blown 540-ci big-block Chevy has all the eye candy a street rod would ever want. An 8-71 BDS Blower, BDS Bugcatcher Hat, and Nitrous Oxide Systems Blower Injector Plate round out the induction. A Big Stuff 3 system performs engine management. This blown big-block makes more than 950 hp on 91-octane fuel without the nitrous. Beck Racing Engines built and tuned this engine.

Roots-style blowers have the injectors in the intake runners. The blower itself sits atop the intake manifold and creates boost when the engine is under load. No fuel passes through the blower. These installations often include intercoolers in the intake manifold to cool the charge.

On the other hand, muscle cars and hot rods typically use a draw-through application in which the fuel passes through the blower (which helps to cool the charge). The most common aftermarket EFI installations with Roots-blown draw-through applications use throttle bodies and injectors above the blower. When the engine is under load, the boost exists only in the intake manifold, which is under the blower. This requires a system designed specifically for such applications.

Some engine builders like to also include a set of injectors under the blower and in the individual runners of the manifold. This allows them to address the challenge of the blower pushing the fuel forward in the manifold, fine-tuning the cylinders to achieve the perfect mixture. This is exactly why the blower on a Top Fuel engine sits so far rearward (set back) on the manifold.

Turbochargers: Turbochargers are, for all practical purposes, just like centrifugal superchargers, as far as an

Fig. 3.21. If too much is just right, this 14-71 blown 582-ci big-block Chevy with nitrous should fit the bill. The induction package includes a 14-71 Kobelco Blower, Enderle Birdcatcher Hat, and Nitrous Oxide Systems Blower Injector Plate. A Big Stuff 3 controller performs engine management. Note the additional injectors in the intake runners under the blower, providing the ability to fine-tune the mixture for each cylinder. Beck Racing Engines built and tuned this engine.

Fig. 3.20. Turbos are all the rage these days, and this twin-turbocharged 427-ci LS3 delivers performance in spades. The GM factory ECU from a 2011 Camaro provides engine management. This combination was good for more than 1,350 hp. Beck Racing Engines built and tuned this engine.

Fig. 3.22. Packaging is tight in the engine bay of this 2011 Camaro. Modern turbo, engine, and EFI technology provide excellent drivability and power that no supercar can match. (Photo Courtesy Lamb Chevrolet)

EFI system is concerned. However, some EFI systems allow you to manage the wastegates electronically. If you're a diehard turbo guy, this can be a huge help in tuning your combination.

Water/Methanol Injection

This is one of the oldest power adders used in the internal combustion engine. In recent years it has gained momentum for several reasons. The quality of the fuel available at the pump is questionable at best for performance applications. It's also inconsistent from one brand to another. Turbochargers and superchargers are more popular today than ever before. Both increase cylinder pressure when making boost and this necessitates higher-octane fuel to prevent detonation.

The objective is to increase the effective octane rating of the fuel. The unique thing about water/methanol injection is that it is compatible with naturally aspirated as well as boosted applications. When using it in naturally aspirated engines, you can increase the ignition timing in an effort to gain horsepower. When used in boosted applications, it isn't necessary to retard the timing as much as the boost comes on and this can have significant effects on horsepower and torque.

Water methanol injection is also referred to as a liquid intercooler because it reduces the temperature of the charge before it enters the intake manifold (although not to the extent of nitrous oxide). As air is compressed its temperature increases, proving once again that there is no such thing as a free lunch. A side benefit of using water/methanol injection is that the combustion chambers are steam cleaned, so to speak, in the process of using it. With gasoline combinations it cleans the carbon deposits with regular use of your right foot.

Water/methanol injection is the least-expensive power adder and it's easily managed. A wide range of kits is offered. They can be activated progressively via a MAP or MAF signal, allowing you to introduce the correct amount of the mixture based on actual engine requirements. At the time of this writing, the Holley HP and Dominator ECUs are the only units I'm aware of that allow you to manage water/methanol injection via the software, which is not only incredibly cool, but allows tuners to get the most from it.

Tuning with Power Adders

Tuning EFI systems with power adders is significantly simpler than tuning similar carbureted setups, but this is something better left to

Fig. 3.23. Many of the factory guys I work with are gearheads. Case in point: Doug Flynn's Nova. Doug is the Product Development Manager for Holley. This 364-ci turbocharged LS engine, equipped with all of Holley's latest, allowed Doug to average 9.57 seconds at 142.8 mph. He ran this average during 2013 Drag Week when the temperatures averaged 95 degrees. That's pretty insane for a 3,850-pound vehicle. (Photo Courtesy Doug Flynn)

experienced tuners. Detonation is the enemy of all engines, but with power adders it can have immediate and devastating effects. In addition, any engine with a power adder is typically capable of serious horsepower. For these reasons, I recommend that an experienced tuner in a controlled environment perform this tuning. Most tuners also employ the use of a correctly calibrated knock sensor to prevent engine damage during the tuning process.

You should now know how to select the correct EFI system if you are using a power adder. As the EFI category in general is somewhat like the computer business, with new and improved software and hardware being introduced often, you're well advised to consult directly with the manufacturer of a given system to review your specific needs to ensure a given system serves them.

After you've selected the system and it has been installed, you may elect to farm the tuning out to a shop equipped with a chassis dyno

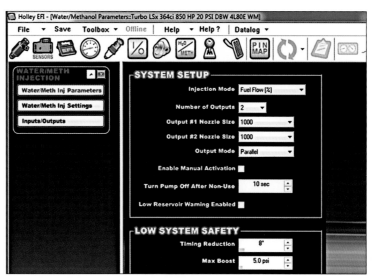

Fig. 3.24. The Holley EFI software allows you to set up the water/methanol system. You can choose to manage injection based on a percentage of actual fuel flow or duty cycle of the water/methanol solenoids. Holley offers matching solenoids in three different flow rates that can be driven directly off any available fuel injector output of either the HP or Dominator ECU.

operated by an experienced tuner. I did. I prefer to work with tuners who tend to be a little conservative.

Both of my vehicles are fuel injected and both have superchargers. My daily driver, a 2003 Ford Mustang GT, has had a centrifugal supercharger and water/methanol injection on it for the past 70,000-plus miles and it runs as well today as it did the day it was tuned on the chassis dyno. My Olds (see Chapter 4) has an old-school Weiand 6-71 blower and 13,000 miles on the clock. Both are equipped with EFI and the tunes are maximized to provide the best performance and drivability with 91-octane fuel.

Fuel Flow (%)

MAP (PSIA)	2000	2400	2800	3200	3600	4000	4400	4800	5200	5600	6000	6400	6800	7200	7600	8000
24.7	10.0	10.0	10.0	10.0	10.0	10.0	10.0	10.0	10.0	10.0	13.5	13.5	13.5	13.5	13.5	13.5
23.0	10.0	10.0	10.0	10.0	10.0	10.0	10.0	10.0	10.0	10.0	13.5	13.5	13.5	13.5	13.5	13.5
21.4	10.0	10.0	10.0	10.0	10.0	10.0	10.0	10.0	10.0	10.0	13.5	13.5	13.5	13.5	13.5	13.5
19.7	10.0	10.0	10.0	10.0	10.0	10.0	10.0	10.0	10.0	10.0	13.5	13.5	13.5	13.5	13.5	13.5
18.1	10.0	10.0	10.0	10.0	10.0	10.0	10.0	10.0	10.0	10.0	13.5	13.5	13.5	13,5	13.5	13.5
16.4	10.0	10.0	10.0	10.0	10.0	10.0	10.0	10.0	10.0	10.0	13.5	13.5	13.5	13.5	13.5	13.5
14.8	10.0	10.0	10.0	10.0	10.0	10.0	10.0	10.0	10.0	10.0	12.0	12.0	12.0	12.0	12.0	12.0
13.2	10.0	10.0	10.0	10.0	10.0	10.0	10.0	10.0	10.0	10.0	10.0	10.0	10.0	10.0	10.0	10.0
11.5	9.0	9.0	9.0	9.0	9.0	9.0	9.0	9.0	9.0	9.0	9.0	9.0	9.0	9.0	9.0	9.0
9.9	8.0	8.0	8.0	8.0	8.0	8.0	8.0	8.0	8.0	8.0	8.0	8.0	8.0	8.0	8.0	8.0
8.2	7.0	7.0	7.0	7.0	7.0	7.0	7.0	7.0	7.0	7.0	7.0	7.0	7.0	7.0	7.0	7.0
6.6	5.6	5.6	5.6	5.6	5.6	5.6	5.6	5.6	5.6	5.6	5.6	5.6	5.6	5.6	5.6	5.6
4.9	4.2	4.2	4.2	4.2	4.2	4.2	4.2	4.2	4.2	4.2	4.2	4.2	4.2	4.2	4.2	4.2
3.3	2.8	2.8	2.8	2.8	2.8	2.8	2.8	2.8	2.8	2.8	2.8	2.8	2.8	2.8	2.8	2.8
1.6	1.4	1.4	1.4	1.4	1.4	1.4	1.4	1.4	1.4	1.4	1.4	1.4	1.4	1.4	1.4	1.4
0.0	0.0	0.0	0.0	0.0	0.0	0.0	0.0	0.0	0.0	0.0	0.0	0.0	0.0	0.0	0.0	0.0

Engine RPM

Fig. 3.25. Holley recommends managing the water/methanol injection based on a percentage of actual fuel flow as a more precise way to achieve your goals.

HOLLEY *HP EFI* SYSTEM INSTALLATION

In this chapter, I discuss the installation of a Holley HP EFI system on my personal hot rod, a 1972 Olds Cutlass with a 6-71 Roots-blown big-block Chevy. This is commonly referred to as a draw-through installation as the fuel is drawn through the supercharger. In addition, the setup I run uses dual throttle bodies. When I selected this system, it was the only TBI system that was designed for such an application.

This system has dramatically increased the drivability, predictability, serviceability, and performance of my Olds. To date, it's by far my favor-ite upgrade. Everyone who rides in the Olds is simply amazed at how docile it is when cruising and how nasty it is when you're in the throttle. Isn't that the balance every enthusiast is after for a street-driven hot rod? It puts a big smile on my face each time I get behind the wheel and it always will.

I spent a considerable amount of time on the front end of this project selecting the components. MSD, Holley, and MagnaFuel really helped to fine-tune my list to ensure that everything worked harmoni-ously together. I also upgraded the charging system on the Olds accord-ingly. The installation couldn't have gone more smoothly, except for a few AN adapters that I needed and didn't order and a few that I did order and didn't need, but that's just par for the course.

Although the HP EFI is a self-learning system, it's really best to do the tuning on a high-horsepower boosted application in a controlled environment such as a chassis dyno versus trying to do it on public roads. Mike "Zippy" King (then of) and Greg LaFontsee of Automotive Diagnostic Specialties (ADS) performed the tuning.

Fig 4.1. Here are the components of the Holley HP EFI system on my Olds. This system is easy to install, easy to tune, offers excellent drivability and perfor-mance, and has performed flawlessly. Not shown is the slave throttle body assembly.

Fig 4.2. Most casual observers assume they're looking at a pair of carburetors. One guy remarked, "Looks like a couple of carburetors on life support. What kind are they?"

Holley HP Fuel Injection System

Holley offers HP EFI systems today with a few improvements over the system I use in my Olds. Holley offers two basic systems, each built from the same throttle-body assembly. The 900-cfm, 75-lb/hr injectors range up to 525 hp. The 900-cfm, 85-lb/hr injectors range up to 600 hp.

Each system offers complete engine management. In addition, the HP ECU has eight PWM outputs. If the ECU is used in a single-throttle-body application, four of the PWM outputs are used for the injectors in the throttle-body assembly, leaving four additional PWM outputs that can be used to drive nitrous solenoids, water/methanol injection, etc. Holley offers a variety of accessories that can be used with these outputs. Utilizing these outputs for nitrous or water/methanol injection allows experienced tuners far more flexibility than using stand-alone controllers.

If you choose a dual-throttle-body application, as I did with the Olds, the extra four PWM outputs are used to drive the injectors in the second throttle body.

These are very capable systems and are compatible with power adders. In addition, the Holley software is very easy to use and offers the utmost control for even the most demanding tuners.

Finally, Holley offers a 5.7-inch full-color touch-screen LCD if you'd prefer to use that versus a laptop computer. ■

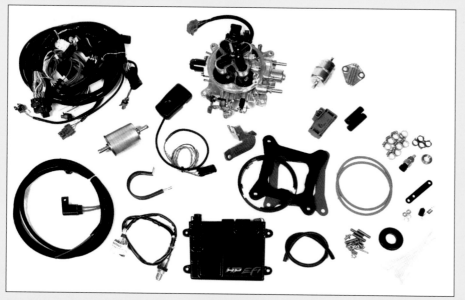

This is the base Holley HP-EFI system on my Olds. It's a twin-throttle-body setup in a draw-through Roots-blown application. It includes the system shown here (PN 550-411) and a slave throttle body (PN 534-187). (Photo Courtesy Holley Performance Products)

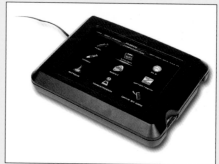

The Holley 5.7-inch LCD touch screen is ideal for those who want to tune the system without having to use a laptop. It offers a full-color display and can act as a virtual gauge panel. (Photo Courtesy Holley Performance Products)

Drivability

Generally speaking, the drivability is excellent and I've put several thousand miles on the Olds since the conversion. Tip-in from idle is a bit of a challenge as there are four return springs to overcome (one for the primary of each throttle body and two standard return springs). Opening 900-cfm worth of throttle blades (the primaries of each throttle body) requires a bit of finesse to keep from accelerating from a stop too aggressively, but I got used to this fairly quickly. The Olds has a TH400 with a manual valve body and shifting through the gears is nice and smooth. It cruises nice in town and on the highway. The engine management works just like that of a modern vehicle, except for a knock sensor that I elected not to use because of the harmonics of the Gilmer-style belt drive for the blower.

Most carbureted Roots-blown applications have a pretty good "blower surge" at idle. This is caused by a lean/rich condition that is common to draw-through Roots-blown applications. This surge gets worse as you increase the drive ratio of the supercharger with respect to the

Olds Conversion Components

I installed the Holley HP EFI system in my Olds in 2010. This system has performed flawlessly and it has really spoiled me. In addition, it has been instrumental in winning over more than one friend to the idea of converting to EFI. Here's a list of the components I chose:

EFI Components

- Holley HP EFI 900-cfm 4-barrel TBI kit* with 75-lb/hr injectors (PN 550-411)
- Holley 900-cfm TBI unit* with 75-lb/hr injectors (PN 534-187)

Also offered with 85-lb/hr injectors

Fuel System Components

- MagnaFuel MP-4302 ProTuner 525 fuel pump
- MagnaFuel MP-9925-C small pump bypass regulator
- MagnaFuel MP-7009 74-micron medium in-line fuel filter
- MagnaFuel MP-7100 10-micron small in-line fuel filter
- MagnaFuel MP-1050 dual-relay wiring harness
- MagnaFuel 10F x 10S, 10F x 8S, and 8F x 8S O-ring to AN-style fittings
- Earl's fuel distribution block: 1/2-inch NPT to (2) 3/8-inch NPT (PN 100183ERL)

- Earl's Perform-O-Flex steel braided hose in -10, -8, and -6 sizes
- Earl's hose ends for -10, -8, and -6 sizes: straight and right angle
- Earl's AN-to-NPT adapters: straight and right angle

Ignition System Components

- MSD 6AL-2 Ignition System (PN 6421)
- MSD GM HEI Distributor (PN 8366)
- MSD 6 Series HVCII Ignition Coil (PN 8253)
- MSD plug wires, etc.

Miscellaneous

- Holley Dual-Throttle-Body Adapter Harness Kit (PN 558-206)
- Holley HEI Ignition Harness (PN 558-304)
- Small Cap HEI Distributor Ignition Module Connector Pigtail (PN 100-00543)
- Holley Throttle Bracket Extender (no part number available)**
- Holley 2 Bar MAP Sensor (PN 538-13)***

** *For dual-throttle-body installations only*
*** *For boosted applications only* ∎

---

crankshaft. The Olds has none. Truth be told, I do like a little blower surge, but I'd prefer not to keep two feet on the brake pedal at a stop sign to keep it from pushing through the intersection. The lack of blower surge with my setup is primarily because the A/F ratio is set to 14.7:1 in the idle area and the blower is underdriven by 13 percent. I'm cool with that.

Throttle response is instantaneous, and I do mean just that. You really have to be careful in a street-driven vehicle with this kind of power on tap.

Diagnosing EFI Running Problems

After you install your EFI system, you may encounter various problems that require some diagnosis and problem solving and mechanical and tuning work to resolve. Certain mechanical problems can manifest themselves as an EFI problem as well. The following are three specific problems I had with my Olds, which is equipped with a big-block Chevy and Holley HP EFI system.

Problem 1

About six months after the installation, the Olds began to run just awful. I pulled out the laptop, connected it to the ECU, and began looking at the Learn Table. Something just wasn't right as it was populated with a bunch of positive numbers in the idle and cruise areas. This indicated that the ECU was

adding a bunch of fuel to achieve the desired A/F ratio, which was the outside of 3-percent margin of acceptability.

As I dug into the problem, I pulled off the driver's side valve cover and found that I could compress the lifter on intake number-1 with very little effort. Uh-oh. A major top-end teardown revealed that the hydraulic lifter for this valve had a very tiny hole worn through the base of it, which rendered it useless. Further inspection showed that 9 of the 16 lifters were badly worn and several cam lobes wiped. When the engine was originally built it had a hydraulic flat-tappet cam and even though I used an oil with a zinc additive it appeared that wasn't enough. It was time to rebuild the top end completely.

My buddy Frank Beck designed a complete top-end package for me built around a custom-ground hydraulic roller camshaft that he spec'd to Comp Cams. Engine builders are typically secretive about their camshaft profiles. But let's just say the old profile had .550 inch of intake lift while the profile Frank spec'd has .664 to .669 inch of lift, more duration, and less overlap.

In addition, I pulled the cylinder heads (iron closed-chamber 3964291s) so that Frank's team could work on them and entirely rebuild them to accommodate the new and lighter 11/32-inch valves and spring package. They upsized the valves to a 2.25-inch intake and 1.90-inch exhaust, from the stock 2.18- and 1.72-inch sizes (yep, 1.72 inches; weird, I know). Given the collectability of these heads, I wouldn't let them cut the intake runners to match the intake, but they did a bunch of work in the chambers that is really hard to detect. When I picked up the heads and new parts from Frank he told me, "It's going to be a radically different animal now."

Now, these are major changes. How would the EFI system adapt? Would I have to take it back for more tuning with the new parts? Once the engine was fully re-assembled, it started right up. The first thing we did was to set the timing via the distributor so that it read identically with a timing light and in the software (per Holley's instructions). No problem.

Incidentally, you *really* want to be sure that your pointer is *dead on* so that when you do this, you'll be spot on. This is easily accomplished with a piston stop.

The idle in open loop was nasty with a *super-nasty* blower surge; it was just the kind of stuff that makes

horsepower guys smile and do a high five. The exhaust tone was radically different, so much so that stuff on the shelves in the garage and in the house was rattling. Nice.

We took it out for a drive and I had accidentally disabled the closed-loop feature in the software. It ran well and sounded even better with a radically louder exhaust tone. We noted that the ECU was making no changes to the Learn Table and showed the A/F ratio to be in the mid-12s as we drove.

The following day, I rectified this and began driving it in closed loop with the learn parameters set at 100 percent. Within 10 or so miles, the ECU had a pretty good handle on all the new parts. Just 10 more miles and it was better yet. Even more drive time was required to get the Fuel Table optimized to achieve the desired A/F ratios in the idle and cruise areas but it was pretty close at this point.

The fact that the ECU was able to optimize the Fuel Table to perform well with all these new parts so quickly was pretty mind boggling. By now the blower surge was gone.

Now it was time to find a nice stretch of road and let the ECU do the same for the part of the tune with some boost. My buddy Bill Surin (owner of the Olds Cutlass featured in Chapter 6) sat in the passenger seat with the laptop, monitoring the A/F ratio as I attempted to ease into the throttle at 25 mph or so. The shift light came on *instantly* (6,200 rpm) as the car blew the tires off so violently it banged the rev limiter, which was set at 6,700 rpm. I was out of the throttle as quickly as I got into it.

Bill scolded me, "Dude! I said easy! What are you doing over there?"

I just had to laugh as my attempt was maybe half throttle . . . maybe. I tried a few more times but we had the same results. We decided the best thing to do was to spin the blower slower and try again another day. I changed the upper pulley to slow the blower from 9 percent under to 11 percent under and drove it a bit like that.

Problem 2

I then took a few friends for a ride, being ever so cautious not to blow the tires off it. No matter how I tried, the new combination overpowered the tires (33x22.5x15s) nearly instantly. It was as if the pulley change never happened.

I took my buddy Marvin for a ride. He's a big-block Chevy guy all the way and he was blown away by how powerful it was. In my best "hold my beer and watch this" moment, I said, "Let's see what it feels like with a few pounds of boost." I feathered into the throttle in first and it blew the tires off so fast they went up into tire shake. I short-shifted it into second, and *boom!* something broke.

We pulled over and found the problem. I had sheared the wheel studs off the passenger-side rear wheel (1/2-inch Moser wheel studs). Luckily, the wheel did not damage the quarter panel. We were able to get the Olds home on a trailer.

Problem 3

After pulling the axles and upgrading the wheel studs to 5/8 inch, spinning the blower even slower (13 percent under), and accidentally banging the limiter a few more times, I lost a pushrod cup in my 1980s vintage "gold" rocker arms.

Hmmm . . . Frank told me to replace them when we rebuilt the top end and I elected to run them to save a few bucks. "Dude, throw those out," he told me. (Words of wisdom as it turned out.)

This minor problem broke numerous parts, scattered shrapnel into the valley, and required a major top-end teardown to retrieve it all. Solution? Get the suspension geom-

etry sorted out and lower the rev limiter to 6,400 rpm until it is. Oh yeah, and listen to Frank.

Interestingly enough, this new combination makes so much more power than the old one, I drove the car two or three more times after this happened, not realizing it was

running on seven cylinders. Then I noticed that the throttle response was less snappy, so I plugged in the laptop and looked at the Learn Table in the ECU. It was again populated with data similar to when the lifter failed.

Pulling the valve cover revealed the rocker arm on the number-3

14- and 16-Volt Batteries

I f you use your vehicle for street/strip or it's strictly used for competition of any kind, you may want to consider using 14- or 16-volt batteries.

After I got the Olds all sorted out, my friends at XS Power asked me if I'd be interested in putting some of their 14-volt batteries in it to replace the aging Diehard Golds. Converting to higher-voltage batteries is popular with racers, so I jumped at the opportunity.

I contacted Holley tech support and verified that their ECUs are compatible with charging systems making up to 18 volts. Perfect, as the alternator had to charge at 16.8 volts to charge the 14-volt batteries.

One of the biggest advantages of doing such a swap in my Olds was weight. The XS Power S1400s weigh 28 pounds each, while my trusty Diehard Gold (Group 27) batteries weigh 49.5 pounds each. That's a reduction of 43 pounds overall for a pair.

If you're a racer, upgrading to a 14-volt or even a 16-volt battery is popular. Furthermore, if you're a racer considering a carb-to-EFI conversion and you already run a 16-volt battery, you're probably wondering if the conversion is even possible.

What are the pros and cons?

The XS Power S1400 is a 14-volt battery with 500 cca. A pair of these will be perfect for my Olds. (Photo Courtesy Scottie Johnson/ XS Power)

Pros

Running higher-voltage batteries allows your cooling fans to spin faster, lights to be brighter, and in some cases reduces the current required of your ignition system. Some racers choose to omit the alternator altogether, mainly to eliminate its weight and parasitic drag on the crankshaft. When doing so, it's popular to switch to 16-volt batteries to power the accessories directly when the engine is running.

Cons

Increasing the voltage to an electric fuel pump causes it to work harder, increasing the fuel pressure as a result.

Reducing that with the regulator is really not the best idea as you are moving more fuel than before and heating it even more in the process. Increasing the voltage to electric fans causes them to work harder (a good thing) but they gulp more current at a higher voltage (see page 59 for solutions).

Remember that a 12-volt battery is really a 12.6-volt battery because it has six 2.1-volt cells wired in series. A 14-volt battery has seven such cells netting 14.7 volts at rest and a 16-volt battery has eight such cells netting 16.8 volts at rest. This makes 16-volt batteries more suited to race applications where an alternator isn't used. But 14-volt batteries are just perfect for both street and strip applications with EFI.

It's commonly accepted that 2.4 volts per cell is the maximum allowable voltage to charge an automotive battery without damaging it over time. The math works as follows:

12-volt battery = 2.4 volts x 6 cells = 14.4 volts
14-volt battery = 2.4 volts x 7 cells = 16.8 volts
16-volt battery = 2.4 volts x 8 cells = 19.2 volts

In the end, 19.2 volts is really a bit too much for many EFI systems on the market, but 16.8 volts falls within the guidelines of many of them. ∎

intake valve was sitting 45 degrees away from the pushrod, the pushrod stuck between the guide and head, and the lock on the stud girdle smashed to bits. I got *really* lucky, and fortunately none of the new parts were damaged in the process.

Troubleshooting with Holley Software

Most of the above is simply attributed to hot rodding. I think it's important to note that in each case where the engine began running poorly, simply plugging into the ECU and looking at the data in the Learn Table showed that there was a lean condition detected by the oxygen sensor that the ECU was attempting to overcome by adjusting the fuel. Thus began the search to find the problem. The feedback available via the Holley software was very valuable as it pointed me in the right direction to find the problem each time. I can tell you that I'm now a believer.

The Olds is a major handful on the street and it still needs some work on the suspension geometry; but only a slick is going to cure the traction issues long term. Since slowing the blower, it's rarely seen more than 5 pounds of boost and it makes that at half throttle. It gets loose *fast*. Honestly, it scares me and this is really a case where the rest of the tuning should be finished on a chassis dyno.

14-Volt Battery Conversion

Before doing a conversion, you must consider three things: increasing the output voltage of the alternator to be able to charge the battery, upgrading the wiring to the electric fan(s) to accommodate the additional current they consume at this higher operating voltage, and

managing the speed of the fuel pump so that you spin it only as fast as required to maintain the desired fuel pressure.

Alternator Output Voltage Increase

Depending on the type and brand of alternator you have, you may be able to increase its output voltage quite easily. I installed a Mechman adjustable voltage boost module on the Iraggi alternator of the Olds to accommodate this voltage increase. The Mechman adapter installed inline on the regulator harness. It has a small potentiometer for adjusting the output voltage. This does so by adding resistance to the sense lead, causing the regulator to think the actual operating voltage is lower than it really is.

In Chapter 2, I discussed choosing an alternator that offers more output than you really need so that you're not working it at 100 percent and creating a bunch of heat in the process. As you increase the output voltage, some accessories such as fans, pumps, and incandescent lights actually consume more current in response.

Electric Fan(s) Wiring Upgrade

An electric fan or pair of them consume current that is directly proportional to the voltage available to them. As voltage increases, current also increases. Remember the Camaro in Chapter 2? That is the

kind of wiring I see most often with electric fans and it's absolutely not up to the task. I typically *only* use 10 AWG wiring to aftermarket electric fans with diameters up to 16 inches. Some OEM-style electric fans, such as the big 18-inch fans from Ford vehicles, require as much as 80 amps. Be sure to wire them accordingly.

I run a pair of 16-inch Spal fans on the Ron Davis radiator. I've measured them at 26 amps each at 14.4 volts, so I know they're going to require even more at 16.8 volts. My current wiring safely accommodates 30 amps per fan, so it's time to upgrade that just to be safe.

Also, I've been itching to build an ECU-controlled two-speed fan setup for the Olds, ever since I did the EFI conversion. I've just never found the time to do it. So, I'm going to kill two birds with one stone.

The Holley ECUs, like most, have dual outputs for electric fans, and each can be set to trigger at different temperatures.

Instead of using one output per fan, I elected to use one output to turn both fans on in low speed at 165 degrees and the second output to switch both fans to high speed at 185 degrees. (See Figure 4.6.)

Of course you can choose any temperature you like. This is a really clever circuit that GM used on the C4 Corvette, so I can't claim it. This circuit is compatible with any ECU that has dual-fan outputs that can be programmed to operate at

Fig. 4.3. The Adjustable Voltage Boost Module from Mechman provides a simple way to raise the output of the alternator from 14.4 volts to 16.8 volts, which is required to properly charge the 14-volt batteries. Mechman offers them for numerous types of alternators.

Fig. 4.4. The Holley Inputs/Outputs Auxiliary Harness (PN 558-400) is required to access the inputs and outputs of the HP-EFI ECU. The harness plugs into the mating connector on the main harness. (Photo Courtesy Holley Performance Products)

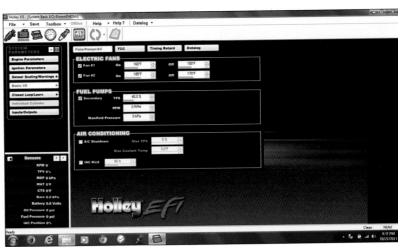

Fig. 4.5. The Basic inputs/outputs tab of the SYSTEM PARAMETERS allows you to configure the ON points for up to two aftermarket electric fans and secondary fuel pump outputs.

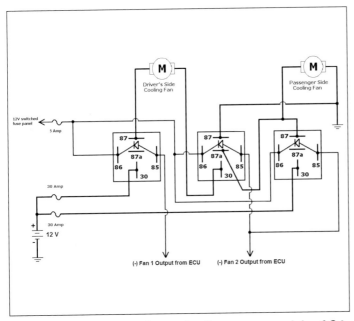

Fig. 4.6. GM used this clever circuit on some models of C4 Corvettes to operate a pair of electric fans in two speeds. I was able to use this circuit in nearly the same way for my Olds. I used A11 for the low-speed output and A10 for the high-speed output from the ECU. Both have negative triggers. I added diodes across the coils of each of the three relays so the outputs of the ECU were protected.

Fig. 4.7. I fabbed-up this power center for the Olds, which includes the waterproof relays shown here for the two-speed fan circuit. I make this kind of stuff from 1/4-inch-thick ABS plastic that I bend to the desired shape with a heat gun. Here, I used a GM Weatherpack connector to provide a simple interface to the wiring in the vehicle. I've left two slots (at the right) for the headlight relays, which are already in the vehicle. Figure 4.6 shows the circuit diagram.

different temperatures, which covers most of them.

Refer to Chapter 7 for in-depth information on how to configure the inputs/outputs of the Holley HP and Dominator ECUs.

High-Volume Fuel Pump Speed Management

Whether or not you plan to use a 14-volt battery in your vehicle, you should consider managing the speed of any high-volume fuel pump. For

that matter, any electric fuel pump benefits from this. By managing the speed of the pump, you'll enjoy several benefits, including increased pump life, decreased pump noise, and reduced heating of the fuel that is

Fig. 4.8. This power center fits perfectly just in front of the passenger-side front wheel. The panel bolts to the inner fender with 1/4-inch hardware.

Fig. 4.9. I mounted the headlight relays to the panel. Waterproof relays are a must for an install such as this because the vehicle has no inner fenders.

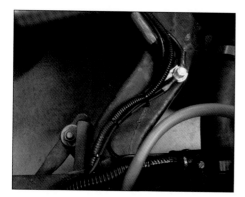

Fig. 4.10. I grounded the fans at the main ground location on the frame rail, which includes the ground upgrade for the alternator. The return path from the fans to the alternator is very short.

Fig. 4.11. I terminated the new harness with the correct fan plugs. I sourced these fan plugs from CE Auto Electric Supply. This provides a perfect fit and finish.

common in a return-style fuel system.

Increasing the input voltage to the fuel pump has an undesirable effect as it pumps a greater volume of fuel and increases the fuel pressure as a result. Reducing the fuel pressure with the regulator further increases the problem of heating the fuel in a return-style system, possibly to the point of cavitation of the fuel pump. All bad things.

The correct way is to reduce the speed, *not the voltage*, of the fuel pump to the minimum at which it can operate and still maintain the

desired fuel pressure. The best way to do this is via pulse width modulation (see sidebar "Pulse Width Modulation" on page 13 for more details).

In the Olds, I elected to use an Aeromotive fuel pump speed controller (FPSC) for this. This controller is suitable for any electric fuel pump. The FPSC utilizes Pulse Width Modulation (PWM) so that it can man-

age the speed of the fuel pump by managing duty cycle (the amount of ON time). It does this by tracking engine RPM. The FPSC uses the minimum amount of duty cycle to maintain the correct operating fuel pressure at idle. The duty cycle progressively increases as engine RPM increases until it reaches 100-percent duty cycle, which is full output. After you've installed the FPSC, it's quite simple to set both of these thresholds using the included instructions.

I've used the FPSC in my Olds for nearly a year and it's worked perfectly. My favorite part is that the pump is really quiet under normal idle and cruising conditions; so quiet that you can't even hear it. Incidentally, if you'd like to see exactly how the FPSC works, watch the following videos on my YouTube channel: "14-Volt Battery Conversion Part 1" and "14-Volt Conversion Part 2: Aeromotive Fuel Pump Speed Controller."

Fuel Pump Speed Controller Installation

This installation was quite simple and the instructions included with it

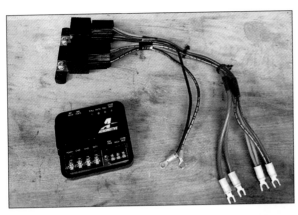

Fig. 4.12. The Aeromotive FPSC is about the same size as the pair of 40-amp relays it replaces. The similarities end there. This is one smart little box. Installation is not much more difficult than connecting the pair of relays that originally powered the fuel pump.

from Aeromotive were very specific. In addition, the kit comes complete with every single part needed to successfully install it.

1 Remove the existing fuel pump relay(s).

Fig. 4.13. I actually installed the relays when I upgraded the fuel system for the project illustrated in my book Automotive Electrical Performance Projects. *Time to make way for the FPSC. This device is intended for aftermarket fuel pumps.*

Fig. 4.14. I love it when I think ahead. Installing the ATC fuse panel and terminal block makes this upgrade a snap. I installed these originally when doing the EFI conversion in my Olds in Automotive Electrical Performance Projects. *Products like these provide far more flexibility if you decide to upgrade components.*

Fig. 4.16. Connecting the Aeromotive FPSC is really no more difficult than connecting the pair of relays that I removed in favor of it. (Illustration Courtesy Aeromotive)

2 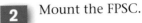 Mount the FPSC.

Fig. 4.15. The FPSC was mounted and in use for about a year when I snapped this photo. The FPSC was easy to set up, has worked exactly as advertised, and I'm very happy with it.

3 Connect the FPSC to the fuel pump.

Connect the PUMP+ output to the fuel pump positive input via the included 10 AWG wiring.

Connect the GND output to the fuel pump negative input via the included 10 AWG wiring.

Note that the negative or ground terminal on your fuel pump now has no connection to ground, only to the GND output terminal on the FPSC. Connecting the fuel pump or GND output of the FPSC to ground can damage the FPSC. If in doubt, follow Figure 4.16 closely.

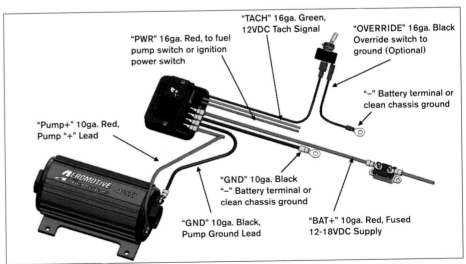

4 Connect the FPSC to the battery.

Connect the GND input to ground via the included 10 AWG wiring.

Connect the BAT+ input to the positive (+) terminal on the battery via the included 10 AWG wiring and the included circuit breaker to protect the FPSC and the wiring.

In the Olds, I connected this to my existing ATC fuse panel and used a UCB-style circuit breaker.

5 Connect the FPSC to the ignition, tach signal, and override switch.

Use the included wire to connect the IGN PWR input to the trigger wire that you used to trigger your fuel pump relay(s).

You really should be using the Fuel Pump Output from your ECU for this as I did in the Olds. In some cases, the ECU harness includes a pre-wired relay designed to directly drive a small fuel pump. If that is the case, you can use the fuel pump output of the relay to trigger the IGN PWR input. If the ECU harness only has a negative output to drive a fuel pump relay, you need to wire a relay to convert this to a positive output to power the IGN PWR input.

Use the included wire to connect the TACH input to the tach output of your ignition system.

If that tach output is also used to drive a tach (and most are!), you

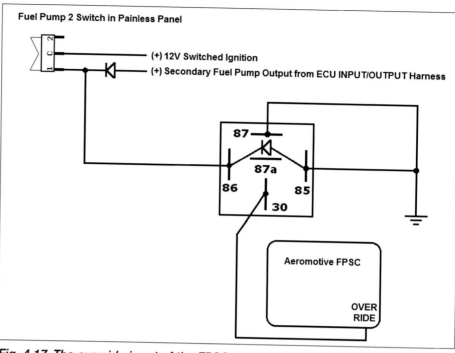

Fig. 4.17. The override input of the FPSC requires a negative trigger. Therefore, it was necessary to invert the output from the switch in the Painless switch panel. I also elected to interface this with the ECU, making the override automatic when the throttle position exceeds 40 percent.

need to run the TACH output of the box to the FPSC first, and then connect the input to your tach to the TACH terminal on the FPSC. In the Olds, I just ran a pair of wires from the TACH input of the FPSC to the front of the vehicle and connected one to the TACH output of my MSD 6AL2 and the other to the input wire of my Auto Meter tach. Aeromotive says this prevents erratic operation of the tach and/or FPSC. I've had no issues.

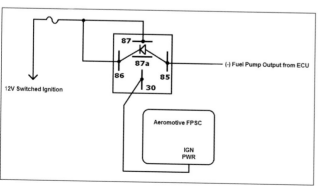

Fig. 4.18. If you're using the FPSC with an ECU that has a negative fuel pump output, it's necessary to use a relay to invert that. The diode across the coil of the relay protects the output of the ECU from damage.

Use the included wire to connect the OVER RIDE input to an optional dash-mounted override switch. This input is negative, so when it is grounded, the FPSC operates the fuel pump at 100-percent duty cycle.

This is a really great feature: you may want to do this when you make a pass down the quarter-mile. I connected this input to the second fuel pump switch in my Painless panel. It was necessary to invert its output from positive to negative to do this, but that was simple. In addition, I used the Secondary Fuel Pump Output of the HP ECU to do this automatically anytime the TPS exceeds 40 percent (see Figure 4.5).

6 Start the engine and verify that the FPSC works correctly.

You should notice the tach LED flashing rapidly to indicate the presence of a tach signal.

7 Adjust the MIN VOLTS per the detailed instructions provided in the manual.

This allows you to reduce the duty cycle and the average operating voltage to the minimum the fuel pump can be driven with to maintain the recommended fuel pressure at idle.

8 Adjust the SET TACH per the detailed instructions provided in the manual.

This allows you to set the RPM point at which the FPSC permits the fuel pump to operate at 100-percent duty cycle.

Volt Meter Upgrade

Like most vehicles, my Olds had an old-school volt meter that was not going to be able to accurately display the voltage of the alternator once it was increased. No problem; a new Auto Meter volt meter fit the bill perfectly.

14-Volt Battery Installation

At this stage, all of the work has been completed to ensure that the 14-volt conversion goes off without a hitch. I now need to remove the 12-volt batteries, install the 14-volt batteries, install the Mechman Adjustable Voltage Boost Module, and set the output voltage of the alternator.

I adjusted the output of the alternator according to the directions included with the Mechman Adjustable Voltage Boost Module. I set the output of the alternator so that I measured 17.0 volts at the batteries after cold starting the engine. This couldn't have been easier. Be sure you connect your DMM to the battery directly when setting the output voltage. See the sidebar Increased

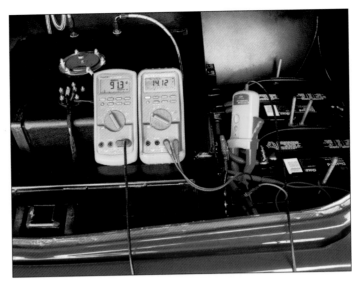

Fig. 4.19. 12-Volt Batteries—With all accessories on and the engine at operating temperature and at idle, I measured 91.3 amps at 14.12 volts. This is the sign of a healthy 12-volt charging system with a proper-size alternator.

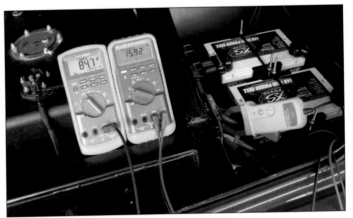

Fig. 4.20. 14-Volt Batteries—With all accessories on and the engine at operating temperature and at idle, I measured 84.7 amps at 15.92 volts. This is the sign of a healthy 14-volt charging system with a proper-size alternator. It's important to note the XS Power AGM batteries require substantially less current to maintain a surface charge than did the Diehard batteries they replaced.

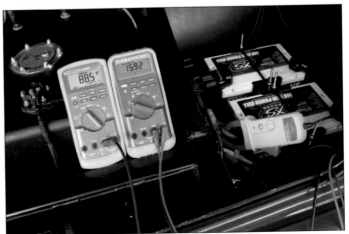

Fig. 4.21. I activated the override switch on the Aeromotive FPSC so that the pump now runs at 100-percent duty cycle. This increases the current required of the pump by 4 amps. The output of the Iraggi alternator doesn't even flinch. The Iraggi alternator, Mechman Voltage Boost Module, Aeromotive FPSC, and XS Power 14-volt batteries work harmoniously together. I'm very happy with how this turned out.

Fig. 4.22. The old Auto Meter volt-meter scale went to only 16 volts. Time to replace it with a newer version that reads up to 18 volts. (Comparing the readings on this to my Fluke 87 DMM reminded me why I'm so fond of Auto Meter gauges.)

Fig. 4.23. The XS Power S1400s are quite a bit smaller than the Diehard Group 27 batteries they replaced. The engine really zings at start-up now.

Voltage to Electric Fans on page 66 to see how the voltage normalizes after the alternator recharges the batteries after a cold start.

Other accessories such as ignition boxes and the ECU consume less current in response. For Olds, here are the measurements before and after the 14-volt battery conversion.

- Output current of the alternator at idle at 14.1 volts, at operating temp, all accessories on: 91.3A
- Output current of the alternator at idle at 15.9 volts, at operating temp, all accessories on: 84.7A

The XS Power AGM batteries require substantially less current to maintain a surface charge than did the Diehard batteries they replaced. This reduces the work load of the alternator.

Low-RPM Rev Limiter Interface

Using a low-RPM rev limiter is common in drag racing. You may have one set up to trigger when

Fig. 4.24. The Mechman Adjustable Voltage Boost Module plugged right in to the existing Iraggi alternator. I elected to extend and loom the sense lead to make the install neat and tidy. For now, I left the adjustment easily accessible.

Increased Voltage to Electric Fans

I was curious to see the effect of additional voltage to electric fans. Ohm's Law says that when you increase voltage to a device such as an electric fan, you also increase the amount of current flowing to it. I started the engine and allowed the alternator to replenish the charge in the batteries. After the charge is replenished in the batteries, voltage settles to a point that is considered the nominal output voltage of the alternator to operate the accessories and keep a surface charge on the batteries.

This 39-percent power increase translates into a substantial increase in airflow from the fans. As a result, they tend to operate only briefly at high speed when I'm driving it around town. ■

	Voltage (volts)	Current (amps)	Power (watts)
12-volt Charging System	13.76	37.8	520.13
14-volt Charging System	16.16	44.6	720.74
Difference	+17%	+18%	+39%

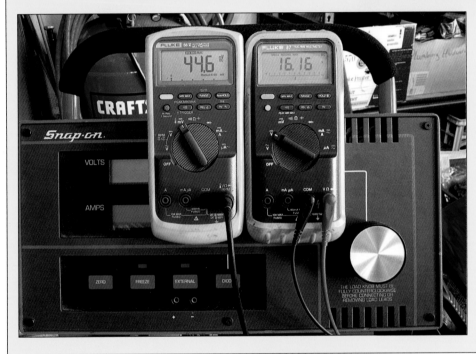

After the upgrade, I have more voltage, more current, and (most important) more power to the electric fans. Measurements are shown at operating temperature. The fans respond to this additional power by moving more air.

you hold down the trans-brake button. Most rev limiters intentionally misfire the cylinders so that you can hold the gas pedal to the floor and sit at a programmed RPM.

Misfiring the cylinders means that there can be unburned fuel entering the exhaust. When operating in closed loop, the oxygen sensor picks that up as a rich condition and the ECU begins to make changes to correct this.

So, you have a few options:

- Run the system in open loop when drag racing
- Run the system in closed loop and reduce the Learn percentage to +/- 5% or less
- Run the system in closed loop and use the low-RPM rev limiter built into the ECU, if it has one

Choosing an ECU with a built-in low-RPM rev limiter is really the way to go. As it is, the Holley HP EFI system has this option and the transmission in my Olds has a trans-brake

that I've never used. (Yeah, like I need that.) Regardless, the interface is simple because you can program this input for positive or negative polarity (see Figure 7.15 page 133 for more details).

Regardless of the specific brand of ECU you elect to run, this interface is simple. Now, when you depress the trans-brake button, the ECU does two things: engage the low-RPM rev limiter (pedal to the floor!) and switch the ECU into open loop.

Fig. 4.25. This Auto Meter wideband A/F gauge kit is the perfect match to the existing 2⅝-inch Sport Comp gauges in the dash of my Olds. Having a wideband A/F gauge in the dash makes it easy to keep tabs on the actual A/F ratio as I cruise around. Installation involves making switched power, ground, and illumination connections in addition to the installation of the oxygen sensor itself.

Fig. 4.26. When the Olds was tuned at ADS, they installed an oxygen bung (see Figure 3.11 on page 46) in the exhaust on the driver's side, just downstream of the collector for their Hariba wideband oxygen meter. After tuning was completed, they plugged it to seal the exhaust. I removed the plug and threaded the oxygen sensor included in the Auto Meter gauge kit right in.

According to Holley, some trans-brakes can create quite a bit of back electromotive force (EMF) when the magnetic field collapses after the trans-brake button is released. This can cause damage to the input of the ECU. At the time of this writing, Holley is working on a module to address this problem entirely.

How cool is that? So, yes, racers really can have their cake and eat it too with EFI.

Wideband A/F Gauge Installation

I also elected to add a wideband A/F gauge to the dash of the Olds. A dash-mounted gauge allows you to easily keep tabs on the actual A/F ratio while driving. I chose an Auto Meter Sport Comp gauge as it matched the gauges already in the dash of the Olds.

The gauge comes complete with an oxygen sensor, weld ring, ring plug, detachable wiring harness, etc. I had a pre-existing plugged oxygen sensor location in my exhaust from the dyno tuning sessions and I elected to use it for the oxygen sensor for the gauge.

I always use Auto Meter gauges in my projects because I'm a stickler for accuracy. I've always found their gauges to be incredibly accurate. Good data is paramount when assessing feedback from the engine and you really shouldn't be looking at a laptop screen when cruising around.

Fig. 4.27. This new gauge looks right at home in the dash. I used my 2⅝-inch hole saw to cut the hole for mounting it. Overall, this installation couldn't have gone any easier and the gauge has been an incredibly useful addition.

MSD ATOMIC SYSTEM INSTALLATION

In this chapter, I cover a complete throttle-body EFI installation, the MSD Atomic EFI system. With the information in this chapter, you will be able to install this or any similar throttle-body system. And by the conclusion of the chapter, you will know the time, tools, and expertise required to complete the task. Could those magazine ads really be true? Is it really possible to convert to EFI so easily and quickly?

When I walked the floor at SEMA (Special Equipment Manufacturers Association) in 2011, and again in 2012, one throttle-body-based EFI system really stood out to me: the MSD Atomic EFI system. When CarTech commissioned me to write this book, I absolutely wanted to include this system. So, what was it about the Atomic EFI system that stood out? Well, first and foremost, the ECU is built into the side of the

1,000-cfm throttle body so you don't have to find a location for it or even mount it.

This product category is growing so incredibly quickly that numerous new examples have likely come to market by the time you have this book in your hands. Other products may be improved. Regardless, the following installation overview is absolutely representative of this category of product. The installation is accomplished by mounting the throttle body to where your carburetor once sat. In addition to the TPS and IAC, the IAT, fuel pressure, and MAP sensors are also built into the throttle-body assembly and all are pre-wired to the ECU. Not only does this mean fewer connections need to be made, the harness itself is more compact and less laborious to install. If wiring isn't your thing, the Atomic requires fewer electrical connections than any other EFI system that I'm aware of.

The Atomic EFI system includes an outboard module that needs to be located under the hood or under the dash: it's your preference. The included harness is plenty long for either choice. MSD calls this the power module, which has a number of outputs:

Fig. 5.1. The main components include a 1,000-cfm throttle body, power module, and handheld controller. Incorporating the ECU into the throttle-body assembly simplifies the installation by eliminating all of the connections normally required between the ECU and the throttle body. (Photo Courtesy MSD Performance)

- Electric Fan 1: low current, designed to drive a relay that powers the fan directly
- Electric Fan 2: low current, designed to drive a relay that powers the fan directly
- Fuel Pump: high current, designed to drive the fuel pump directly (20-amp capability)

In addition, the included handheld controller plugs into the power module.

MSD elected to use CANbus (controller area network) technology between the throttle-body assembly and the power module, as well as between the power module and the handheld controller. Again, this greatly simplifies the installation by reducing the number of wires required between components as a single CANbus cable connects the

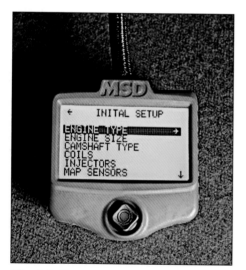

Fig. 5.2. The kit includes a handheld controller that's simple to navigate and easy to use. You use it to configure the system before initial start-up and to fine-tune the system after the vehicle is running. In addition, the handheld controller allows you to monitor numerous engine parameters in real time while the vehicle is running. (Photo Courtesy MSD Performance)

throttle-body assembly to the power module.

The ECU being integrated into the throttle body is the first thing that caught my attention, and likely the first thing that will catch yours.

System Advantages

When MSD representatives gave me the lowdown on the unit, the following things stood out that I thought enthusiasts would appreciate.

PWM Fuel Pump Output

The thing that caught my eye about the fuel pump output is that it has a built-in PWM with three possible settings, depending on the fuel system you elect to use:

- Pulse Width Modulated: returnless system with no regulator
- Non-PWM with Regulator: return-style system with a regulator
- PWM with Regulator: return-style system with a regulator

I'm really fond of using PWM to manage the speed of the fuel pump for a number of reasons. If you elect to use a returnless system with no

regulator with the Atomic EFI system, you *must* locate the fuel pump in the fuel tank and it must be designed to be submerged in fuel. As discussed in Chapter 2, this keeps the pump cool and prevents premature failure of the pump. Furthermore, if you're that guy who refuels 50 miles after the "low fuel" light comes on (guilty . . .), the purpose of locating the pump in the tank to begin with is defeated. Be honest with yourself here.

Engine Management

Allowing the ECU to also manage the ignition timing is the icing on the cake. At the time of this writing, the Atomic EFI system is one of only a few entry-level EFI systems to offer this.

Handheld Controller

The Atomic handheld controller is compact and easy to use. It's chock full of terminology that any enthusiast familiar with carburetors already understands including idle advance, total advance, pump squirt, and power valve enrich.

Nitrous Input

The Atomic EFI system has a nitrous input that can be used to retard the engine timing when the

Fig. 5.3 . Interestingly, MSD uses CANbus cables to connect the ECU and handheld controller to the power module. Given that a single CANbus cable is all that is required to connect the ECU to the power module, wiring between the two is greatly minimized. (Photo Courtesy MSD Performance)

nitrous is engaged. Obviously, the engine management feature *must be* utilized for this feature to work. Adding a 125 shot of nitrous to a 300-hp naturally aspirated engine would be a heck of a lot of fun on the cheap.

System Aspects

MSD Atomic designers and engineers are constantly refining the company's products. At the time of this writing, the following apply.

Camshaft Profile

You need adequate vacuum for an EFI system to operate optimally. If you have a big ol' lumpy camshaft with no vacuum at idle to speak of, many entry-level throttle-body-based EFI systems are incompatible. According to MSD, if the lobe separation angle (LSA) is less than 108 degrees or if the duration is longer than 250 degrees, the Atomic EFI is not suitable for your application.

Sure, who doesn't love the sound of camshaft cut on a 108-degree LSA with a bunch of lift and duration? Although that may get attention when you idle into the cruise, it's the wrong grind for an entry-level EFI system such as the Atomic.

Maximum Horsepower

The maximum horsepower the system is currently capable of supporting is 625 hp when used with the correct fuel system components. In addition, the injector size cannot be upgraded from the stock size (80 lbs/hr at 60 psi).

Power Adders

The Atomic EFI system is compatible with power adders of any type. According to MSD, due to the increased fuel requirement on boosted applications the maximum horsepower that the TBI is capable of supporting can be 20 to 30 percent less.

Because the system cannot add the fuel required of a nitrous system, a wet nitrous kit must be used and the fuel system must be designed accordingly.

Miscellaneous

The MSD Atomic system is not compatible with dual-throttle-body applications, nor it is compatible for marine applications.

It is not UL approved.

MSD Atomic EFI System Installation

So, it's time to get down to brass tacks and see if the Atomic EFI system delivers what it promises. Before beginning a similar installation in your own vehicle, you must have an 18-mm bung in the collector of one of the headers for the oxygen sensor. If you do not already have one, you need to install one before the installation begins.

It is preferable to locate the oxygen sensor upstream of the collector-to-exhaust junction. This

Fig. 5.4. This is Keith Kanak's super-clean 1964 Chevelle. He has driven it on numerous Hot Rod Power Tours. It has a 383-ci Beck Racing Engines small-block Chevy backed by a Tremec 5-speed transmission. (Photo Courtesy Keith Kanak)

Fig. 5.5. Under the hood, the Chevelle is very well detailed. Our goal is to keep the engine bay equally clean with the upgrade.

Fig. 5.6. Keith's 383 was fitted with a Holley HP-series 750-cfm double-pumper carburetor for years and he's been very happy with the performance. Before he and I met, he had actually been considering an EFI conversion to improve fuel economy so this couldn't have worked out better.

prevents unmetered air passing the oxygen sensor in the event of a leaky collector gasket, which can provide erroneous feedback to the ECU and throw off the A/F mixture as a result. Any capable exhaust shop can do this and the bungs (and plugs) are readily available at any speed shop.

I did something here that you are not likely to do. I chose the system first and then had to find a vehicle that allowed me to illustrate a typical installation. You already have the vehicle and you'll choose the system to best suit your application. But my task was easy enough. I found Keith Kanak and his 1964 Chevelle with one phone call.

A 383-ci small-block Chevy from Beck Racing Engines is installed in Keith's Chevelle. It has 10:1 compression and makes approximately 500 hp at the flywheel. The ignition system consists of only a Mallory HEI distributor with vacuum advance (basic enough) and the specs on the camshaft in the 383 are within the guidelines of the Atomic EFI system. In addition, the Chevelle has A/C, has been on The Power Tour multiple times, and Keith drives it everywhere. Long before I met Keith, I spotted this extra-clean Chevelle at a car show just a few miles from my home. Incidentally, Keith had been considering an EFI conversion for some time. Perfect.

I think it's fair to say that most enthusiasts considering an EFI conversion like this one want to do it as inexpensively as possible. To illustrate this, I've split the install in the Chevelle into two stages. Stage 1 is the least expensive way to complete the conversion.

In addition, I've elected to use a factory-style fuel tank and not a custom-built EFI-specific fuel tank. Most owners also choose to use a stock tank in an effort to keep costs down.

In Stage One of the installation, we use the existing ignition system and have the Atomic perform fuel metering only. In Stage Two, we install a new ignition system and configure the Atomic to manage the ignition timing as well as fuel metering. You will learn whether or not this additional cost yields better results.

Here is an overview of the two installation stages:

Stage One: Add EFI, Utilizing the Existing Ignition System

1. Optimize electrical system
2. Install fuel system
3. Install Atomic EFI components
4. Get it to run!

Stage Two: Add Complete Engine Management

1. Upgrade the ignition system
2. Set up the Atomic EFI to manage the timing

Stage One: Add EFI, Utilizing the Existing Ignition System

The electrical system is the backbone of any EFI installation. Before adding a host of new electronic components to Keith's Chevelle, we need to determine if the electrical system is up to the task. If not, we'll optimize it.

1. Optimize Electrical System

When Keith popped the hood of the Chevelle, the first thing I noticed was the run-of-the-mill CS-series alternator and 10 AWG charge lead. Keith did have the engine grounded properly, which was a welcome sight. In addition, the Chevelle has a mechanical fan, which Keith intends to keep as it works perfectly, even in the summer in Phoenix.

So, is the alternator capable of handling the additional load of the MSD Atomic EFI system and electric fuel pump?

I used my Fluke DMMs and accessories and a Snap-on MT3750 Charging System Analyzer to perform all measurements. These are excellent tools and provide excellent data. If you don't have access to such an analyzer, many well-equipped auto service centers have one on hand. Before taking the first measurement, I already knew that at a minimum we'd have to upgrade the wiring to the charging system to get all of the performance the alternator is capable of.

Using the procedure outlined in Chapter 2, here are the steps we used and our readings:

1 Record the resting voltage of the battery with the engine not running: 12.4 volts. (In most cases this denotes a partially charged

battery. However, this vehicle has a red-top Optima battery. Here in the desert, it is all too common to see this particular battery resting well below 12.6 volts, so don't read too much into that.)

2 Start the engine and bring the vehicle to operating temperature.

3 Turn on all of the accessories, including the high-beam headlights, A/C, electric cooling fan(s), audio system at a common listening level, etc.

4 After the engine has reached operating temperature, record the voltage at the battery: 14.0 volts

5 Record the output current of the alternator: 30 amps.

6 Load the alternator with the carbon-pile load in the Snap-On analyzer to determine how much output the alternator is capable of at 800 engine RPM.

7 Record the voltage at the battery: 12.0 volts.

8 Record the output current of the alternator: 61 amps.

This leaves us with 31 amps of reserve that can be used to power the EFI system and fuel pump. Even though this should be plenty, I know we can improve upon it and I'm

Fig. 5.7. The Snap-on AVR charging system analyzers are expensive tools. However, many automotive service centers have them and can perform the required measurements for you. Shown here is the output voltage and output current of the alternator with the Chevelle idling with all of the accessories turned on.

Fig. 5.8. Using the carbon-pile load in the Snap-on analyzer, we determined that the alternator can make a maximum of 61 amps at idle, as it is currently wired.

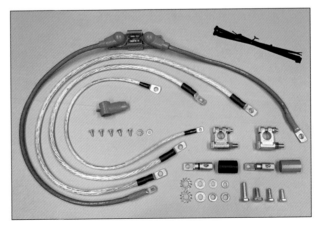

Fig. 5.9. A charging system upgrade kit, such as the 4 AWG kit pictured here, makes it easy to properly wire a 100-amp or larger alternator. This kit from CE Auto Electric Supply is inexpensive and simple to install. They offer them for alternators making up to 300 amps of output.

going to show you how. We elected to upgrade the charging system accordingly.

This vehicle has a stock ammeter in the cluster and Keith wanted to retain it so I kept the stock wiring configuration for the charge lead. The ammeter in the Chevelle has a shunt wired in parallel so it was possible to keep it. In many cases, you are not able to retain the functionality of a stock ammeter when upgrading the charging system, especially when upgrading the alternator to a higher-output unit.

In short, I upgraded the charge lead, the return path of the alternator, and the return path of the bat-

tery. While I was at it, I assembled some new battery cables to replace the ones that were an eyesore to an otherwise clean engine bay.

Because of the wiring scheme of the Chevelle and the fact that we

Fig. 5.10. Correctly grounding the alternator is key to getting all of the output any alternator is capable of. This typically yields 10 to 20 percent more output from the alternator. Note the use of a star washer to get a good bite into the metal.

Ammeter Basics

An ammeter is a device that is designed to measure the flow of current in a circuit. Automotive ammeters typically have both a positive and a negative scale and they indicate the flow of current in two directions. Generally speaking, the following is true of an any such ammeter:

- A positive reading on an ammeter indicates current flow from the alternator to the battery, an indication of a correctly functioning alternator when the vehicle is running.
- A negative reading on the ammeter indicates current flow from the battery to the accessories, an indication of an alternator that is either not large enough or one that isn't working.

With a correctly working alternator, current also flows from the alternator to the accessories, but that isn't displayed on the ammeter.

Wiring Schemes

There are two types of common wiring schemes for ammeters in an automobile: wired directly in-line and wired in parallel with a shunt.

In-Line

This scheme is commonly found on older Chrysler, Dodge, and Plymouth vehicles, as well as some older Ford, Lincoln, and Mercury vehicles. The ammeter is connected in-line, directly between the output of the alternator and the battery. Depending on the state of charge of the battery, significant current can pass through the ammeter.

The wiring between the alternator and the ammeter and between the ammeter and the battery is typically 10 AWG. Depending on the vehicle, this can pass through the bulkhead connector. Today, this wiring scheme is considered somewhat unsafe. Here's why: As the vehicle ages, so does the wiring, connections, and bulkhead connector. As connections age, they break down, increasing resistance through them. Increased resistance causes heat and heat can cause a fire.

If the ammeter in your vehicle is wired in this fashion and you elect to upgrade the alternator, you must bypass the ammeter or you risk a fire. For example, if your vehicle was originally equipped with a 40-amp alternator and you desire

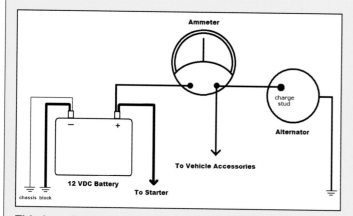

This is a diagram of an ammeter wired directly in-line between the alternator and battery. Significant current can flow through the ammeter depending on the charge state of the battery.

Ammeter Basics CONTINUED

to upgrade it to a 100-amp unit, the ammeter, wiring, and connectors were only designed to safely pass a maximum of 40 amps of current.

The ammeter must be removed from the circuit entirely and the wiring scheme changed or you risk severe damage to the wiring harness, the bulkhead connector, the ammeter, or all three. You can always replace the ammeter with a volt meter if you want to keep tabs on your charging system as you drive.

In Parallel with a Shunt

Many older GM vehicles use this wiring scheme, including Keith's Chevelle. Quite simply, a shunt is connected between two points and the ammeter is connected across the shunt at these two points. This places the ammeter in parallel with the shunt.

Because the ammeter has higher resistance than the shunt (by design), only a small amount of current passes through the ammeter. The shunt can be a short length of solid metal or even a length of wire. Either way, the shunt has a known resistance across its length and the ammeter is calibrated to display the current passing across it.

This is a diagram of an ammeter wired in parallel with a shunt. The shunt bears the brunt of the current, and only a small amount of current flows through the ammeter itself.

This is a far safer way to wire an ammeter because the wiring to the ammeter itself is of a much smaller gauge. Kudos to GM for employing this scheme.

Upgrade Tips

If your vehicle is equipped with an ammeter, it's imperative that you know what kind of wiring scheme is used before you upgrade the alternator, its wiring, or both. Obtain a wiring diagram of the vehicle's charging system from a company such as Mitchell1 to make the determination.

If in doubt, I recommend that you contact a qualified shop that specializes in automotive electrical systems. ∎

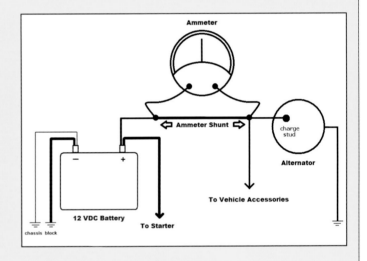

were retaining the ammeter, I elected to use 8 AWG wiring for the wiring upgrades to the alternator (I normally use 4 AWG). All parts were obtained from CE Auto Electric Supply.

Assessment After Charging System Upgrades

After the upgrades were finished, we again used the procedure outlined in Chapter 2 to take new readings to see the fruits of our efforts. Here are the steps and our readings:

1 Record the resting voltage of the battery with the engine not running: 12.4 volts.

Fig. 5.11. For a very long time GM used the horn relay as a point of commonality for power connections, including the charge lead from the alternator. We retained the stock wiring scheme, even as we upgraded to 8 AWG wiring. This allowed us to retain the function of the stock ammeter in the cluster. In some vehicles, that isn't possible.

2 Start the engine and bring the vehicle to operating temperature.

3 Turn on all of the accessories, including the high-beam headlights, A/C, electric cooling fan(s), audio system at a common listening level, etc.

Fig. 5.12. We grounded the alternator directly to the frame rail in the Chevelle, also with 8 AWG cable. I built some new battery cables for the Chevelle at the same time we rewired the alternator (see Figure 5.41 on page 82) where we included a 4 AWG cable from the battery negative to the frame. This provides a low-resistance return path for the alternator and the yet-to-be-installed electric fuel pump.

Fig. 5.13. The Snap-on analyzer shows the fruits of our efforts. We're rewarded with higher-output current and higher-output voltage at idle with all of the accessories turned on. Keith reported brighter headlights on his drive home as a result.

Fig. 5.14. Correctly wiring the charging system produced an 11-amp increase in alternator output current, which was a gain of 18 percent over what we started with. The 11-amp increase was previously lost in the form of heat in the old 10 AWG wiring and high-resistance return path.

4 After the engine has reached operating temperature, record the voltage at the battery: 14.4 volts.

5 Record the output current of the alternator: 36 amps.

6 Load the alternator with the carbon pile load in the Snap-on analyzer to determine how much output the alternator is capable of at 800 engine RPM.

7 Record the voltage at the battery: 12.0 volts.

8 Record the output current of the alternator: 72 amps.

Charging System Results

Our efforts paid off and we got a substantial improvement. Let's consider our results as percentages in the charts below.

Now, these numbers alone don't tell the full story as accessories respond to power, which is the product of voltage and current. So, let's compare that in the charts below.

This "free power" was simply the result of wiring the alternator correctly and with the correct gauge of wire, eliminating the voltage drop caused by resistance in the process. I'll take those gains all day long and I'm confident that this alternator now has enough reserve to power the ECU and fuel pump.

Disconnect the negative (-) battery terminal before proceeding.

2. Install Fuel System

Keith had recently replaced the 50-year-old fuel tank in his Chevelle with a new factory replacement tank from Impala Bob's. He added a -6 male bung to it before installing it, anticipating that he would be upgrading to EFI at some point down the road. He capped it in the meantime. That paid off in spades for us here.

Description	Before	After	Percentage Gain
Resting voltage of battery	12.4 volts	12.4 volts	none
Voltage at battery, vehicle idling and all accessories on	14.0 volts	14.4 volts	2.9
Current required by all accessories at idle	30 amps	36 amps	20
Maximum output current of alternator, loaded with MT3750	61 amps	72 amps	18

Description	Before	After	Percentage Gain
Total power available to accessories at idle (watts)	420	518.4	23
Total power available from alternator at idle (watts)	732	864.0	18

Fig. 5.15. Keith added a -6 male fitting to the Impala Bob's stock replacement fuel tank to facilitate a return-style fuel system. (Photo Courtesy Keith Kanak)

Before choosing the exact components for this system, we first determined the size of line required based on the chart on page 24 in Chapter 2. Because MSD recommends a 3/8-inch inside-diameter (ID) fuel line to the inlet of the throttle body, this is what we came up with:

We used push-lock–style hose and fittings for this installation to keep cost down and reduce installation time. It is worth noting that MSD specifically points out that hard fuel lines are not compatible with the Atomic EFI system. We elected to run a return-style fuel system, as we're using a fuel pump that is not located in the fuel tank (see Figure 2.6 on page 22). We chose components from Holley for this fuel system.

Holley has a document on their website called the *Holley Fuel System Selection Chart* that makes it easy to determine the correct components for any fuel system. Also, Holley now offers EFI fuel system kits on their website, which include a pump, pre-filter, post-filter, regulator, lines, and fittings.

In Keith's Chevelle, it simply isn't possible to mount the tank and pump rearward of the fuel tank. So Keith fabricated a really slick bracket to mount the pump and pre-filter to just forward of the tank, which is equipped with a pick-up to supply the pump. Keith mounted the assembly to the floor of the trunk just forward of the tank.

Although the exhaust doesn't run particularly hot in this area, Keith is in the process of modifying the over-axle assembly to relocate this part of the exhaust. This ensures the heat from the exhaust isn't an issue.

We found a nice place inside the frame rail just behind the front passenger wheel to locate the post-filter.

Okay, now that a bunch of the hard work is complete, it's time to remove the carburetor and install the throttle-body assembly. Once the installation is complete, you have to look closely to see that this isn't a carburetor.

We located the regulator along the firewall, behind the inner fender and as far away from the headers as possible. This mounting location doesn't satisfy NHRA regulations for fuel system components. That's not an issue with this Chevelle, but it may be for you, so be sure to take the rules of any sanctioning body into consideration when choosing a place for the components.

Fuel Line	Size	ID (inch)	Fuel Line	Size	ID (inch)
Tank to Pre-Filter	-8	1/2	Throttle Body to Regulator	-6	3/8
Pre-Filter to Pump	-8	1/2	Regulator to Tank (return)	-6	3/8
Pump to Post-Filter	-6	3/8			
Post-Filter to Throttle Body	-6	3/8	Tank Vent	-6	3/8

Description	Part Number	Rating
Fuel Pump	12-890	76 gph* at 43 psi, up to 900 hp naturally aspirated
Pre-Filter	162-564	100-micron, fuel-injected applications
Post-Filter	162-554	10-micron, fuel-injected applications
Regulator	12-846	return-style, fuel-injected applications
* Gallons Per Hour		

Fig. 5.16. Keith built a really slick metal bracket to mount the pre-filter and fuel pump just forward of the fuel tank. He painted it the same color as the tank. (Photo Courtesy Keith Kanak)

Fig. 5.17. We utilized the latest and greatest fuel system components from Holley for this installation. This series of Holley fuel pumps is incredibly quiet: so quiet, you can barely hear them with the engine running.

Fig. 5.18. The pre-filter and fuel pump fit nicely in front of the fuel tank. Note that there is plenty of space around the exhaust.

Fig. 5.19. We located the post-filter along the frame rail, just under the regulator. The 45-degree fittings allow the lines to make a smooth entry into and exit from the filter.

Fig. 5.20. MSD went out of their way to make the throttle-body assembly look like a carburetor. I'm sure this will fool a lot of folks at the car shows.

Fig. 5.21. We located the regulator as out of the way as possible in the corner of the engine compartment to keep things clean and tidy. We mounted it with the included bracket and hardware.

Fig. 5.22. We routed the fuel lines neatly up and out of the way of the exhaust and suspension components. This keeps them away from heat and out of harm's way.

Fig. 5.23. We used Adel clamps, also obtained from CE Auto Electric Supply, to anchor the fuel lines properly on their way to the front of the Chevelle.

Fig. 5.24. More of the same as the fuel lines pass over the control arm and emergency brake cable.

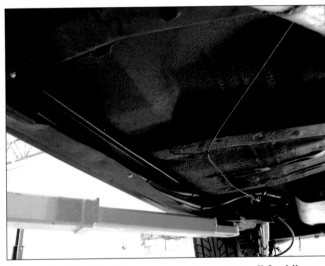

Fig. 5.25. Take the time to properly secure all fuel lines under your vehicle. It just takes one damaged fuel line for you to have a really bad day.

Fig. 5.26. Keep filters and fuel lines tucked up as close as possible to frame rails to minimize the risk of damage via flying debris, etc.

The feed and return lines were then routed along the frame rails and up to the throttle body and regulator. We anchored these with Adel clamps and cable ties to keep everything secure and out of harm's way.

Although the vent tube is hard to see, it is located to the left of the return, about an inch higher.

The return line and feed lines are now connected to the regulator and throttle body, respectively.

Fig. 5.27. All return-style regulators are installed between the outlet of the throttle body and the return inlet of the fuel tank. Follow the provided diagram closely.

Fig. 5.28. We connected the fuel feed line to the rear port on the throttle-body assembly and the return line from the front port of the throttle-body assembly to the regulator. These can be connected in reverse if your particular application calls for it as they are not input or output specific.

Fig. 5.29. The throttle linkage connected exactly as before.

Now that all the fuel lines are connected, we elected to connect the existing linkage to the throttle body. As the throttle body is nearly identical in this respect to the carburetor, this took all of two seconds.

3. Install Atomic EFI Components

Next, we located the CTS in the intake manifold. You may choose to locate it in either cylinder head as well. Either way works. We elected to put the CTS in the manifold to avoid the possibility of breaking off the plug in the head when trying to remove it, which is all too common. If the plug breaks off in the head, it makes for a long day to remove it.

It is necessary to drain the top 1/3 or 1/2 of the radiator before doing this so that the level of coolant in the radiator is below the location you choose for the CTS. After draining the coolant, we marked a location on the manifold, and drilled and tapped the hole without removing the thermostat housing. The CTS included in the Atomic EFI is a 3/8-inch NPT thread, which calls for a 37/64-inch hole. Any real car guy has both in his toolbox!

We used plenty of grease on the drill bit and tap to minimize the amount of shavings that fall into the water passage. I also held the shop vac while Keith drilled. After the tapping was done, we vacuumed the inside of the water passage to get every last shaving out. This was actually quite simple.

Next up is the oxygen sensor. Keith already had an 18-mm bung welded into the collector on the passenger-side header for a handheld wideband A/F meter, so this was greatly simplified. MSD, as all others, recommends that you locate the oxygen sensor in such a way that it is mounted at an angle of at least 10 degrees above horizontal.

The Chevelle is equipped with a Mallory HEI distributor with vacuum advance. I'm a huge fan of vacuum advance for street-driven vehicles because it promotes lower engine temperatures at idle and increases fuel economy and throttle response, all of which provide better drivability.

We connected the vacuum advance to the base of the throttle body, which has three ports on the front. Two are manifold vacuum ports and one is ported vacuum. We connected the vacuum advance to the manifold vacuum port on the driver's side.

The power module is the remaining component of the Atomic EFI that needs to be installed. It can be located either in the passenger

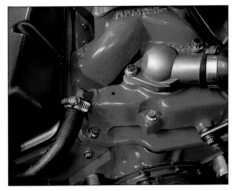

Fig. 5.30. We installed the CTS without removing the thermostat or thermostat housing in just a few simple steps. Be sure to drain an appropriate amount of coolant first.

Fig. 5.31. Keith drilled and tapped the hole (3/8-inch NPT) while I held the vacuum cleaner to catch the shavings. After the hole was tapped, Keith also vacuumed the debris out of the water passage.

Fig. 5.32. Done. My favorite part is that we didn't have to re-seal the thermostat housing. Great idea, Keith!

compartment or in the engine compartment. We chose a location just inside the passenger side of the firewall.

This leaves everyone's favorite part: the electrical connections. The connector on the throttle body includes the connections to the tach output of the ignition system (we use this in the first stage of this installation only) and the A/C compressor for the fast idle input. (Figure 5.36 shows the specifics.)

The power module includes the connections to the fuel pump, battery, and switched ignition. Figure

5.36 also shows the specifics for the wiring from the power module.

Even though this Chevelle doesn't have electric fans, your vehicle may. The power module requires relays to operate electric fans, so Figure 5.45 illustrates how to wire them properly.

If you have a pair of electric fans, each controlled by a relay, you're well advised to have each relay independently controlled by each of the fan outputs as illustrated in Figure 5.44. This allows you to set one fan to come on at a

lower temperature and the second to come on at a higher temperature only when it's necessary. This reduces fan noise and strain on the electrical system when you're cruising around. (The connection to the switched ignition is not shown.) Be sure that you connect the switched ignition input to a point that measures +12V with the key in the RUN and START positions.

It's important to note that the BATTERY (+) and BATTERY (–) connections connect directly to the battery positive and negative, not to the stud of the starter, the fuse box, etc. (See Chapter 2 for more details.)

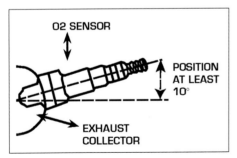

Fig. 5.33. All of the aftermarket EFI companies are on the same page in the preferred angle of orientation of the oxygen sensor in the exhaust. This prevents condensation from damaging the sensor. (Illustration Courtesy MSD Performance)

Ported versus Manifold Vacuum

So, what's the difference and which is best? The difference is simple. Manifold vacuum is generated at the base of the throttle body, which is below the throttle blades. Ported vacuum is generated above the throttle blades. With the throttle blades closed, the ported vacuum port has no signal.

When connecting the vacuum advance of a distributor to the throttle body, I typically connect it to a manifold vacuum port and not to a ported vacuum port. If you connect it to a ported vacuum port, the vacuum advance is rendered useless at idle because the timing is a sum of initial and centrifugal only. Ported vacuum was originally intended as a crutch in early vehicle emissions efforts. Vehicles that used it also had radically different timing curves than were used in any performance application. Sometimes on stock engines or engines with big-cam/automatic combinations, ported has its benefits but, in most cases, people starting fresh plan and curve for a manifold. ∎

Fig. 5.34. Keith located the power module up high on the passenger kick panel to keep it inside and out of sight. The power module is designed so that it can also be mounted in the engine compartment.

Fig. 5.35. Always use a rubber grommet or plastic snap bushing when running cables and/or harnesses through the firewall, even if they're loomed like these.

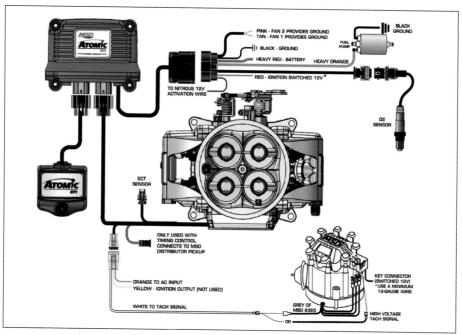

Fig. 5.36. Interfacing the Atomic EFI system with Keith's Mallory HEI distributor was a snap. MSD provides excellent diagrams in their manuals and on their website. (Illustration Courtesy MSD Performance)

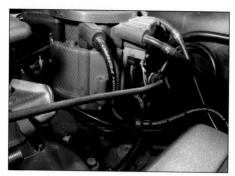

Fig. 5.37. I connected the TACH output of the Mallory distributor to the 18-gauge white wire in the harness on the throttle-body assembly per Figure 5.36.

Fig. 5.38. I connected the A/C compressor to the 18-gauge orange wire in the harness on the throttle-body assembly per Figure 5.36.

Fig. 5.39. We loomed and routed the 12-gauge orange wire from the power module to the fuel pump. We anchored it along the fuel lines and inside the Adel clamps.

Fig. 5.40. Using 12-gauge wire, we grounded the fuel pump to the frame rail. Note the use of a star washer to get a good bite into the metal.

Fig. 5.41. I grounded the 18-gauge black wire from the power module directly to the negative terminal of the battery. These side-post accessory adapters make short work of that, also available from CE Auto Electric Supply.

Fig. 5.42. I connected the 12-gauge red wire from the power module to a small ATC fuse panel connected directly to the battery positive terminal using a short length of 4 AWG. We installed this when we re-wired the alternator and fabbed up new battery cables. We fused this with a 30-amp fuse.

Fig. 5.43. I tied up the wiring to the power module. You may elect to do this after you've successfully started the engine.

4. Get It to Run!

At this point, you need to do a few things before you can start the engine: flush the fuel system, set the fuel pressure, configure the Atomic EFI, and adjust the throttle blades. Reconnect the negative battery cable before proceeding.

Flush the Fuel System

This ensures that any debris in the lines is flushed into a catch can and not into your new components. Simply disconnect the inlet to the throttle body and place it into a catch can. Then temporarily disconnect the pump from the power module, and power the pump directly from the battery via a jumper. Repeat this process for the line from the throttle body to the regulator (at the regulator) and the return line (at the tank).

After flushing the fuel system, re-connect all fuel lines and tighten the fittings accordingly. Then pressurize the system via the jumper to the fuel pump to check it for leaks. Check all fittings, including the ones under the vehicle. Address any leaks before proceeding.

Set the Fuel Pressure

I used the 1/8-inch NPT port in the regulator for this. MSD recommends between 42 and 48 psi of fuel pressure. I again used the jumper to connect the fuel pump directly to the battery as we adjusted the regulator

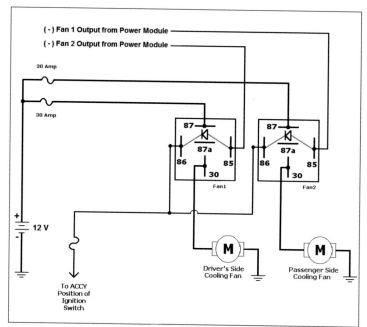

Fig. 5.44. Keith's Chevelle doesn't have electric fans, but your vehicle may. If it does, this is the proper interface. The diodes across the coils of the relays prevent back EMF from damaging the low-current outputs from the power module when the fans are turned off.

Fig. 5.45. I used my trusty Fluke 87 DMM and PV350 pressure/vacuum transducer to set the fuel pressure via the fuel pressure gauge port on the Holley regulator. The Fluke PV350 connects to the regulator in the same way as any standard gauge and provides incredibly accurate readings. MSD recommends between 42 and 48 psi, so we set it at 46 psi.

to 46 psi. After setting the fuel pressure, check all fittings for leaks.

The Atomic EFI actually has a fuel pressure sensor built into the throttle body and the results are displayed on the handheld controller. You can use this to set the fuel pressure as long as you use a jumper to run the fuel pump continuously when doing so. The particular unit we installed displayed approximately 2 psi greater fuel pressure on the handheld than on my trusty Fluke 87.

Configure the Atomic EFI

Here, we simply configure the Atomic EFI to work with the engine combination in the Chevelle. Using the handheld controller we access the INITIAL SETUP menu.

This entire process takes just minutes to complete.

Here are the data items that you enter:

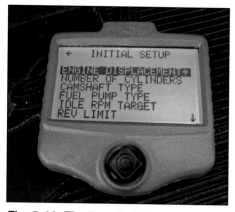

Fig. 5.46. The handheld controller makes it a snap to set up the Atomic prior to starting the engine.

ENGINE DISPLACEMENT
NUMBER OF CYLINDERS
CAMSHAFT TYPE
- Stock = Less than 210 degrees of duration
- Medium = 211 to 230 degrees of duration
- Large = 231 to 250 degress of duration

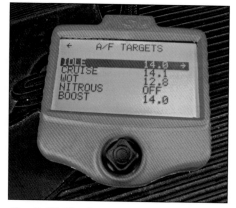

Fig. 5.47. The handheld controller allows you to easily change the A/F targets for idle, cruise, and WOT.

FUEL PUMP TYPE (more accurately, fuel system type)
- Returnless
- Return with a regulator
IDLE RPM TARGET: Input the RPM at which you'd like the engine to idle at operating temperature
REV LIMIT: Set a high-speed rev limiter

TIMING CONTROL: Choose Disabled for now

Once you've input the basics, you need to input the following in the ADVANCED SETUP:

FANS: Set the ON temperature for each electric fan
A/F TARGETS: Set the target A/F ratio at idle, cruise, and WOT
TIMING CONTROL: You address this in Stage Two
PUMP SQUIRT: Leave the factory setting for now
POWER VALVE ENRICH: Leave the factory setting for now

Adjust the Throttle Blades

The final step before attempting to start the engine is to set the throttle blades. This process is done based on the camshaft in the engine. According to the Atomic installation manual, the Chevelle's camshaft qualifies as *Large* so we set each of the throttle blades at "1½ turns from the point at which the blades first move."

Start the Engine

Now it's time to start the engine. Keith turned the key from the RUN to

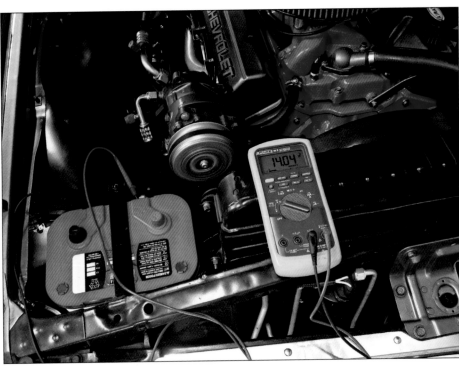

Fig. 5.48. After the Chevelle got to operating temperature, I wanted to look at how well the alternator was performing with all accessories operating at idle; this includes the spinning A/C compressor. Remember, we need a minimum of 13.4 volts to operate the accessories and charge the battery.

the START position, and the engine started immediately, and I do mean immediately. Nice!

Take a Test Drive

Before going for a drive, we allowed the engine to reach operating temperature and made a few final adjustments to the throttle blades and Idle RPM Target setting on the handheld. We also verified that the alternator was indeed producing enough current to keep up with the demands of the ECU, fuel pump, and

Measuring Fuel System Performance

In Chapter 2, I discussed some of the secrets of the fuel system gurus being too well kept. Well, this is a case in point. The following methods that Tom Kise of Holley outlined to me allow you to confidently determine just how well any fuel system is working. This requires a few tools that are readily available:

- -6 male-to-female adapter with 1/8-inch NPT port (Earl's PN 100199ERL)
- 1/8-inch NPT to -4 adapter
- Short length of -4 line
- Fuel pressure gauge

You may also elect to grab an -8 male-to-female adapter with 1/8-inch NPT port (Earl's PN 100200ERL). That way, you're covered for nearly any type of system you measure.

The Fluke PV350 is definitely the cat's meow here, but the Auto Meter gauge gets you pretty close and it costs a whole lot less.

Here are the steps:

1 Temporarily disconnect the feed line to the throttle body.

2 Insert the male-to-female adapter in-line and reinstall the feed line.

Measuring Fuel System Performance *continued*

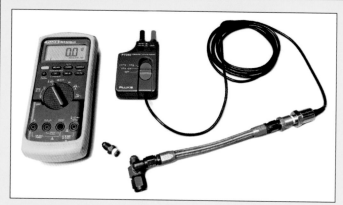

A mechanical gauge, like this one from Auto Meter (PN 4312), gets you close if you don't have access to the Fluke tools. Although it is not extremely accurate below 10 psi, you can use a low-pressure gauge to measure the return.

I fabricated a quick T-line for the fuel system so that we could use the Fluke DMM and PV350 anywhere in the fuel system to analyze it. I have to give Tom Kise at Holley credit for this idea, as it worked flawlessly.

3 Start the engine and measure the fuel pressure.

4 Turn off the engine.

5 Repeat the above process for the return line between the throttle body and regulator, as well as the return line between the regulator and fuel tank.

In the Chevelle, we measured the following:

- Pressure at inlet of throttle body: 46.0 psi
- Pressure at return outlet of throttle body: 44.8 psi
- Pressure at return side of regulator: 0.6 psi

In the case of the Chevelle, pressure at the return outlet is 3 percent lower than the inlet, which is absolutely fine. The pressure measured on the return line should be no more than 4 to 5 psi.

You can also determine whether the vent in a given fuel tank is a restriction. To do so, connect the AN adapter assembly on the inlet side of the pump. With the pump running at full speed, ensure you have no vacuum present on the inlet of the pump. Even an inch or two of vacuum indicates that the vent isn't adequate and is restrictive. Fortunately, the Fluke PV350, which retails for about $400, permits vacuum measurements as well. Tom uses a large industrial vacuum gauge for that.

Spend the extra ten minutes here to evaluate the effectiveness of the fuel system you just installed so that you know with certainty that it's flowing freely and free of restrictions. You'll thank me later! ■

Remove the fuel feed to the throttle body and install the adapter to read fuel pressure at the inlet of the throttle body. Repeat this at the outlet of the throttle body and the return outlet of the regulator. This is simple and takes seconds.

injectors as we estimated it would. No problem.

After we were happy with the idle, it was time for a victory lap. We took ours on a 119-degree day in June, which just happened to be a record for that day in Phoenix. The Chevelle ran flawlessly. I held the handheld controller and monitored the A/F ratio as the Atomic was mapping the fuel tables to hit the pre-programmed targets. Wow, this process is fast, so fast that it's hard to detect that it's even happening.

The Chevelle never ran anything but smooth from the time we pulled it out of the shop until we returned, but it continued to get progressively smoother with each additional mile. Keith had a big smile on his face and was very happy with how the Chevelle ran.

Drivability Report

Keith drove the vehicle for a bit. Its engine was equipped with the existing Mallory HEI distributor. He noticed that the Chevelle tended to surge between 2,500 and 3,000 rpm at a steady speed after he had driven it for a few weeks. Keith had slightly changed the A/F targets in the Atomic's fuel map to the following in an effort to resolve this:

Idle: 13.8:1
Cruise: 14.5:1
WOT: 12.8:1

In addition, he increased the fuel pressure by 2 psi. Neither resolved the problem. After discussing this with him at length, I asked him to provide these details on the specifics of the timing in the engine:

Initial: 16 degrees
Total: 32 degrees

Fig. 5.49. Peek under the air cleaner and still most people wouldn't realize that they're looking directly at the heatsink of the ECU. If you're after stealth, this is the system for you.

Vacuum Advance: 10 degrees
Timing All In: by 3,000 rpm

We decided to get together the following week to analyze the problem. In preparation, Keith installed a second bung in the exhaust so that we had a convenient place to connect my Innovate LM-2 handheld wideband oxygen meter.

After driving the vehicle 30 miles to my place, Keith took me for a ride and it ran perfectly. According to the Atomic handheld, coolant temperature was 200 degrees F and incoming air temperature 108, which is to be expected on a 108-degree Phoenix evening. Try as he may, Keith was simply unable to get the Chevelle to surge or exhibit any problems. It ran perfectly at any speed and any RPM.

We decided to move forward with our original plans to collect some data in hopes that we could replicate the problem. To that end, I wanted to monitor some things *over time* as Keith attempted to replicate the problem. These included the A/F ratio and the fuel pressure (so we could rule out a fuel delivery issue).

Yes, the Atomic handheld provides real-time data on both. However, datalogging the above as Keith drove the Chevelle allowed us to closely analyze the data after the drive in an effort to pinpoint the problem. I typically assume ESO (equipment smarter than operator) until I find otherwise. Acquiring data is an excellent way to remove the guesswork and get down to solving the problem and that's just what we intended to do.

We connected my Fluke 87 DMM/Fluke PV350 and Innovate LM-2 wideband oxygen meter. Both the Fluke 87 and the Innovate have datalogging capability. The Fluke 87 datalogs via the MIN/MAX mode. You simply press the MIN/MAX button to begin datalogging and press it again to end datalogging. Then, pressing the MIN/MAX button repeatedly allows you to scroll through MIN(minimum), AVG (average), and MAX(maximum) readings during the time lapsed. The Innovate LM-2 datalogs via the internal SD Card by pressing the RECORD button once to start the datalog and a second time to stop the datalog.

In the time it took us to connect the equipment, air temperature dropped to 95 degrees and coolant temperature dropped to 180 degrees. We didn't make it too far before we noticed the Chevelle running differently in the cruise area and sure enough it surged just like Keith had reported. The cause was immediately obvious on both the LM-2 and the Atomic handheld. The A/F ratio was jumping up and down from 12.0 to 16.0 as Keith held the throttle at a constant RPM between 2,500 and 3,000. The Chevelle ran perfectly under nearly every other condition, including WOT.

While driving around, fuel pressure was rock solid at 47.8 psi on the Fluke, even when the Chevelle was surging. At WOT, the log in the Fluke showed that fuel pressure dropped to 45.8 psi (a decrease of only 4 percent), which is perfectly logical considering how much fuel the engine is consuming. The fuel pressure remained sufficient with this nominal 4-percent drop. This data allowed us to rule out a fuel delivery issue. We didn't need to make a log with the LM-2 as the problem was obvious. I think it's worth mentioning that the Atomic handheld displayed similar data, so a passenger paying very close attention should be able to obtain similar information.

I'm not an expert in tuning but you don't need to be one to install and set up one of these systems. That's why I took on this project and documented the process. My buddies Bill Surin and Frank Beck are both excellent tuners and excellent resources. In the following days, I discussed Keith's Chevelle with them and came to the conclusion that the likely cause of the surging was too much ignition timing, too lean of a mixture, or both.

Frank recommended we lower the target A/F ratio in the cruise area to 13.5:1 and disconnect the vacuum advance of the distributor and report back. Guess what? This solved the surging immediately.

Reducing the amount of vacuum advance (the Mallory canister is adjustable) and slowly leaning the mixture to achieve the best fuel economy without surging was the next move. As I suspected earlier, all of the installed components were indeed working properly.

Fuel is an important aspect that must be considered because it is somewhat inconsistent from one gas station to another. In addition, some brands of fuel use detergents or additives while others don't have the same chemistry. These inconsistencies can certainly play a role in drivability of an aftermarket EFI system. I recommend picking a brand of fuel and sticking with it. When possible, refill at the same station. That way if a problem does arise, you know that it is less likely to be a result of fuel inconsistencies.

With the surging issue behind us, we elected to proceed to Stage Two (configuring the Atomic to manage the ignition timing). This allows us to easily tune the timing and A/F at a cruise via pressing buttons on the handheld controller to achieve our goals.

Stage Two: Add Complete Engine Management

In this stage, we upgrade the ignition system so that the Atomic system can also manage the engine timing. This allows us to use the Atomic to its fullest capabilities. This upgrade permits complete control of the ignition timing parameters via the handheld, automatic timing retard when coolant temperature and/or intake air temperature reach a certain point, and automatic timing retard when a nitrous system is engaged.

1. Upgrade the Ignition System

The Mallory HEI Distributor needs to be removed and a completely different ignition system installed for us to allow the Atomic to manage the timing. The distributor needs to be matched to the requirements of the Atomic EFI system because it acts as the trigger for the ECU and the ECU in turn triggers the ignition system. Fortunately, the Atomic system has been designed to interface with all MSD Pro-Billet (magnetic trigger) or MSD Ready-to-Run distributors. Either way, you need an outboard ignition box. (MSD provides excellent diagrams for either scenario on their website.)

Keith's Chevelle is the exception rather than the norm because most of the cars I see at the cruises have one of the above distributors and a 6AL ignition box. We elected to use an MSD Pro-Billet distributor and referred to Figure 5.50, which is printed in the Atomic EFI installation manual.

In addition, you need an adjustable rotor and the balancer must be degreed. If your balancer isn't degreed, you can use timing tape (MSD PN 8985). Finally, you need a timing light.

We elected to use the following ignition components from MSD:

Description	Part Number
MSD Digital 6AL Ignition Box	6425
MSD Pro-Billet Distributor	85551
MSD Adjustable Rotor	84211
MSD HVC Coil	8252

The Digital 6AL ignition box has a detachable plug and this greatly simplifies installation and troubleshooting. I wish all ignition boxes had this. In addition, the rev limiter of the Digital 6AL doesn't require pills, is right in plain view, can be adjusted with a screwdriver, and has a water-resistant cover. I'm also a huge fan of MSD's HVC series of coils (see chart on page 89).

The HVC coil has more than double the output current of the Blaster 2 and double the output power. I've had really good luck with MSD's HVC and HVC II coils and I enthusiastically recommend them both. Sure they're a bit more money, but well worth it.

The installation of these components is really simple and most enthusiasts have experience with all of them. The most difficult part is installing the distributor, which really isn't all that difficult. I have to give MSD props here for the incredibly well-written installation manuals. If you follow them step-by-step, you simply cannot get lost.

If you've already got an MSD Ready-to-Run or Pro-Billet Distributor, a CD-style ignition box, and a coil, you save a bunch of time at this stage.

Position Engine

Position the engine at 15 degrees BTDC on the compression stroke before proceeding regardless of whether you remove your existing

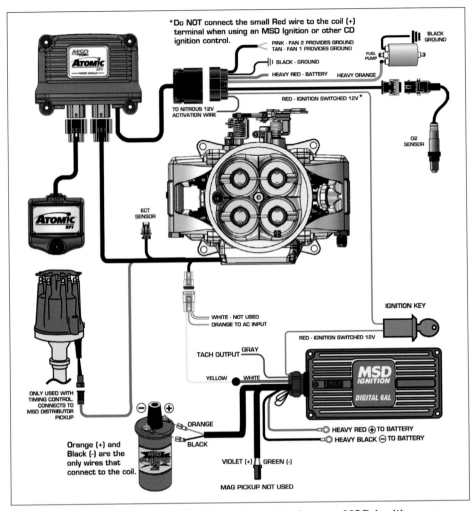

Fig. 5.50. Interfacing the Atomic EFI system with the new MSD ignition components was simple and straightforward. Note that the distributor's magnetic pickup plugs into the ECU and not the ignition box.

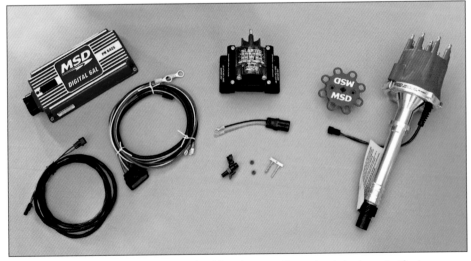

Fig. 5.51. Here's the distributor, ignition box, coil, and related parts that we used for the electrical system upgrade.

HVC and Blaster 2 Comparison

Description	HVC	Blaster 2
Maximum Output Voltage	42,000 volts	45,000 volts
Peak Output Current	300 mA	140 mA
Total Output Power (Voltage * Current)	12,600 watts	6,300 watts
Spark Duration	200 µS	350 µS

Fig. 5.52. Disassemble the distributor, remove the weights and springs, and lock it out per the instructions included in the installation manual. This is simple.

Fig. 5.53. Install the adjustable rotor cap, adjust it to 15-degrees retarded, and install the distributor in the engine.

distributor or replace it altogether. Pull the driver-side valve cover and note the position of the number-1 exhaust and intake valves to determine advance. The compression stroke occurs after the intake valve event and both valves are fully closed during the compression stroke. I typically use a 27-inch-long-handle 1/2-inch ratchet with all the spark plugs in to turn the engine over; just like you see the guys do in the pits of any Top Fuel team.

You may elect to mark the orientation of the rotor before removing the distributor, especially if you want your existing plug wires to go back on the same way they came off. You can now remove the existing distributor.

On small-block and big-block Chevys, I typically orient the cap so that the number-8 and number-1 terminals are at the very front and point the rotor at the number-1 cylinder when installing the distributor, but that's personal preference. It's another excellent trick I picked up from Frank Beck.

Lock Out Distributor

Because the Atomic EFI ECU controls the timing, it's necessary to lock out the distributor, thereby eliminating any centrifugal and/or vacuum advance. This process is outlined fully in the Atomic EFI installation manual as well as in the distributor manual so I'll not repeat it here.

Install Adjustable Rotor

Install the adjustable rotor in place of the rotor provided with the distributor. Two screws anchor it in place. Phase the rotor by retarding it by 15 degrees. Note that the MSD rotor has up to 20 degrees advance or 20 degrees retard and the rotor is marked accordingly. To retard the rotor, you move the rotor in the *opposite* direction that the distributor rotates. Think about that for a second and it will absolutely make sense.

Use red thread locker on the set screw for the rotor; you do not want it to come loose.

Install Distributor

You may now install (or re-install) the distributor in the engine. Ensure that the rotor ends up pointing at the number-1 terminal of the cap. On small-block and big-block Chevys, it can be an arduous process to get the rotor pointing exactly where you want it because you most likely have to manually rotate the oil pump driveshaft to permit it.

The Chevelle didn't disappoint, and we spent a few minutes with a long flat-blade screwdriver getting the shaft exactly where we needed it to be. Leave the hold-down clamp just loose enough to move the distributor to set the timing.

Install Ignition Box

Keith constructed a small steel plate for the ignition box that allowed us to mount it up high on the passenger side. This plate also permitted us to use the rubber isolators on all four corners of the box.

Fig. 5.54. Keith fabricated this slick metal panel so that he could mount the Digital 6AL with the included rubber isolators. Note that the complete wiring harness is removable via a single plug, and the rev limiter is easily adjustable with a flat-blade screwdriver.

Install Coil

We chose a location on the firewall toward the driver's side of the brake components to install the coil. This location permitted us to use the rubber isolators on the HVC coil on all four corners, which are an integral part of the mounting scheme of this (and the HVC II) coil.

Wire Components

This is actually *very* simple and not much more is involved than installing the ignition box on its own (see Figure 5.50 for more details). Notice that the distributor's magnetic pickup plugs into the red pigtail on the ECU and *not* into the matching input of the ignition box as you may expect. This allows the distributor to trigger the ECU and in turn trigger the ignition box via its points-style input. This is accomplished by connecting the yellow wire from the ECU to the white wire on the box.

We elected to cover all of the wiring in split-braide tubing, which was the most time-consuming part of the wiring job. The HVC coil includes a pigtail with a Weatherpack plug on it. It also includes the mating con-

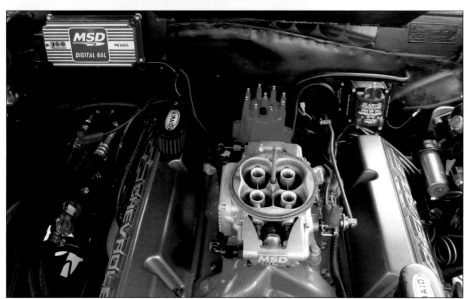

Fig. 5.55. We went out of our way to install the ignition box and coil in such a way that they didn't attract a lot of attention.

Fig. 5.56. The HVC coil install kit includes a Weatherpack-style pigtail, which is shown in Figure 5.51. We used it and I terminated the other end, also included, on the end of the harness from the Digital 6AL. This requires that you have the correct Weatherpack terminal installation tool.

Fig. 5.57. I routed the red and gray wires to the harness we disconnected from the Mallory HEI distributor, as it contained both a +12V switched wire and the trigger wire to the aftermarket tach.

Fig. 5.58. I made these connections with heat-shrinkable butt connectors, as they were both low current, and then slid the heat shrink (left) over the connections to insulate them. Yes, I realize that the number-3 plug wire is in the wrong location. Keith swapped it with number-6 and all was good.

nector for the harness from the ignition box. We used both.

Once all of the components were mounted, I had all of the wiring completed in less than one hour. While I worked on the wiring, Keith grounded the coil to the firewall via the included ground lead, fabricated a plug wire between the coil and distributor, and connected all the plug wires as before.

Fig. 5.59. I routed the power wiring from the Digital 6AL through the inner fender and to the battery. I connected the heavy black 12 AWG ground directly to the battery negative.

Fig. 5.60. I connected the heavy red 12 AWG power wire from the Digital 6AL to the fuse panel and fused it with a 25-amp fuse.

Fig. 5.61. I tied up all harnesses to be as inconspicuous as possible. Only the Digital 6AL stands out.

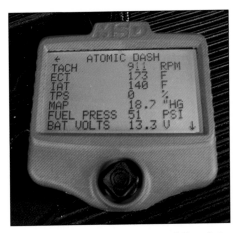

Fig. 5.62. This is just some of the data available via the Atomic Dash menu of the handheld controller when the engine is running.

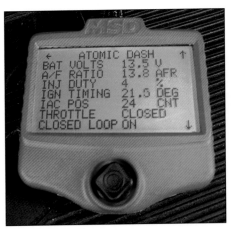

Fig. 5.63. The Atomic Dash shows you every parameter the Atomic monitors. This takes a dashboard full of gauges to replicate.

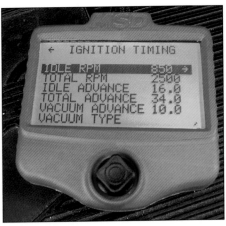

Fig. 5.64. Setting up the ignition timing via the handheld controller is a snap.

2. Set Up Atomic EFI to Manage Timing

Now that the ignition system is installed, we're minutes away from firing the engine. Before doing so, we need to make a few changes via the handheld controller. We use it to calibrate the timing settings. The process is covered in the Atomic EFI installation manual, but you should follow these steps to perform the initial setup:

1 Turn the ignition ON

2 Using the handheld controller, select INITIAL SETUP
- Select TIMING CONTROL
- Select ENABLE
- Exit INITIAL SETUP
- Select ADVANCED SETUP
- Select IGNITION TIMING

3 Select IDLE RPM: Set the RPM at which the advance begins to come in—think centrifugal)

4 Select TOTAL RPM: Set the RPM at which all of the advance is in

5 Select IDLE ADVANCE: Set the initial timing

Ignition Timing Settings

Idle RPM	850*
Total RPM	2,500
Idle Advance	16 degrees
Total Advance	34 degrees
Vacuum Advance	10 degrees

* Keith wanted this to begin with, but he may elect to raise it slightly in the future.

---

6 Select TOTAL ADVANCE: Set the total timing

7 Select VACUUM ADVANCE: Set additional advance for idle and cruise, based on vacuum via the MAP sensor

We chose the above timing settings (to start, at least), based on the original ignition curve of the Chevelle.

Lock the Timing via the Handheld Controller

Next, cycle the ignition key OFF and then back ON.

Once back ON, go to ADVANCED

SETUP, select IGNITION TIMING, and then select LOCK TIMING.

This allows you to lock the timing in the ECU to 15 degrees BTDC. Locking the timing in the ECU allows you to set the distributor properly after you've started the engine.

Start the Engine

Have your timing light connected and ready. Keith turned the key and the Chevelle cranked for a few seconds and then came to life.

Once the engine is running, rotate the distributor so that you read 15 degrees BTDC on the balancer and then tighten the hold-down clamp to lock it in place.

Exit the LOCK TIMING screen via the handheld controller.

The Atomic EFI is now managing the timing as you've programmed it. This whole process took Keith and me about 5 hours and that included taking all of the photos you see here. This was an incredibly easy upgrade and MSD's instructions were very well written.

Victory Lap!

After buttoning everything back up, reinstalling the air cleaner, and

---

Fig. 5.65. Keith elected to paint the ignition box and coil black after the installation was completed to prevent the components from detracting from his clean engine bay. (Photo Courtesy Keith Kanak)

Fig. 5.66. Keith also replaced the existing plug wires with MSD black plug wires. Little touches like this make the difference when it comes to achieving the look Keith was after. (Photo Courtesy Keith Kanak)

we drove it some more. It surged the slightest bit at first and then settled in nicely very shortly.

Overall, Keith and I were very happy with how the Chevelle ran.

The best fuel economy comes with the A/F ratio closest to stoichiometric and the most timing you can get within the cruise area. Each engine combination is a little different in this regard, and Frank always tells me, "Give it what it wants."

Allowing the Atomic to manage both engine timing and fuel metering makes it extremely easy to arrive at this for any applicable engine combination by making changes on the handheld, even while the engine is running.

Drivability Report

After driving the car for a few weeks with the ignition upgrade, Keith was very happy with the overall performance of the system. He made a few tweaks to fine-tune the drivability.

So, was the ignition upgrade worth the cost of the components? Absolutely, and I do mean absolutely! Being able to manage all of the ignition parameters and all of the fuel metering parameters from the handheld controller couldn't be simpler. This allows you to quickly fine-tune the system to work optimally with your combination. Finally, you can make very fine adjustments to the total timing in the quest for the best performance.

Any EFI system is only as good as the weakest link. The combination of parts we chose for Keith's Chevelle were instrumental in delivering the exact kind of performance expected from such an EFI conversion. I'm blown away by how easy this conversion was and how well it performs. More important, so is Keith.

Final Fuel Metering		Final Engine Timing	
Idle	14.2:1	Idle RPM	1,100 rpm
Cruise	14.2:1	Total RPM	2,600 rpm
Wide Open Throttle	12.8:1	Idle Advance	15 degrees
Pump Squirt	25%	Total Advance	36 degrees
Power Valve	25%	Vacuum Advance	12 degrees

putting the tools away, it was time to take the Chevelle for a spin. For now, we left the target A/F ratio in the cruise area at 13.5:1. The Chevelle ran perfectly and climbed through the RPM smoothly.

We pulled over and I nudged the target A/F ratio in the cruise area to 14.0. We drove it some more with the same results.

I then nudged the target A/F ratio in the cruise area to 14.1 and

HOLLEY DOMINATOR SYSTEM INSTALLATION

Multiport fuel injection systems deliver the ultimate in adjustability and tuning capability to extract maximum performance from an engine for a particular application. So if you desire the ultimate in tuning and flexibility for your fuel system, a custom-designed MPFI system is certainly for you. Among the many MPFI systems on the market, the Holley Dominator proved to be a leader.

Most engine builders have a favorite throttle body, favorite injec-

tor brand, favorite ECU brand, etc. Over the years, they've refined their formula to deliver results that are predictable in performance and offer them the utmost in flexibility in tuning. Pull any tuner aside and ask them what makes or breaks a particular EFI combination and they will tell you it's the software. The software simply must be able to allow them the control they desire.

For the past three SEMA shows, I've paid very close attention to the EFI systems available. The Holley Dominator system continues to be a real stand-out. As this book became a reality, I definitely wanted to include it, but first it had to pass the "Bill" test. Bill Surin owns the Olds in this chapter.

Bill is a hard-core enthu-

siast who lives and breathes by the time slip. He assembles his own engines and does his own tuning and he's quite good at it. He's got the largest selection of Holley carburetor parts of anyone I know and is constantly tuning to achieve the best performance in the current weather. He's also been talking for a while about converting to MPFI, especially since he's seen firsthand how well the TBI setup on my Olds performs.

Bill's Olds was featured in my book *Automotive Electrical Performance Projects,* so you may recognize it. In that book, we optimized the performance of the charging system and correctly wired the relocated battery. Once this was complete, we were then able to optimize the performance of the electric fans and headlights.

Define Your Objective

Before selecting components for a project of this scale, it's important to define what you intend to accomplish. Holley offers two ECUs that can be used as the basis for a custom

Fig. 6.1. This Holley 2,000-cfm throttle body (PN 112-578) has a Dominator flange. It is the latest version of the throttle body. This CNC-billet throttle body flows all the air the 620 hp Olds 455 can ingest. (Photo Courtesy Holley Performance Products)

Fig. 6.2. Bill's 1970 Olds Cutlass is his pride and joy. When people see and hear it, they think it's a 13-second car. Actually it runs 10.6 at 125 mph in the quarter-mile under Olds power.

Fig. 6.3. At the car shows, most don't pay this Olds 455 much attention, but It makes about 620 hp. It's bored .030 over, has a 950-cfm QFT E85 carb sitting on a port-matched Edelbrock Victor manifold, Edelbrock Performer cylinder heads, hydraulic roller, and custom billet main girdle.

MFPI system: the HP and the Dominator. Both use the same software, same harnesses, have a similar feature set, and are compatible with the following:

- TBI installations (single or dual throttle body)
- MPFI installations
- GM LS conversion installations, compatible with EV6-style injectors and coil-on-plug ignition systems
- GM HEI/Ford TFI/CD-style/Holley DIS (distributorless ignition systems)
- Crank trigger/cam trigger
- Holley's water/methanol injection driver and associated components
- Holley's nitrous-oxide solenoid driver
- Traction control via Davis Technologies' Holley Module

The Dominator ECU adds the following features:

- Dual oxygen-sensor inputs (the HP ECU has a single oxygen-sensor input)
- Built-in control for GM 4L60E and 4L80E automatics
- GM drive-by-wire compatibility (pedal and throttle body)
- 12 injector drivers, capable of driving up to 24 low- or high-impedance injectors (the HP ECU has 8 injector drivers)

- More than 50 user-configurable inputs/outputs (the HP ECUs has 8 user-configurable inputs/outputs)

The main reasons we chose the Dominator ECU for Bill's Olds are that Bill wants to be able to add a single stage of nitrous (dry) and have the ECU manage it: add the nitrous progressively (via one of the four spare injector drivers), richen the mixture accordingly, and retard the timing accordingly. Also, Bill may add an overdrive transmission later.

If your priorities don't include the above, you can use the HP ECU for a similar MPFI installation and save a few bucks.

Component Selection

The main difference between the Holley MPFI system and every other system previously discussed is that you choose the components specific to your particular application, thereby assembling an MPFI system from scratch. Holley has done a good job of making this process painless

via the EFI Selection Chart on their website. In short order, Bill and I were able to determine the parts required.

Here are the options we had available:

- Throttle Body (4500 or 4150 flange)
- ECU (Dominator or HP)
- Main Harness
- Injector Harness
- Ignition Harness
- Transmission Control (if using a GM 4L60/65/70/80/55E automatic transmission)

Injector Selection Math

Selecting the correct-size fuel injectors for a given engine combination is critical to unlock the engine's performance potential as well as prevent engine damage. Fortunately, it's just math and the formulas are pretty simple.

Brake Specific Fuel Consumption

Brake specific fuel consumption (BSFC) is a representation of how much fuel (in pounds) is required per hour for each brake horsepower produced by an engine.

Naturally Aspirated at WOT

Gasoline: .38 to .52 lb/hr, depending on efficiency
E85: .63 to .75 lb/hr, depending on efficiency

Forced Induction at WOT

Gasoline: .55 to .65 lb/hr, depending on efficiency
E85: .84 to .95 lb/hr, depending on efficiency

Here's the formula for calculating your fuel flow requirement for each injector:

Fuel Flow Requirement = (brake horsepower x BSFC) ÷ number of injectors

For example, using a naturally aspirated 400-hp V-8 engine with .50 BFSC gasoline, you plug in the numbers:

400 hp x .50 lb/hr = 200 lbs/hr of fuel
200 lbs/hr ÷ 8 injectors = 25 lbs/hr per injector

This assumes 100-percent duty cycle of the injector, which is not ideal (the reasons for which are outside of the scope of this book). Most recommend a maximum duty cycle of 85 percent for injectors, so let's compute that for our example:

25 lbs/hr ÷ 85% = 29.41 lbs/hr

So, choosing 30-lb/hr injectors for this application is ideal.

Now, let's do the math for Bill's Olds, given that it makes 620 hp on E85. Let's also assume the highest BFSC of E85 just to be safe.

Fuel Flow Requirement = (brake horsepower x BSFC) ÷ number of injectors

620 hp x .75 lb/hr = 465 lbs/hr of fuel
465 lbs/hr ÷ 8 injectors = 58.12 lbs/hr
58.12 lbs/hr ÷ 85% = 68.37 lbs/hr

We chose 83-lb/hr injectors for Bill's Olds as Bill wants to add a little nitrous down the road and we'd like to have enough injector for that as well.

Now, please keep in mind that BFSC numbers may vary slightly from what I've outlined, so you're well advised to consult the manufacturer of the fuel components, your engine builder, or both to get their input. ∎

- GM Drive-By-Wire Harness (if applicable)
- Auxiliary Harness (to facilitate connections to INPUTS and OUTPUTS)
- Fuel Injectors
- Sensors (oxygen, MAP, CTS, IAT, fuel pressure, oil pressure)
- Crank Trigger (optional)
- Cam Trigger (optional here; required for sequential fuel injection)
- Distributorless Igniton System (DIS; optional)
- Accessories

As you can see, this is a substantially different system from the MSD Atomic System discussed in Chapter 5. You have so many more options at your disposal; you can truly assemble a system that offers you exactly what you're after in the way of operation, performance, and tuning.

We were faced with a challenge in the parts selection process because Bill's Olds runs E85 and not gasoline. E85 has a different stoichiometric ratio (9.8:1) than gasoline (14.7:1). In addition, E85 has a lower energy content than gasoline, which means quite simply that a given mass of E85 has less power potential than the same mass of gasoline. So, we knew right away that we needed to supply a greater mass of E85 to the engine than with gasoline. This affected the selection of fuel system components, including the fuel injectors.

After taking all variables into consideration, we chose the components for this installation (see top chart).

In addition, Holley recommended some fuel components for our application (see bottom chart).

You also need a laptop computer to communicate with the ECU. You don't need a laptop with the latest processor, a lot of RAM, or the latest operating system. Windows XP works fine, as does Windows 7. However, Windows 7 requires a few simple tweaks to allow the datalogger and other write functions to work.

You need to document your current engine timing setup *before* removing the carburetor for an installation like this one. Specifically, you need to know:

- Base Timing: Disconnect any vacuum advance, plug the vacuum port, read at idle
- Idle Timing: Reconnect any vacuum advance, read at idle
- Total Timing
- At what RPM the timing is all in

You may also want to look at the timing at cruise RPM to see just how much timing is in the engine when you're cruising down the freeway in high gear. Document everything and keep the information in a place where you won't lose track of it. You will need it when setting up your base tune later in the project.

For Bill's combination, he runs an MSD Pro-Billet distributor with no vacuum advance and has the distributor locked out, bypassing the centrifugal advance. Bill determined that his combination works best with 31

Project Components

Description	Part Number
Edelbrock Victor Intake Manifold with 4500-series flange	2811
Holley 2,000-cfmThrottle Body with 4500-series flange	112-578
Holley Dominator ECU	554-114
Holley ECU Main Power Harness	558-308
Holley Universal MPFI Harness	558-104
Holley V-8 Injector Harness	558-200
Holley ECU Auxiliary Harness (with secondnd oxygen-sensor input plug)	558-401
Holley J2A, J2B, J3, J4 Connector; and Pin Kit	558-408
Holley 83 PPH Injectors (8 pack)	522-838
(2) Bosch Wideband Oxygen Sensors (via Holley)	554-101
Holley 1 Bar MAP Sensor	538-24
Holley Coolant Temperature Sensor	534-10
Holley Air Temperature Sensor	9920-107
(2) Holley 100 PSI Stainless Pressure Sensors (fuel/oil pressure)	554-102
Holley Big-Block Chevy Crank Trigger Kit	556-111
Holley Nitrous Solenoid Driver	554-111
Holley Throttle Linkage Bracket	20-32

Fuel Components

Description	Part Number
Dominator In-Line Billet Fuel Pump	12-1400
Dominator Billet Fuel Pressure Regulator, EFI bypass style	12-848
100 Micron Pre-Filter, EFI style	162-572
10 Micron Post-Filter, EFI style	162-570

Fig. 6.4. Here are the parts we selected from Holley for this conversion. The throttle body is a 4500 flange and it flows 2,000 cfm and is more than double that of the carb it replaces. A 1,000-cfm version is available in a standard 4150 flange. Not shown are the fuel injectors.

degrees of timing both on the engine dyno and chassis dyno. Finally, he uses the *Start Retard* function of an MSD Digital-6 CD-style ignition box to retard 20 degrees of timing during start. All of these parts are fully compatible with the Holley system.

Holley Dominator System Installation

An installation such as this one can be intimidating. By separating the installation into stages, you can simplify the process and ensure you complete each stage fully before proceeding to the next. Here is an overview of the four installation stages:

Fig. 6.5. Holley recommended their Dominator series 12-1400 fuel pump and matching filters and regulators. The fit and finish on these components is just jaw dropping.

Stage One: Pre-Installation

1. Load the software
2. Install fuel injectors
3. Install oxygen sensor bungs

Stage Two: Electrical and Fuel Systems

1. Optimize electrical system
2. Install fuel system

Stage Three: Holley Dominator Components

1. Install throttle body and linkage
2. Choose component location
3. Install sensors
4. Install wiring harnesses
5. Interface ECU to ignition system
6. Install ECU

Stage Four: Get It to Run!

1. Flush system and set fuel pressure
2. Build or adjust a base tune
3. Load base tune into ECU
4. Perform calibrations before engine start
5. Start engine
6. Final Calibrations and test drive

Before beginning, I strongly encourage you to plan accordingly. This is not a project that you can do in a weekend. To achieve the results a system like this is capable of, it's imperative to spend the effort required to perform each of the steps to the best of your ability. If in doubt, call in a friend to help before proceeding to the next step.

Stage One: Pre-Installation

You need to complete the following steps to correctly install the software, oxygen sensor bungs, oxygen sensors, and fuel injectors. In order to maximize functionality and performance of the system, you must perform or have a professional-quality installation performed.

1. Load the Software

The very first thing you want to do is to load the Holley EFI software on your laptop and desktop PC. This is because Holley does not include any printed instructions with the Dominator EFI systems and you're going to want to print out several documents (likely from your desktop PC). Holley includes a CD-ROM (with the software on it) with the ECU, but you may elect to check the Holley EFI website for the latest version of the software before installing it from the disc (holleyefi.com > TECHNICAL > Resource Documents & Downloads > Fuel Injection).

Once you have the software loaded, open it. When the *CHOOSE OPENING OPTION* menu comes up, click on *Cancel* at the bottom of the window. All of the instructions are located in the Help Menu of the software.

- Click on *Help* on the toolbar at the top
- Select *Contents*
- Expand the *READ FIRST! HELP/ Instructions Overview*, click on the document of the same name and print it
- Expand the *Quick Start Guide*, click on the document of the same name and print it
- Expand the *Step-By-Step Beginners*

Tuning Guide, click on the document of the same name and print it
- Expand the *Wiring Manual and Diagrams*, click on the document of the same name and print it

I recommend that you print the pages two-sided if your printer allows it, three-hole-punch them all, and put them in a binder for easy reference if you have questions along the way. (The Contents section of the Help menu has all of the documents you may need for a particular installation.)

It's also not a bad idea to read through these documents before beginning the installation so that you can familiarize yourself with the big picture of how the system works and the terminology that Holley uses with the system and software.

As you perform the installation of various components, you may also elect to three-hole-punch any included instructions and put them in your binder.

2. Install Fuel Injectors

Many enthusiasts have a professional shop complete this work. We did. In fact, we had a shop install the fuel injectors on the aluminum manifold because neither Bill nor I is a welder. If you're an accomplished welder and an expert TIG welder, you may elect to tackle this part on your own.

We farmed this job out to local fuel injection specialist Bob Ream. He took our bone-stock Edelbrock Victor manifold and welded bungs in the intake runners for the injectors. In addition, he cut fuel rails to length,

Fig. 6.6. We chose the Edelbrock Victor manifold with a 4500-series flange to mate perfectly with the throttle body. The injectors are mounted low in the runners so they have a straight shot into the intake port of the cylinder head.

constructed mounts for them to attach to the manifold, and threaded the ends for -8 straight-cut fittings. His pricing was very reasonable and the end result looks quite good.

After Bob completed this work, Bill spent an afternoon and evening with a die grinder and port-matched the intake runners to the Edelbrock cylinder heads on the 455 to ensure maximum airflow between the manifold and cylinder head.

3. Install Oxygen Sensor Bungs

Bill has more oxygen sensor bungs in the headers on his Olds than any three people I know. Long before we started this project, he had already paid a local exhaust shop to install oxygen bungs in each primary and two in each collector of each header: that's 12 in all. Bill had plans to purchase an Innovate LM-2 dual-channel wideband A/F meter and wanted to take advantage of all the data acquisition the unit offers.

Stage Two: Electrical and Fuel Systems

This stage of the project is easily the most arduous and time consuming. It is also the most critical because the electrical and fuel systems collectively determine the performance potential of the installation.

1. Optimize Electrical System

You need to optimize the charging system so that you can accommodate the additional current required by an EFI system. As I mentioned earlier, we had already done this in Bill's Olds. However, I suspected we were right at the maximum output Bill's alternator was capable of making at idle (87 amps). Bill has since converted his Olds to run on E85, upgraded to a larger Fuelabs multi-speed pump, and added the Innovate LM-2 dual-channel wideband A/F meter and numerous oxygen sensors. I suspected this was the tipping point for the existing 12SI alternator, as Bill noted voltage was in the low-13s on his dash-mounted volt meter when cruising around.

We know we have to upgrade the alternator first. Because the charge lead and return path were already upgraded, we just need to swap out the alternator.

However, the underdash of Bill's car has needed attention since we met. We can't even start on this project before addressing this and honestly, I had not been looking forward to fixing this mess despite Bill's repeated attempts at bribing me to do so. It was time to pay the piper, so I bit the bullet and got busy.

Correcting this took me the better part of an entire weekend. The benefit of owning an auto electric supply company is that I have parts on hand for a job like this.

Fig. 6.7. Bill has been after me for a long time to help him get his underdash wiring sorted out. So I ripped it all out and redid everything. Don't even consider taking on a project of this scale if the wiring under the dash of your vehicle looks anything like this.

Fig. 6.8. I always try to do as much of the work as I can on the bench. This neatly wired power center mounts to the firewall in place of the disaster shown in Figure 6.7.

If you have a similar mess under the dash of your prized possession and want to convert that to a sensible, orderly, and safe installation, I illustrate the process fully in *Automotive Electrical Performance Projects*. This process is lengthy and outside of the scope of this book.

Fig. 6.9. This BILLET-TECH alternator from Mechman replaced the antique 12SI. I've been preaching for years that you simply cannot get the output claimed from any alternator without properly grounding it. This unit came out of the box with a 2 AWG cable already affixed to the case for just that purpose. It also has a 5/16-inch output stud and a much newer regulator.

Fig. 6.10. The GM 12SI unit we removed has served Bill well. Notice the difference in the size of the output stud when compared to the Mechman unit in Figure 6.9. Also, note the diode in-line on the exciter wire required to prevent run-on. The new-style regulator didn't require it.

Install Alternator

We chose a BILLET-TECH alternator from Mechman in the black hard-anodized finish for Bill's Olds. Based on our needs, they recommended the 170A Model, rated to deliver 140 amps at idle (800 engine RPM) and 170 amps at cruise (2,000 engine RPM) with a standard 3:1 pulley ratio. I was pleasantly surprised when I noticed that the BILLET-TECH 170A output at cruise RPM was actually measured at 1,800 engine RPM according to the sheet provided with it. It should be perfect.

Using the methods outlined in Chapter 2, here are the steps and our readings:

1 Record the resting voltage of the battery with the engine not running: 12.5 volts.

2 Start the engine and bring the vehicle to operating temperature.

3 Turn on all of the accessories, including the high-beam headlights, A/C, electric cooling fan(s), audio system at a common listening level, etc.

4 After the engine has reached operating temperature, record the voltage at the battery: 13.1 volts.

5 Record the output current of the alternator: 82 amps.

The first problem here is that our running voltage is below 13.4 volts, which confirms the Fuelabs pump, the Innovate LM-2, and the array of oxygen sensors were indeed the tipping

Fig. 6.12. Installing the new alternator was really not that big a deal. We simply had to enlarge the opening in the custom front engine plate to clear the charge stud and regulator harness. Note the 2 AWG charge lead.

Fig. 6.13. We made use of the 3/8-inch bolts on the engine plate bracket to ground the circuits properly. The clear 2 AWG lead is the return path for the starter and connects to the block. The brown 2 AWG lead is the return path for the alternator.

Fig. 6.11. With the Olds idling and all accessories turned on, the alternator was putting out 82 amps of current, but only at 13.1 volts. We need 13.4 volts to power all the accessories and charge the battery so this must be improved. This measurement was taken at approximately 800 engine RPM.

point for the existing 12SI alternator. Output current dropped from 87 to 81 amps as a result of this drop in voltage.

For fun, I put my Fluke i410 current clamp around the battery positive cable while the vehicle was running (separate from the charge lead in this installation), and recorded only 1 amp of current flowing back into the battery at idle. This explains the lower-than-ideal 12.5 resting voltage of the battery.

There's no need to load the alternator with the carbon pile load in the Snap-on analyzer as we know it isn't big enough.

Typically, an alternator swap like this is a piece of cake. However, Bill's Olds has a front engine plate and we had to modify it slightly to accommodate the larger output stud and larger regulator plug.

While we were installing the alternator, we put my trusty Schumacher battery charger on the battery to charge it fully (this is outlined fully in the instructions included with the alternator).

1 Once the BILLET-TECH alternator was installed, we started the engine, allowed it to reach operating temperature, and then again turned on all of the accessories.

2 Record the voltage at the battery: 14.7 volts.

3 Record the output current of the alternator: 90 amps.

4 Load the alternator with the carbon pile load in the Snap-on analyzer to determine how much output the alternator is capable of at 800 engine RPM.

5 Record the voltage at the battery: 11.9 volts.

6 Record the output current of the alternator: 139 amps.

Fig. 6.14. The Mechman unit definitely delivers the goods. It produced more than enough power to operate all of the accessories and charge the battery. This is what you want to see from a properly performing alternator. Once again, this measurement was taken at approximately 800 engine RPM.

Fig. 6.15. The Mechman unit also has plenty of current to spare at idle when loaded with the carbon pile load in the MT3750. In fact, it has 49 amps of reserve over the base requirements of all accessories. That comes in handy for the second stage of the fuel pump, additional current required by the fuel injectors at WOT, nitrous driver and solenoid, nitrous bottle heater, etc.

Now that's not bad, considering the distance between the alternator and battery is approximately 20 feet. We fell only 2 amps short of the 141 amps reported by Mechman on the test certificate included with the alternator. This is to be expected in an installation like this where the battery is so far from the alternator. This certainly illustrates the importance of using the correct-size charge lead (2 AWG in this Olds) and a proper return path for the alternator (also 2 AWG).

Again, our efforts paid off and we got a substantial improvement. Let's consider our results as percentages (see chart below).

Now that the charging system is in order, we can move on to the

Description	Before	After	Percentage Gain
Resting battery voltage	12.4 volts	12.7 volts*	2.4
Voltage at battery, vehicle idling, all accessories on	13.1 volts	14.7 volts	12.2
Current required by all accessories at idle	81 amps	90 amps	11
Maximum idle output current of alternator	Not Tested	139 amps	a lot
Total power available to accessories at idle	1,061 watts	1,323 watts	24.6
Total power available from alternator at idle	Not Tested	1,654 watts	a lot

* Measured after we charged the battery and then depleted the surface charge by turning the headlights on for 30 seconds. This shows the battery is healthy and it made a full recovery.

fun stuff. In addition, we are able to rest easy knowing that the newly installed alternator is capable of making all the power our new components will ever need. This ensures they live a long and healthy life.

2. Install Fuel System

Bill's Olds has always had a solid fuel system, for a carbureted application. He removed the factory tank, had a baffled sump installed with a pair of -8 bungs (one for the outlet and one for the return), and he uses the factory vent. The fuel lines are -8 Aeroquip push-locks for the feed and return. An Aeromotive 100-micron filter with shut-off valve, Fuelabs multi-speed fuel pump, and Mallory regulator rounded out the carbureted fuel system. It is basic, but very functional. We elected to retain the Aeromotive pre-filter as the shut-off valve is handy, especially considering that we could simply turn it off and make all of the upgrades you see here without draining the tank.

Plumbing a fuel system that includes fuel rails is really not that difficult. There are two popular methods. We chose the simpler of the two for Bill's Olds (see Figure 6.17), which is illustrated in the installation manual included with the Holley fuel pumps. The other is illustrated in the sidebar "Plumbing High-Horsepower Applications" on page 106.

I mounted the Holley fuel pump to the frame rail, using the bracket I had previously made for the Fuelabs fuel pump. In addition, we re-used several of Bill's existing fuel lines. Hey, sometimes you do get lucky! It was necessary to purchase numerous -12 O-ring to -8 AN fittings, -8 O-ring fittings, and -8 straight-cut fittings for this installation.

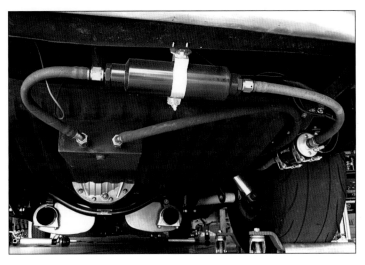

Fig. 6.16. The fuel system is pretty simple. Upgrading it gives me the perfect opportunity to clean up all of Bill's wiring.

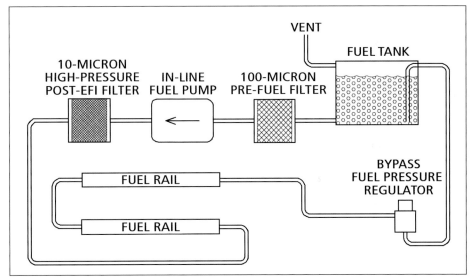

Fig. 6.17. This is one of two methods used for plumbing fuel rails to a return-style fuel system. We used it in Bill's Olds.

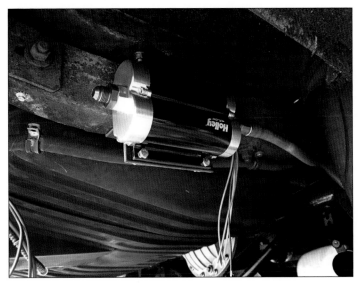

Fig. 6.18. I was able to use the bracket I originally fabbed-up for the Fuelabs pump to mount the Holley pump. It's mounted along the frame rail, as close to the bottom of the tank as possible.

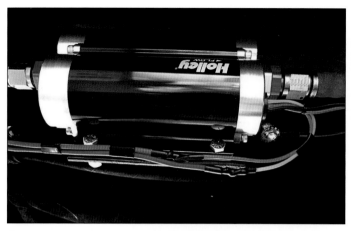

Fig. 6.19. I took an extra five minutes to solder and heat shrink all connections to the fuel pump, including the eyelet for the ground. I used a star washer under the ground eyelet to get a good bite into the metal.

Fig. 6.20. I loomed up the wiring for the fuel pump to keep it clean and protected. The black line behind the pump is the return.

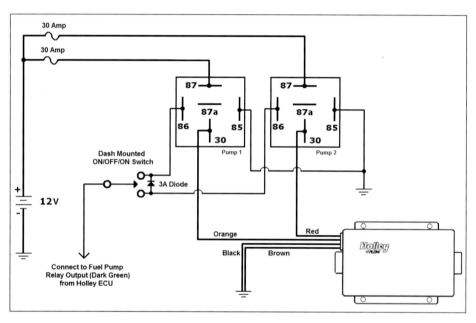

Fig. 6.21. I used a single SPDT center-off switch to control both halves of the Holley Dominator fuel pump. In one position, only one half of the pump is used. In the other position, both halves of the pump are used. (In Chapter 7, we interface the ECU to this to automate the circuit.)

The Holley 12-1400 and 12-1800 fuel pumps are somewhat unusual. Each has two pumps in a common housing and they share the inlet and outlet. Only one pump is required for cruising, and both are required for WOT in an effort to maintain fuel pressure. Therefore, each has independent power and ground leads for each of the internal pumps. I connected each of the internal pumps to its own 30-amp relay as shown in the installation manual. In addition, I fed each pump with 10 AWG and soldered all connections for the best performance and reliability.

Bill already had a pair of Bosch 30-amp relays mounted in sockets for the Fuelabs pump, each connected to the three-position ATC fuse panel we installed in his car in *Automotive Electrical Performance*

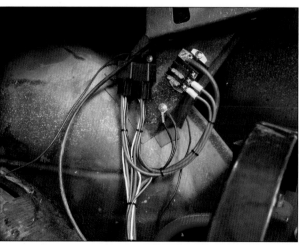

Fig. 6.22. I made use of the pre-existing Bosch 30-amp relays. I simply re-wired the sockets with 10 AWG TXL for the power and pump connections, which are connected to terminals 87 and 30.

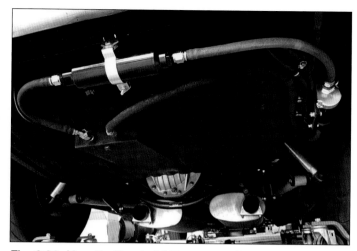

Fig. 6.23. Now that's what I like to see. Nice and clean, no exposed or unprotected wiring anywhere, and everything properly anchored. No need to rush a job like this; take your time and it will pay off.

Fig. 6.24. We mounted the post-filter and regulator to the inner fender. As they're plastic in the Olds, we used 1/4-inch hardware with washers, split washers, and nuts.

Monitoring and Datalogging Fuel and Oil Pressure

A quality fuel pressure gauge is a critical component to any high-performance installation. EFI systems are designed to operate with between 20 and 80 psi of fuel pressure, depending on their design. This is outside of the range of any fuel pressure gauge intended for carbureted applications so this is an upgrade that you should plan on. Given that an electronic fuel pressure gauge is expensive, why even run a dash-mounted gauge if the ECU can monitor fuel pressure? Good question.

A dash-mounted gauge is ideal to set fuel pressure (something that must be done before starting the engine after the installation) and to monitor it safely while driving. Connecting the Holley ECU to the optional fuel pressure transducer allows you to datalog fuel pressure during a run. After you make a run, you can go back and look at the datalog and note dips or spikes in the fuel pressure, possibly indicating a shortcoming in the fuel system that should be addressed. This may not be possible to see on a dash-mounted gauge and is certainly not possible to do safely from the driver's seat while under throttle.

The same applies to oil pressure. You can never have too much data at your disposal. I recommend taking full advantage of these features of any ECU that offers them. ∎

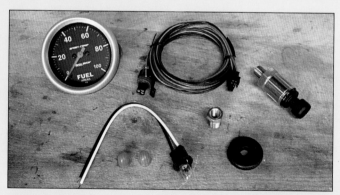

I've had really good luck with Auto Meter products over the years. This fully electronic fuel pressure gauge comes with everything you need and the wiring harness is plug-and-play with only switched and ground connections.

This was definitely a case of good luck. We used a single 1/8-inch NPT brass T and a single brass elbow for the perfect fit. The wrench flats on the sending units barely cleared one another.

Projects. Even though the instruction manual included with the 12-1400 pump suggests wiring each of the internal pumps with 12 AWG, I elected to use 10 AWG to further min- imize voltage drop, which included re-wiring the relay sockets with 10 AWG. For now, I've wired the fuel pump so that it can be controlled directly from Bill's dash-mounted fuel pump switch (in Chapter 7, we automate it).

We mounted the Holley regulator in nearly the same position the Mal- lory regulator had occupied, and the

Plumbing High-Horsepower Applications

On higher-horsepower applications you may elect to use a Y-block to split the fuel feed to feed each of the fuel rails. Then, each of the fuel rails can be plumbed back to the regulator independently. Many engine builders prefer this method. ■

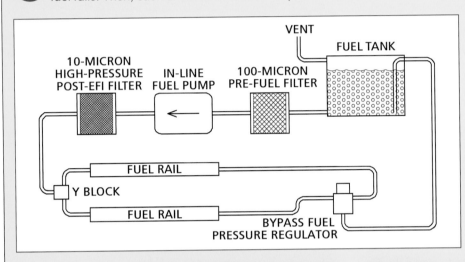

In higher-horsepower applications, it's advisable to use a Y-block to split the inlet to each of the fuel rails. Each of the rails can then be connected to a dual-input return-style regulator.

Look closely at the plumbing on this LS3-powered 1965 'Vette. A single -10 line feeds a MagnaFuel Y-block (pur- ple), which feeds both fuel rails. The returns from the rails (on the front side of the engine) feed into separate ports on the Aeromotive return-style regulator.

In this example, an Earl's Y-block feeds twin throttle bodies, each of which return back into a MagnaFuel return-style regulator.

Fig. 6.25. We fabbed-up the rear crossover line between the fuel rails so that it easily clears the distributor cab and the cap can be easily removed without having to remove the crossover line.

Fig. 6.26. We fabbed-up the feed and return lines from the fuel rails. The Aeroquip push-lock hose and ends are easy to assemble. Lubricate the ends with engine oil to reduce friction when assembling them. Also, avoid sharp bends or turns in the lines.

Holley 10-micron post-filter just above that on the inner fender. The component location complies with NHRA rules. Since the inner fender on the Olds is plastic, we used 1/4-inch hardware (bolts, washers, lock washers, nuts) to mount the components securely.

We also connected a brass T and a brass 90-degree elbow (both 1/8-inch NPT) to the fuel-gauge port on the regulator to provide locations for the Holley fuel pressure transducer as well as the transducer that came in the new Auto Meter electric fuel pressure gauge

(see the sidebar "Monitoring and Datalogging Fuel and Oil Pressure" on page 105 for more details).

We fabricated the remaining fuel lines to and from the fuel rails. This really is a simple fuel system. At this point, the fuel system is completed and we're ready to move on to Stage Three.

Stage Three: Holley Dominator Components

Now that the electrical system has been appropriately upgraded and the fuel system is installed, it's time to install the throttle body, sensors, and wiring harness. In addition, we need to interface the ignition system and install the ECU.

1. Install Throttle Body and Linkage

Okay, I admit it. Immediately upon receiving the actual components, Bill and I took about seventeen seconds to get the intake manifold and throttle body unboxed and mated together. Let the cell phone picture blasts begin. After we got that out of our system, the throttle body went back into its box and now it's finally time to install it for real.

At this point, it's really hard to not get a little bit excited as we're on the downhill stretch. We're already thinking about how folks are going to react when they see this new jewelry under the hood at the next car show. Time for round two of cell phone picture blasts.

That was the easy part. Now it was time to get the linkage dialed in and this took a few hours to get right. We ended up fabbing a short bracket out of 1/4-inch-thick flat-steel stock to mount the Holley throttle cable linkage bracket to. The challenge is to get the linkage to work properly without binding, permit WOT, and fit under the air cleaner assembly. Patience here is definitely a virtue.

2. Choose Component Location

Before mounting any of the other components or sensors, you need to first determine their installed locations. Specifically, you want to choose a location for the ECU, each of the sensors, and lay the main harness loosely in the vehicle to be sure that everything reaches.

When choosing a location for the ECU, be sure to locate it away from sources of noise, such as ignition system components and their harnesses. In addition, it's preferable not to have a big length of "extra" harness that you've got to bundle somehow as a result of locating the ECU too close to the engine.

I've often mounted ECUs behind the dash on the passenger side, which solves both problems, but in this Olds that's quite a busy (and electrically noisy) location. In addition, the Dominator ECU is the largest ECU I've yet seen so it requires a fair chunk of real estate and should have good airflow around it. We elected to mount it under the hood. Specifically, we chose to locate it at the front of the passenger-side inner fender. This offered plenty of room, as well as the ability to route the main harness up through the area between the inner fender and fender, totally out of sight.

According to the thick red warning sheet wrapped around the ECU, Holley cautions us not to mount the ECU in such a way that its chassis is "shorted" to the vehicle chassis in any way, which made the plastic inner fender even more attractive. The ECU has nylon bushings in each of the mounting tabs and includes

Fig. 6.27. This Holley billet throttle body flows 2,000 cfm and is car-guy jewelry. I've long suspected the 950-cfm carburetor was a bottleneck at high RPM. We'll soon see.

Fig. 6.28. We used a piece of 3/16-inch flat-steel stock to fabricate a standoff for the Holley throttle linkage bracket, which is located at the rear of the throttle body. This was necessary for the throttle cable to fit under the air cleaner assembly and not bind when in motion.

Fig. 6.29. Holley includes this weather-tight USB cable with the ECU. The USB cable is permanently installed and it routes through the firewall. You don't have to worry about moisture entering the ECU.

Unterminated Harnesses

Holley offers the main harness for their ECUs in an unterminated fashion, as they do most of their other EFI harnesses (injector harness, ignition harness, etc.). The unterminated version comes with the plugs to the ECU pre-terminated and is 15 feet long. It's up to you to cut all sub-harnesses to the perfect length, terminate each one, and then wrap the harness as an assembly. This allows you to build an EFI harness specific to your application, which is ideal for engine builders and car builders. This process is time consuming and requires special tools to properly install each of the open-barrel terminals.

In Chapter 7, I illustrate the process of building a vehicle-specific EFI harness. ■

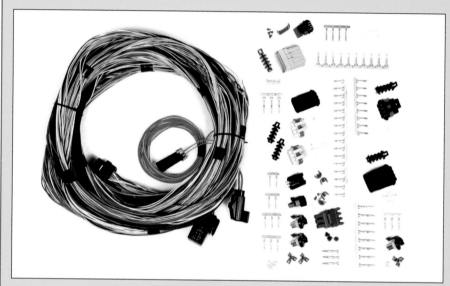

Custom car builders and super enthusiasts take note: Holley offers their harnesses un-terminated so that you build them to suit the exact routing that you require for an ultra-clean, finished look. Pins and bodies at the ECU end are pre-assembled; the rest is up to you. Overall harness length is 15 feet. (Photo Courtesy Holley Performance Products)

stainless mounting hardware to prevent an electrical connection between the chassis of the ECU and the chassis of the vehicle, even when mounting it to a metal panel.

Holley even includes a weather-tight USB cable that's plugged into the ECU when mounted under the hood and then routed through the firewall. I verified that it was long enough before settling on this location.

Before choosing locations for each of the sensors, I recommend that you have a good look at all harnesses for the ECU and familiarize yourself with how much length each of the sensor sub-harnesses offers you. I mention this because you most likely prefer to avoid extending any of these and you may be able to determine locations for each of the sensors that work perfectly with the harness as it is. In some cases, there is one location for a given sensor. In other cases, such as with CTS, IAT, and MAP sensors, you may have multiple locations to choose from.

After we settled on a location for the ECU and each of the sensors, I laid the harness over the passenger-side fender and routed it along the firewall and to the intake manifold to be

sure that everything reached. In this installation, I had to extend a few of the sensor sub-harnesses, which was not difficult, so don't fret if you need to do this.

3. Install Sensors

We've already installed the pressure transducers for the fuel pressure input of the ECU and the Auto Meter fuel pressure gauge. Next in line was

the crank trigger. The Holley big-block Chevy Crank Trigger Kit required a few simple modifications to work on the Olds 455. Bill runs an ATI Olds balancer, which has a bolt pattern for a big-block Chevy crank pulley. Even so, it was still necessary to modify parts of the kit slightly to achieve a good fit. A qualified machine shop should perform this work.

Bill recruited Precision Research to help make the installation a

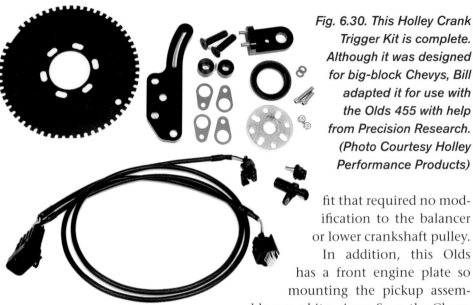

Fig. 6.30. This Holley Crank Trigger Kit is complete. Although it was designed for big-block Chevys, Bill adapted it for use with the Olds 455 with help from Precision Research. (Photo Courtesy Holley Performance Products)

snap. Specifically, Precision Research opened up the centering adapter by a few thousandths so that it fit perfectly around the harmonic balancer locating pilot. They also made a .090-inch-thick aluminum spacer that fits between the trigger wheel and the balancer.

The spacer was installed first, then the trigger wheel, and the centering adapter. They netted a perfect

fit that required no modification to the balancer or lower crankshaft pulley.

In addition, this Olds has a front engine plate so mounting the pickup assembly was a bit unique. Sure, the Chevy guys get all the cool parts, but that didn't stand in our way here.

We located the CTS in the stock thermostat housing, which had a plugged 3/8-inch NPT threaded hole

ready to accept the sensor. Before removing such a plug, drain the coolant in the radiator to below its level. You only forget to do that once . . .

We located the transducer for the oil pressure input of the ECU just below the transducer Bill had already mounted for his Auto Meter electric oil pressure gauge. Thankfully, Bill had installed the brass T when installing the other sending unit many years ago, so all we had to do was remove the plug and thread the transducer in. Simple.

We located the MAP sensor on the firewall, just under the cowl. When mounting a MAP sensor, you should always mount it in such a way that the barb points downward.

We mounted the IAT sensor in the air cleaner assembly mainly because Bill intends to use nitrous

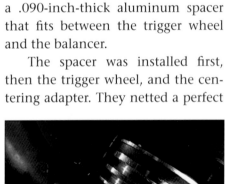

Fig. 6.31. Alignment of the pickup to the reluctor wheel is critical. In addition, it's important to locate the pickup on a given tooth of the reluctor wheel with the engine resting at TDC.

Fig. 6.32. We installed the CTS in an available 3/8-inch NPT port in the front of the thermostat housing. We installed the oil pressure transducer in the available 1/8-inch NPT port in the pre-existing brass T.

Fig. 6.33. I mounted the MAP sensor under the lip in front of the cowl with the nipple pointing downward. This is a 1 bar sensor, which is all you need for a naturally aspirated combination.

Fig. 6.34. Bill mounted the IAT sensor in the rear of the new K&N air filter assembly. The sensor is threaded and doesn't include a nut to hold it in place as shown here. Luckily, I had the perfect nut to secure it. We also could have located it in the manifold itself, which is pre-tapped for this, but we'll be spraying a small shot of nitrous via a plate system. We want the option of having the IAT in fresh air.

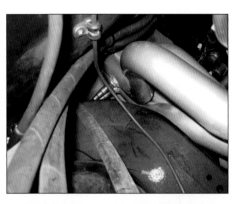

Fig. 6.35. These are two of the oxygen sensors on the driver's side for the Innovate LM-2. The oxygen sensors for the Holley ECU are directly after these in the collector.

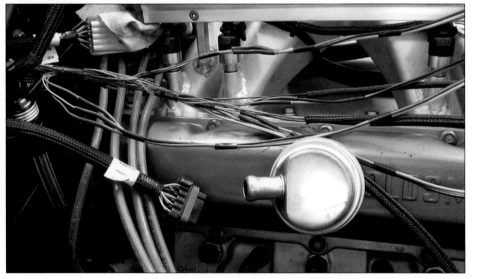

Fig. 6.36. I elected to order the pre-assembled main harness rather than the un-terminated harness. As a result, I had to lengthen a few of the sensor sub-harnesses, but none by more than 2 feet. All connections were soldered and insulated with adhesive-lined heat-shrink tubing. Afterward, I re-loomed these sub-harnesses with split-braid tubing.

via a plate system. The IAT can also be mounted in the intake manifold. Holley labels this connector MAT (manifold air temperature). In boosted installations, it's preferable to mount the IAT in the intake manifold because the temperature of the ambient air rises when the supercharger compresses the air. Nitrous is just the opposite so we wanted to keep the IAT out of the manifold for now. The Edelbrock Victor manifold has a 3/8-inch NPT threaded boss in the rear if we elect to change this in the future as Bill perfects his nitrous tune.

As I discussed earlier, Bill had a spare bung in each collector for the oxygen sensors. So installing them was a snap.

Based on the location for the ECU and for each of the sensors, I had to extend the following sub-harnesses: fuel pressure, CTS, oil pressure, and MAP.

This is really a simple process. I began by unwrapping the sensor pigtail of the main harness, untaping the gathered wires, and separating them so that I could easily work on each individually. I extended each with 18 AWG GPT, which is one size larger than the size used in the harness.

After each of the sub-harnesses was extended, I re-wrapped the harness with split-braide tubing.

4. Install Wiring Harnesses

I began by installing the injector harness. To keep the connections clean and out of sight, I spun each of the injectors around so that their plugs faced the throttle body. I routed the injector harness into the center of the manifold, under the runners, from the rear to keep it out of sight as much as possible.

Then I installed the crank sensor harness. Now that the injector harness, crank sensor harness, and all of the sensors have been installed, we can begin installing the main wiring harness.

The injector harness simply plugs into the mating connector on the main harness.

The crank sensor harness plugs into the mating connector on the main harness.

Fig. 6.37. I routed the injector harness from the rear of the intake and under the runners for cylinders 5, 6, 7, and 8. This allowed me to neatly tie up the harness on the rear side of the injector rails.

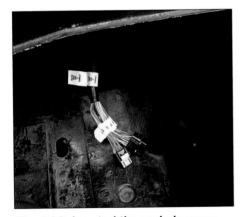

Fig. 6.38. I routed the main harness through the fender and inner fender from the rear forward. The fuel pump relay and switched ignition fuse harness are just out of sight. I tied them securely to the harness.

Fig. 6.39. I routed the sub-harnesses to the oil pressure transducer, CTS, IAC, and TPS tightly inside the fuel rails and along the injector harness to keep it as neat and out of sight as possible.

Fig. 6.40. Note that I spun the injectors so that their connectors were out of view from either side of the engine. This allowed me to route the injector harness through the center of the manifold.

Fig. 6.41. I anchored the main harness neatly along the firewall. Notice the crank sensor harness and harnesses to the fuel pressure transducers tied neatly to the return line, which we properly anchored to the inner fender.

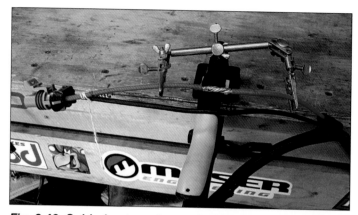

Fig. 6.42. Soldering two pieces of 10 AWG wire together end to end like this is actually pretty easy. I use a Craftsman 400-watt soldering gun (PN 27320) for this kind of stuff.

Fig. 6.43. I insulated this connection with two layers of adhesive-lined heat-shrink tubing.

Fig. 6.44. I keep the correct terminals in stock for the weather-tight fuse holders that Holley uses. I was able to reuse the fuse holder body and save Bill a few dollars in parts. The negative lead connects directly to the battery negative terminal.

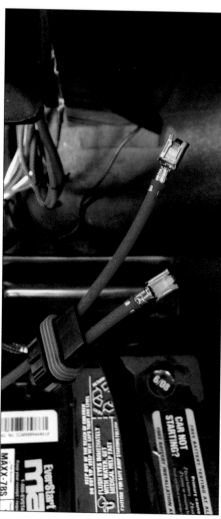

Fig. 6.46. Bill must have bumped his head just before choosing a battery with side-post terminals only. No matter; I keep adapters on hand to make correct connections to the side posts. I also mounted the fuse holder in the battery box.

Fig. 6.45. I always crimp and solder all 10 AWG open-barrel terminals for maximum current transfer. After the wires cool, they can be snapped back into the housing.

Then I pugged in the TPS and IAC on the throttle body, and each of the sensors. I routed the oxygen sensor harness in the main ECU harness across the top of the bell-housing to the oxygen sensor on the driver's side; it was the perfect length.

Next up was the auxiliary harness for the passenger-side oxygen sensor. It also was the perfect length. CAUTION: Do not plug the oxygen sensors into the harness at this time. They must be set up in the ECU first or they will be damaged when you power up the ECU.

The included power harness was just a few feet short, given the location we chose for the ECU and the fact that the Olds has a rear-located battery, albeit on the same side as the ECU. I extended the harness by 5 feet with 10 AWG TXL.

I also elected to remove the ATC fuse holder from the ECU end of the power harness and relocate it to the rear of the vehicle near the battery for safety reasons. For now, leave the fuse out of the fuse holder.

This leaves only the following "loose wires," as Holley refers to them, to connect:

Wire Color	Application
Black	Clean chassis ground
Red/White	+12V switched ignition
Green	+12V fuel pump output (from fuel pump relay)
Yellow	Not used in this installation
White	Ignition trigger output for CD-style ignition boxes

I connected the black wire to the frame on the same side of the frame where the battery is grounded. This ground should be all alone, with no other grounds tied to it.

Fig. 6.47. The loose black wire goes to a clean ground all by itself. The frame of this Olds is the return path for the charging system, so this is the perfect place. Note the use of a star washer and lithium grease.

Fig. 6.48. I passed the remaining loose wires through the snap bushing (to the left and below the grommet), along with several of the oxygen harnesses Bill had already routed for the Innovate LM-2.

Fig. 6.49. Bill fabricated this switch panel when he was in high school (he's had the Olds a long time) and it has a bit of sentimental value to him. I removed it and wired it up neatly for him. I used an SPDT center-off switch for the fuel pump. Center is off, down is Pump 1, up is Pump 1 and Pump 2.

I routed the other four wires through the firewall and into the passenger compartment. I passed them through a plastic snap bushing to protect them, of course.

The red/white wire connects to a +12V switched source. I connected that to one of the fused switched outputs on the power panel. (Any power wire that passes through the firewall must be fused with a foot or so of its source of power. Keep that in mind if you elect to connect this wire to the ignition switch, etc.) For now, leave the fuse out.

I routed the green wire to the switch panel in Bill's dash. He's had this same switch panel for nearly 20 years, but I helped him to wire it correctly. I always recommend using the fuel pump output of the ECU because it primes the system when the key is turned to run position. In addition, the Holley software allows you to adjust the length of time the fuel pump primes. That's cool. Even though we've already installed a pair of 30-amp relays for the Holley Dominator fuel pump, they're switched positively, so the output

Fig. 6.50. The fuel pump output of the ECU (dark green wire on the left) powers the fuel pump relays via the fuel pump switch. You need to refer to the provided diagram for specifics. The loose terminal is actually a switched ignition lead that can be easily swapped for the trigger wire from the ECU.

Fig. 6.51. The wiring and electrical system is now sorted out and much more sensible to work with than what Bill had under the dash when we started. The red/white wire from the ECU connects to one of the switched fuse locations on the 15-position switched fuse panel (on the left). The white wire from the ECU (points output) connects to the white wire (points trigger) on the MSD Digital 6AL box.

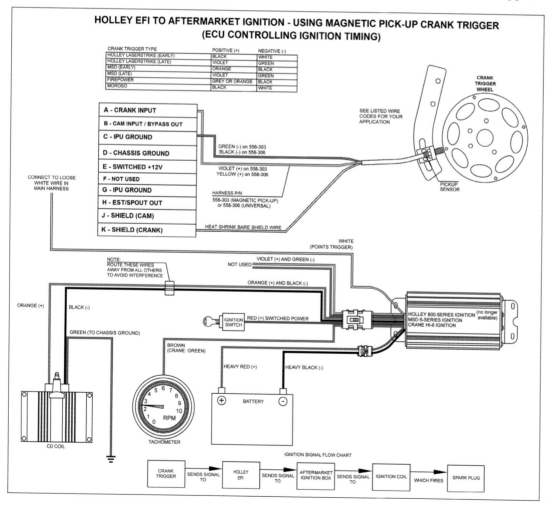

Fig. 6.52. The crank trigger is simply plug-and-play with the main harness. The ECU fires the ignition box via its points input. Note the block diagram at the bottom that clearly shows how the spark is fired. (Photo Courtesy Holley Performance Products)

Fig. 6.53. Time to plug in the ECU. The USB cable, main harness, secondary oxygen harness (which doubles as an IN/OUT harness), and the power harness round it out.

Fig. 6.54. We mounted the ECU with the stainless hardware Holley included. This is obviously the number-one giveaway that Bill's Olds is now fuel injected.

from the ECU is correct for us (see Figure 6.21).

You must be able to power the fuel pump directly (not via the ECU's fuel pump output) to check the fuel system for leaks and to set the fuel pressure. In Bill's Olds I left the fuel pump switch wired as it was (manual), for now, for this reason.

5. Interface ECU to Ignition System

This is really pretty simple if you're running a stand-alone CD-type ignition box. The Dominator ECU sends a trigger out that is connected to the points input of the ignition box. Look at it like this: the crank trigger tells the ECU where the crankshaft is. The ECU triggers the ignition box based on the location of the crankshaft, which coincides with the location of the rotor in the distributor. Remember that the rotor makes one full rotation for every two rotations of the crankshaft. It was as simple as connecting the white wire from the ECU to the white wire of the MSD Digital 6AL. Done.

6. Install ECU

By this point, Bill was foaming at the mouth: "Dude, plug that in and let's start it!" Not so fast, we've got a ways to go yet. Before mount-

ing the ECU, you need to install the Holley EFI software on the laptop you intend to use with the vehicle (if you have not done so already), including the USB bridge. Then establish a connection between the laptop and the ECU via the included USB cable.

This step is imperative so that you can communicate with the ECU from your laptop via the USB. This process is simple, can be done on the bench without the ECU powered up, and is outlined clearly in the instructions included with the ECU.

We used the stainless hardware Holley included to mount the ECU to the inner fender. It was far easier than I thought it would be.

Stage Four: Get It to Run

Before starting the Olds we need to flush the fuel system, set the fuel pressure, build a base tune, load the tune into the ECU, and perform a few final calibrations. Each of these final steps is critical to ensure the Olds fires up and runs correctly.

1. Flush System and Set Fuel Pressure

Anytime you assemble a fuel system from scratch, as we did here, you want to blow out each assembled line with compressed air as you're assembling them. Even then, it's always a great idea to flush the lines with some fuel before final assembly. Before doing so, ensure that all fittings are tight from tank to pre-filter, pre-filter to pump, pump to post-filter, and at the outlet of the post-filter.

Undo the fitting for the line at the inlet to the fuel rails and let this line hang free.

If your pre-filter has a shut-off valve, like the Aeromotive filter in this installation does, be sure that it is in the FLOW position before proceeding.

Also, install the fuse for the fuel pump at this time.

Have a helper hold the free line in a catch can and manually turn on the fuel pump to flush some fuel into the catch can, just enough to flush any debris out of the lines. In the Olds it was easy to power up the fuel pump manually via the dash-mounted switch with the ignition key in the RUN position.

Then reinstall the fitting on the fuel rail and remove the return line from the other fuel rail to the regulator (at the regulator).

Repeat.

Now that the fuel system has been flushed, reconnect any disconnected lines and tighten all fittings appropriately.

Power the fuel pump back up to pressurize the system and check all fittings for leaks. Address any leaks at this time.

After you've verified the system is leak free, power the fuel pump and set fuel pressure via the dash-mounted gauge. You can do this via an external fuel pressure gauge such as the Fluke (illustrated in Chapter 5). With this Holley system, we set fuel pressure to 43 psi per Holley's instructions.

Remove the fuse for the fuel pump before proceeding.

2. Build or Adjust a Base Tune

It's time to build the tune you will load into the ECU. You have two choices: build a base tune from scratch or tweak one of the base tunes Holley has provided.

If you're an advanced tuner, you may elect to build a base tune from scratch. We elected option number two, and loaded a base tune that was close to the Olds' parameters. You really should know your camshaft profile, etc. before proceeding here.

To tweak one of the base tunes follow Holley's section 3.3.2, "Creating an Initial Calibration" in the *Step-By-Step Beginners Tuning Guide* (found in the Help menu). The process for building a base tune from scratch is explained in section 2.2.2, "Creating an Initial Calibration" in the *Experienced User Tuning Manual* (also found in the Help menu).

Holley has included a number of base calibrations that can be loaded into the ECU so why not take advantage of that? We did. You can find a complete listing of the included base calibrations in the Help menu (Help > Contents > Base Calibration Information). Each has a brief description, and they are separated into TBI and MPFI base calibrations.

After looking a few of them over, we settled on the 496_650HP base calibration for the Olds, found in the Custom Calibrations section. Because we're using E85 fuel and not a DIS ignition system, we need to change those things in the base calibration. This is easy: We simply followed section 4.0 in the in the *Step-By-Step Beginners Tuning Guide*, "Step-By-Step INITIAL STARTUP INSTRUCTIONS."

The Holley software stores tunes in Global Folders. A Global Folder has the following discrete files at a minimum:

- Fuel File (.fuel)
- Idle File (.idle)
- I/O (input/output) File (.io)
- Sensor File (.sensor)
- Spark File (.spark)
- System File (.system)

Our tune also has a Nitrous File (.nitrous); we add that after we get the Olds running the way we want it to naturally aspirated. Each of these files is created (or tweaked) by the user in the software by choosing the appropriate icon in the title bar.

Holley Software Setup for Windows 7 Users

If you're running Windows 7 on your laptop, you need to perform the following to prevent errors in saving files with the Holley software. This also prevents errors later in creating datalogs.

1 Click on the START button.

2 Select Computer. Double-click on Drive C.

3 Double-click on Program Files [or Program Files (x86) if you don't find a Holley Folder in Program Files].

4 Double-click on Holley.

5 Right-click on EFI > Select Properties > Select Security.

6 Look at the group or user names; Select the group or user that is running the EFI software (likely the user's name), and then look at the Permissions for Users box below it.

7 Is Write checked to allow? If not, click on the Edit tab, and choose Allow Full Control.

8 Click Apply.

9 Click OK. ■

Although the software has a seemingly endless array of adjustments, the objective here is to get the vehicle running (we fine-tune it in Chapter 7). Build the tune on the laptop that will be used with the vehicle.

At this point, the laptop is not plugged into the ECU. The objective here is to get you comfortable with the software, navigating it, etc. so have fun!

The following 10 steps apply to the V2 software.

1 Launch the Holley EFI software from the icon on your desktop.

2 Choose Open Global Folder.

3 Double-click on the Custom Calibrations (Cals) folder.

4 Double-click on the 496 650HP Global Folder.

To prevent making changes to this tune, make a copy of this global folder, which is specific to your application, before proceeding. (To do that, click on File > Save Global Folder As and choose your folder name. Type an appropriate name for your tune, and click Save. Save your tune in the Custom Cals folder to make it easy to find later.)

5 From the Toolbox menu, select Preferences.

Check Display Pressure as PSIA if

System Parameters

The SYSTEM PARAMETERS settings allow you to set specifics about the engine, fuel delivery, ignition triggering, how the ECU processes the feedback from the oxygen sensor, etc. ∎

you'd like to see MAP readings in PSI versus kPa. If you are using an HP EFI ECU, you also select that here.

6 Click on the System ICF icon on the taskbar (looks like an ECU). This brings up the *SYSTEM PARAMETERS* box in the left column.

7 Let's begin with Engine Parameters. We need to make the following changes for this installation:

• Change Engine Displacement to 462 ci
• Change Fuel Type to E85
• Change Wideband Oxygen Sensor to Bosch
• Change Number of Sensors to 2; this brings up a Sensor Averaging window, and for now we select Average
• In the FUEL SYSTEM box, change

System Type to 83LB Holley 522-838; this automatically triggers the low-impedance setting in the Injector Type selection in the INJECTOR SET 1 box.

8 Click on Ignition Parameters in the SYSTEM PARAMETERS box on the left.

We need to make the following changes for this installation:

• Change Ignition Type to Custom, which brings up the CRANK SENSOR window
• Sensor Type default should be DIGITAL FALLING; if not, select it
• Set TDC Tooth Number to 11, which is how Bill set it up when he installed the crank sensor
• Change CAM SENSOR type to Not Used
• Change OUTPUT SETUP type to Points Output, which allows the

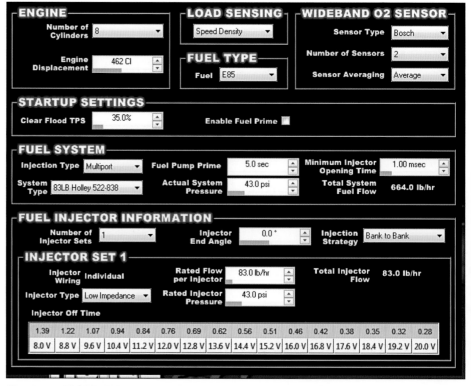

Fig. 6.55. ENGINE PARAMETERS: You need to set up the engine parameters in the Holley V2 software. This basic information is necessary for the ECU to function correctly with your specific engine combination.

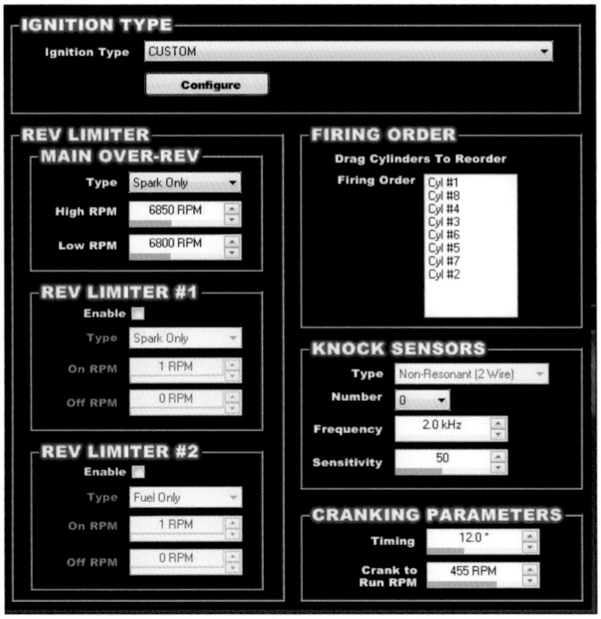

Fig. 6.56. IGNITION PARAMETERS: Setting up the type of ignition system you'll be using is accomplished here. In addition, this is where you'll later set up rev limiters. For now, you simply choose the type of ignition system and the cranking timing. Clicking on the Configure button at the top brings up the box shown in Figure 6.57.

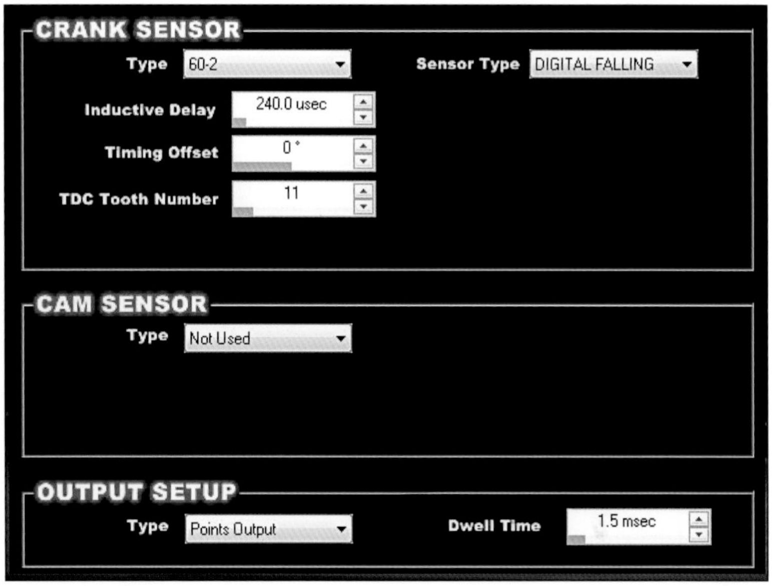

Fig. 6.57. When using a crank sensor, you need to define its type as well as which tooth rests nearest the pickup with the engine at TDC. In addition, you need to provide specifics as to which type of cam sensor you have (we're not using one on the Olds) and how you'd like the ECU to trigger the ignition system.

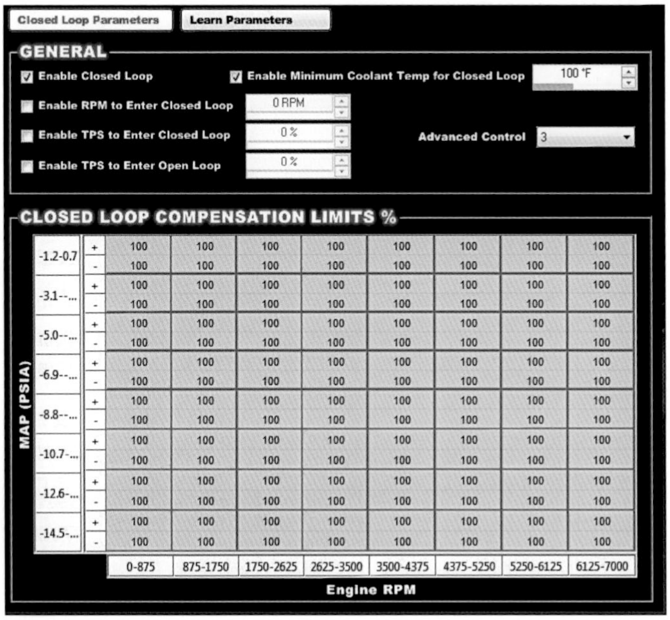

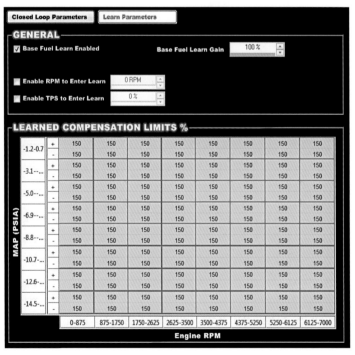

Fig. 6.58. CLOSED LOOP/LEARN: Enable the closed-loop feature. Also, set the minimum coolant temperature for the system to enter closed loop. Setting this incorrectly is one of the most common reasons the system doesn't enter closed loop. The table allows you to fine-tune the closed-loop mode. Leave it as is for now.

Fig. 6.59. LEARN PARAMETERS: For now, enable the Base Fuel Learn Mode and the set the Base Fuel Learn Gain to 100%. The table allows you to fine-tune the Learn Mode. Leave it as is for now.

Sensors Parameters

The SENSORS PARAMETERS settings allow you to choose specific sensors. In this installation we used all Holley-supplied parts, but the ECU is compatible with a wide variety of sensors for multiple applications. ■

ECU to trigger the MSD Digital 6AL box

- Click again on Ignition Parameters on the left
- Set CRANKING PARAMETERS timing to 12.0 degrees
- Set the MAIN OVER-REV REV LIMITER as you see in Figure 6.56

9 Click on Closed Loop/Learn in the SYSTEM PARAMETERS box on the left. Then:

- Select Enable Closed Loop
- Click on the Learn Parameters box at the top

Fuel Settings

The FUEL SETTINGS allow you to develop a Target Air/Fuel Ratio Map, which is a function of both engine RPM and MAP. The software also offers advanced settings that can be made to the fuel settings to improve startup, eliminate bogs on throttle transitions, etc.

In addition, the software allows you to enrich the mixture based on coolant temperature and/or air temperature as well as during acceleration and deceleration.

Finally, you can also fine-tune that rate of change of enrichment with respect to numerous variables. ■

- Select Base Fuel Learn Enabled (for now, leave the Base Fuel Learn Gain at 100 percent)
- Click Save and close the SYSTEM PARAMETERS box before proceeding

10 Click on Sensors ICF Icon

We used a 1-bar MAP sensor in this installation, which is the default. All of the other sensors in the software are also set to default to the Holley sensors we used in the installation. It's never a bad idea to verify this, though.

- Click Save
- Close the SENSORS box before proceeding

11 Click on the Fuel ICF Icon.

- Modify the Target Air/Fuel Ratio Table (from gasoline to our use of E85) as follows:

14.7:1 (1 Lambda) is stoichiometric for gasoline
9.8:1 (1 Lambda) is stoichiometric for E85

1 Lambda = 14.7:1
X A/F ratio/14.7 = Lambda
Lambda x 9.8 = correct E85 value

For example, consider a cell with 13.6:

13.6/14.7 = .925 Lambda
.925 Lambda x 9.8 = 9.06

This measurement represents the conversion of the gas value to value for E85.

Each of the cells in the table has a resolution to one-tenth. Round up to the nearest tenth to make the

Target Air/Fuel Ratio

MAP (PSIA)	700	900	1100	1400	1800	2200	2500	3000	3500	4000	4500	5000	5500	6000	6500	7000
0.7	9.8	9.8	8.1	8.1	8.1	8.1	8.1	8.1	8.1	8.1	8.1	8.1	8.1	8.1	8.1	8.1
-0.3	9.8	9.8	8.1	8.1	8.1	8.1	8.1	8.1	8.1	8.1	8.1	8.1	8.1	8.1	8.1	8.1
-1.3	9.8	9.8	8.1	8.1	8.1	8.1	8.1	8.1	8.1	8.1	8.1	8.1	8.1	8.1	8.1	8.1
-2.3	9.8	9.8	8.7	8.5	8.5	8.5	8.5	8.5	8.5	8.5	8.5	8.5	8.5	8.5	8.5	8.5
-3.3	9.8	9.8	9.0	8.7	8.7	8.7	8.7	8.7	8.7	8.7	8.7	8.7	8.7	8.7	8.7	8.7
-4.4	9.8	9.8	9.8	9.8	9.8	8.9	8.9	8.9	8.9	8.9	8.9	8.9	8.9	8.9	8.9	8.9
-5.4	9.8	9.8	9.8	9.8	9.8	9.1	9.1	9.1	9.1	9.1	9.1	9.1	9.1	9.1	9.1	9.1
-6.4	9.8	9.8	9.8	9.8	9.8	9.8	9.8	9.8	9.8	9.8	9.8	9.8	9.8	9.8	9.8	9.8
-7.4	9.8	9.8	9.8	9.8	9.8	9.8	9.8	9.8	9.8	9.8	9.8	9.8	9.8	9.8	9.8	9.8
-8.4	9.8	9.8	9.8	9.8	9.8	9.8	9.8	9.8	9.8	9.8	9.8	9.8	9.8	9.8	9.8	9.8
-9.4	9.8	9.8	9.8	9.8	9.8	9.8	9.8	9.8	9.8	9.8	9.8	9.8	9.8	9.8	9.8	9.8
-10.4	9.8	9.8	9.8	9.8	9.8	9.8	9.8	9.8	9.8	9.8	9.8	9.8	9.8	9.8	9.8	9.8
-11.5	9.8	9.8	9.8	9.8	9.8	9.8	9.8	9.8	9.8	9.8	9.8	9.8	9.8	9.8	9.8	9.8
-12.5	9.8	9.8	9.8	9.8	9.8	9.8	9.8	9.8	9.8	9.8	9.8	9.8	9.8	9.8	9.8	9.8
-13.5	9.8	9.8	9.8	9.8	9.8	9.8	9.8	9.8	9.8	9.8	9.8	9.8	9.8	9.8	9.8	9.8
-14.4	9.8	9.8	9.8	9.8	9.8	9.8	9.8	9.8	9.8	9.8	9.8	9.8	9.8	9.8	9.8	9.8

Engine RPM

Fig. 6.60. TARGET AIR/FUEL RATIO: We set the values in each of these cells based on E85. Since we began with a tune that was originally developed on the gas scale, we converted the existing values to E85 values using a Lambda multiplier as shown in the math above. You can achieve smooth transitions from cell to cell by highlighting multiple cells, right clicking, and using the Fill Column Values and Fill Row Values functions.

Idle Settings

The IDLE Settings allow us to set the idle speed relative to coolant temperature, set the type of IAC, and adjust the functionality of the IAC. ■

Spark Settings

The SPARK SETTINGS allow you to build a Base Timing Table relative to RPM and MAP, manage retard for an optional knock sensor (electronic spark control, ESC), and set up modifiers for the timing based on coolant temperature and/or air temperature. ■

mixture leaner; round down to make it richer.

Changing the values in the Target Air/Fuel Ratio Table is easy; click and drag all of the cells with the same value, type in the value you desire, and press Enter. All cells are updated accordingly.

Bill converted all values that were listed at 14.0 to 9.8 to achieve 1 lambda with E85 in the all-important idle and cruise (drivability) areas, which is what he previously determined works best for his combination in the Phoenix climate when it was carbureted.

After the conversion, the Target Air/Fuel Ratio Table looked like the one in Figure 6.60.

Remember, we just need to get a base tune in the ECU so we can start the engine. Additional tuning may

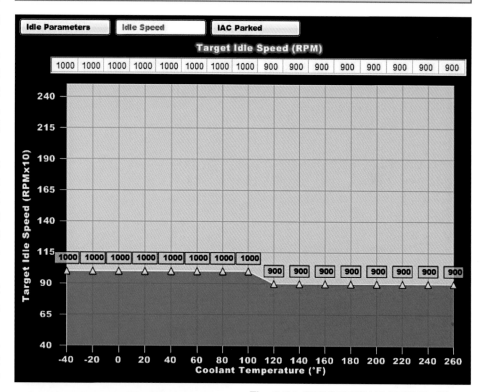

Fig. 6.61. TARGET IDLE SPEED: We set the idle according to Bill's preferences. This is a simple adjustment that can be made at any time.

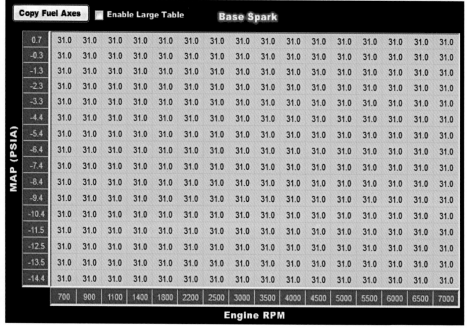

Fig. 6.62. BASE SPARK: Recall the data you logged at the beginning of this project for ignition timing for your combination. From that data, enter values in the table that coincide with what you ran at idle, cruise, and WOT. You can achieve smooth transitions from cell to cell by highlighting multiple cells, right clicking, and using the Fill Column Values and Fill Row Values functions. For now, we've set all values to 31 degrees as that is what Bill ran. He'll build a timing table for his Olds after we get it running as he wants.

alter these values. There are many additional FUEL SETTINGS, but for now, we can leave them as is from the tune we're tweaking.

- Click Save
- Close the FUEL box before proceeding

12 Click on the Idle ICF icon.

- Click on the Idle Speed tab at the top. (Idle speed is pre-set at 1,000 rpm. We tweaked this a bit for when the engine warms up. You can either enter the values in the white boxes at the top and press enter, or click and drag the yellow boxes to the desired values.) (See Figure 6.61.)
- Click Save
- Close the IDLE box before proceeding

13 Click on the Spark ICF icon.

Pull out the notes that you took earlier regarding the timing your vehicle had before you removed the carburetor.

- Click on Base Timing Table
- Modify the table according to your combination (in the case of Bill's car, we set all cells to 31 degrees, which is exactly how his timing was set up before we began the conversion. Later, we add some timing in the idle and drivability areas to improve the burn of the mixture, improve fuel economy, lower exhaust temperatures, etc.) (See Figure 6.62.)

- Click Save
- Close the SPARK Box before proceeding

3. Load Base Tune into ECU

Now that the base tune has been tweaked, we can load it into the ECU. Fortunately, that's simple. Before proceeding, it's time to install the fuses for the ECU. Also, ensure that the fuse to the fuel pump is still removed so that it's inactive during the following steps.

1 Plug the USB cable into the port of the laptop that you set up to work with the ECU when you installed the USB bridge at the end of Stage Three (see page 116).

2 Open the Holley software and choose OPEN GLOBAL FOLDER.

3 Find your tune in the Custom Cals folder and click Open.

4 Turn the ignition power on, ensuring the USB cable is connected.

The Communication mode is just to the right of the Toolbox on the Menu bar. It should now say USB Link.

5 Click on the USB Link button; this starts a sync between the Global Folder you currently have open and the ECU.

Because the ECU has no Global Folder in it currently, select Send to ECU. The Communication mode shows Online while you are communicating with the ECU or looking at the settings within the Global Folder stored within the ECU.

Now that the Global Folder has been sent to the ECU, I recommend that you surf through all of the settings you've made (while online) to be sure that everything is accurate. Pay close attention to the oxygen sensor settings in the *SYSTEM PARAMETERS* to be sure that you have set it correctly.

While online, you'll notice that several of the parameters of the Global Folder can be manipulated in real time (even when the engine is running), while others can only be manipulated when you are not online (shown as grayed out). If you have to make any changes to any grayed-out parameters within the Global Folder in the ECU, simply switch the ignition off, make the change, switch the ignition back on, click on the USB Link button, allow it to sync, and then follow the instructions to send your changes to the ECU.

Finally, switch the ignition off and then back on to cement the change. Incidentally, the process of turning the ignition key off and then back on is referred to as cycling the key.

4. Perform Calibrations Before Engine Start

This is the final step before starting the engine. Each of the following steps is critical to ensure a successful start-up.

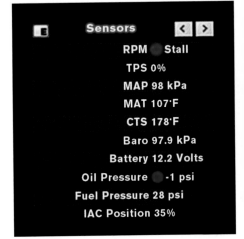

Fig. 6.63. DATA MONITOR: The data monitor is at the lower left corner of the software and displays live data while the key is in the RUN position. You can use the right and left buttons to scroll through ten such monitors.

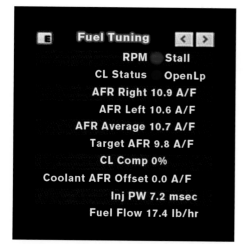

Fig. 6.64. The Data Monitor, found on the lower left-hand side of the screen, provides a verification that each of the sensors/inputs is functioning properly.

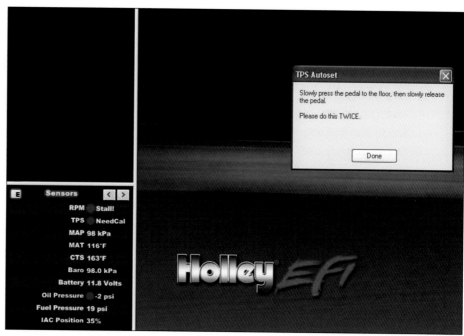

Fig. 6.65. TPS AUTOSET: The ECU does not permit the engine to start until a TPS Autoset has been performed. This calibrates the throttle to the TPS.

Ignition Check

Ensure all components are properly installed and wired. Compare your work to the diagrams to ensure accuracy.

We manually rolled over the engine in Bill's car to ensure that we had the rotor pointing at cylinder number-1 with the timing on the balancer at 31 degrees BTDC to ensure a quick start. This was off by 180 degrees so we rotated the engine one full time.

Before proceeding, install any fuses for any ignition components.

Throttle-Body Idle Settings

The throttle blades need to be open enough to allow the engine to idle. Adjust the idle setting for the throttle blades on the throttle body to achieve this. If the throttle blades are open too far, it simply causes a fast idle, which is easily corrected after the engine is started.

Verify Sensor Functionality

After you're happy with the tune in the ECU, switch the ignition off and plug in the oxygen sensors. Turn the ignition key back on, click on the USB Link, and allow it to synch.

After the synch, look at the Data Monitor box in the lower left. The first view is Sensors and you should have readings for TPS (move the throttle to be sure that it changes), MAP, MAT, CTS, battery, oil pressure, fuel pressure, and IAC position.

Click on the right arrow at the top of the box to scroll to the next window (Fuel Tuning) and verify readings for the oxygen sensors. If you do not have readings for all sensors, remedy it before proceeding.

The *Step-By-Step Beginners Tuning Guide* has a place for you to document each of the sensor readings if you choose to do so.

Perform a TPS Autoset

You must perform this or the ECU does not allow the engine to start. The purpose is to calibrate the TPS to the ECU based on your linkage setup, etc. With the ECU online, click on the down arrow next to the Sync with ECU icon (the two arrows in the shape of a circle) on the menu bar and select TPS Autoset (or simply press Ctrl + T). Follow the directions on the screen.

Check Cranking Timing

Unplug the fuel injector harness. (Obviously, the engine will not start with the fuel injector harness unplugged and the fuse for the fuel pump removed.) Connect a timing light and verify the timing while a helper cranks the engine.

Keep in mind that you may need to crank the engine for a while to get the timing light to flash even once, so ensure your battery is fully charged. The timing you read on the balancer should be close to the value you have set in the SYSTEM PARAMETERS > Ignition Parameters > Cranking Parameters > Timing in the Global Folder. If this is off by a little bit with a crank trigger (as in this installation), it can be adjusted in the

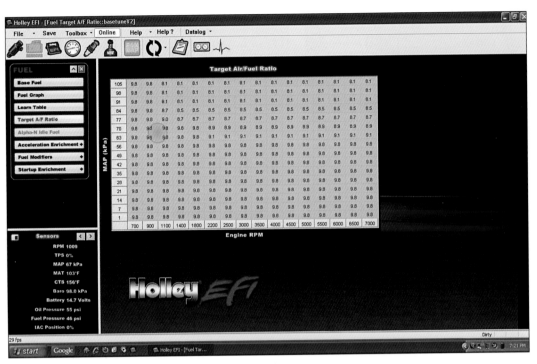

Fig. 6.66. TARGET AIR/ FUEL RATIO LIVE: While online, you can actually watch the orange dot swirling about in the Target Air/Fuel Ratio Table. The dot moves based on RPM and MAP. It is a good tool in fine-tuning the targets to achieve smooth transitions as you drive. Obviously, this is something that should be done from the passenger seat while the driver focuses on the road.

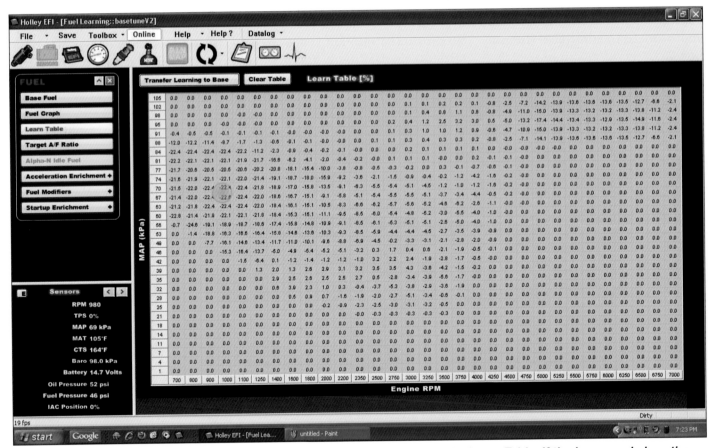

Fig. 6.67. LEARN TABLE LIVE: While online, the orange dot swirls around in the Learn Table. If the learn mode is active, values are plotted in each of the cells the dot hovers over. These values correspond to the percentage of fuel the ECU must add or subtract from the value in the Base Fuel Table to achieve the targets in the Target Air/Fuel Ratio Table. This is interesting to watch. Again, this should be done from the passenger seat while the driver focuses on the road.

software after fire-up so don't sweat it. If this is off by a lot, you should verify the proper installation of the pickup of the crank trigger sensor.

When you're happy with the value, plug the fuel injector harness back together.

Check Engine Cooling

At this point, we've not connected the ECU to the electric cooling fans in Bill's Olds. For now, they are activated as before, manually. Consider this before attempting to start your vehicle.

5. Start Engine

If you made any changes to the settings in the Global Folder between the last time you performed a sync and now, you must cycle the ignition key (turn it off and then back to the IGN/RUN position) and perform another sync.

You're now ready to start the engine. Ensure that your software is up and the ECU plugged in before proceeding.

- With the ignition off, reinstall the fuse for the fuel pump
- Turn the ignition on, and allow the ECU to prime the fuel system
- Without touching the throttle, start the engine; it should immediately start (Bill's did)

If the engine does not start, refer to the "Basic Tuning" section (Chapter 5.1) in the *Step-By-Step Beginners Tuning Guide* before proceeding.

Assuming the engine does start, press the USB Link button to establish communication between the ECU and laptop so that you can utilize the Data Monitor in the lower left.

Press the right arrow to scroll to Idle Tuning.

Verify that the fuel mixture isn't excessively rich, which could damage the engine or catalytic converters. If the engine is running excessively rich, turn it off and refer to the "Basic Tuning Section" (Chapter 6.1A) of the *Step-By-Step Beginners Tuning Guide* before proceeding.

If the engine runs smoothly and isn't excessively rich, allow the coolant temperature to climb until the ECU switches to closed loop.

Press the right arrow in the Data Monitor to scroll to Fuel Tuning so you can monitor whether the system is operating in open loop or closed loop. Once the system is in closed loop, the ECU begins adding/subtracting fuel to achieve the target air/fuel ratio. At this point, you can watch the following happen live:

- Click on the Fuel ICF icon
- Click on the Target A/F Ratio (notice the dot swirling about)
- Click on the Learn Table (the ECU plots +/- changes to the Base Fuel Table to achieve the Target Air/Fuel Ratio)

6. Final Calibrations and Test Drive

Before taking the Olds for a victory lap, we have two final calibrations to make: ignition timing and idle calibration. We do the ignition timing first, because changes to the timing can affect the idle.

Ignition Timing

We use a crankshaft trigger in this installation so turning the distributor by hand does nothing to affect timing. Rather, all timing changes are

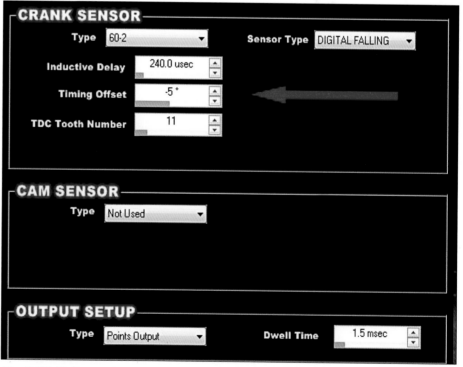

Fig. 6.68. Before going on the victory lap, we need to calibrate the timing read on the balancer to that shown in the Data Monitor (Scroll to Idle Tuning). This is easily accomplished with a timing light.

---

made in the ECU via the software. We need to ensure the reading on the balancer matches the reading in the ECU so that the values in the Base Timing Table are absolutely accurate. Have a helper connect a timing light and be ready to observe the timing reading on the balancer. Then:

- Start the engine and allow it to idle
- With the ECU online, scroll to Idle Tuning in the Data Monitor and note the Ignition Timing reading

If the timing on the balancer is not identical to the timing shown in the Data Monitor, it is easily adjusted in the software. To do so, note the difference (e.g., 34 on the balancer and 30 in the Data Monitor; the difference is 4 degrees). Now, shut the engine off and move the ignition switch to the off position. The ECU is now offline.

- Click on the System ICF icon > SYSTEM PARAMETERS > Ignition Parameters > IGNITION TYPE > Configure
- Adjust the Timing Offset up or down by the difference that you've noted
- Turn the ignition switch to the IGN/RUN position, click the USB Link button and allow the ECU to sync

As the tune on the laptop has been changed, it does not match the tune in the ECU so follow the on-screen instructions to update it.

After you've sent the changes to the ECU, cycle the ignition key and then start the vehicle.

With the ECU online, compare the timing reading on the balancer to the timing reading in the Data Monitor again to be sure that it's correct. Bill and I took a few times to get this perfect. We had to drive the vehicle for a bit first before we could verify this at different RPMs as the ECU is mapping the Fuel Tables according to the Target Air/Fuel Ratio Map. Therefore, a constant RPM (say, 3,000) is not achievable until this has been done.

But it is good enough for a test drive.

Idle Calibration

Allow the engine to reach normal operating temperature. Then the idle can be evaluated. If the engine idles higher than the Idle Speed setting (Idle ICF) you set in the Global Folder, you need to adjust the throttle blades manually to reduce it.

Anytime you make a mechanical modification to the throttle linkage or throttle blades, you need to perform another TPS Autoset so that the ECU and throttle are properly calibrated.

Once you're happy with the idle, these final calibrations are done.

By now the vehicle should be idling smoothly and the ECU should be busy mapping the Learn Table according to the Target A/F Ratio Table. Ready to go for a ride? I thought you might be.

First, it's a good idea to give every line and fitting in the fuel system a second check for leaks. We had one *very* minor leak at the input of the fuel rails and actually had to remove the line and clean the mating surfaces with Scotch Brite to solve it.

The Victory Lap

Bill drove the Olds for 30 minutes or so while I sat in the passenger seat with the laptop and LM-2. It's always a good idea to have a buddy go along for the test drive to monitor the live data available as the ECU maps the Learn Table while you keep your eyes on the road.

I monitored the mapping of the Learn Table, the actual A/F ratio as compared to the target A/F ratio (CL Comp in the Idle Tuning of the Data Monitor), TPS percentage, fuel pressure, oil pressure, etc. In addition, I had the LM-2 set to display Lambda so Bill could see at a glance how close to perfect the A/F ratio really was while he cruised around (1.0 Lambda is stoichiometric for E-85 at 9.8:1).

Bill was beside himself. He was immediately impressed by how dead-on the A/F ratio data in the Data Monitor was, compared to his trusty LM-2. "Dude, they're spot on." He was also amazed that he was able to cruise at 1 Lambda nearly immediately (the ECU mapping is incredibly fast) and this was maintained throughout all of the drivability area. "I was *never* able to achieve this kind of drivability with the carburetor. Never!" The LM-2 confirmed this.

Okay, I'm more than a bit familiar with the Holley EFI products as I've had an HP EFI system on my own vehicle for more than two years now and it works excellent. That doesn't mean I can't be impressed. I'm blown away by the engineering it took to allow us to achieve our goals so quickly with Bill's Olds. It's such a versatile system and we've barely scratched the surface on its capabilities.

As an author, I do my best to remain neutral and unbiased. As an enthusiast, this sometimes proves to be difficult. The Holley Dominator system is easily one of the coolest aftermarket products I have touched.

Bill and I smiled for the rest of the day.

FINE-TUNING THE
HOLLEY DOMINATOR SYSTEM

Between the time we completed the installation on the 1970 Olds and the writing of this chapter, 30 days have passed. This time has afforded the opportunity to assess the system's performance. In that time the Holley Dominator system has performed flawlessly. So, is Bill equally impressed with its performance? That

would be an understatement. Bill is a tuner at heart. The Holley system allows him to spend his time doing just that, not pulling the fuel bowls, not drilling out air-bleed blanks, not calling me asking if I have some red accelerator pump cams lying around (I don't), etc. Basically, not getting his hands dirty.

During this time, Bill and I have spent a few hours fine-tuning his Olds to achieve the best fuel metering possible. We had only a single problem crop up: the gap between the pickup and reluctor wheel of the crank trigger was too large. This caused the timing to drift slightly when we made adjustments to it via the software and then looked at that on the balancer with a timing light. We reduced the gap of Holley's spec and the problem was solved.

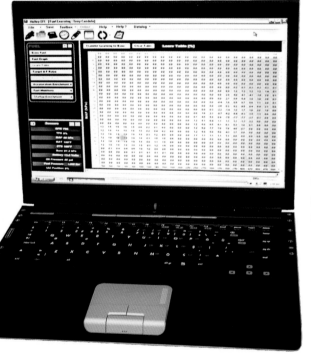

Fig. 7.1.
Windows-based PC software allows you to monitor the performance and status of the Holley HP and Dominator EFI systems. You can quickly identify problems and adjust your fuel and timing maps to arrive at the best tune for your engine.

Fuel Mixture

Because Bill had been monitoring the A/F ratio via his LM-2 when driving around, he noticed two things: The mixture was a bit lean as he accelerated (not WOT) and the right bank was slightly leaner than the left bank. We decided to fix both.

Acceleration Enrichment
The Holley software provides numerous parameters to enrich the mixture during acceleration. We focused our efforts on two of them:

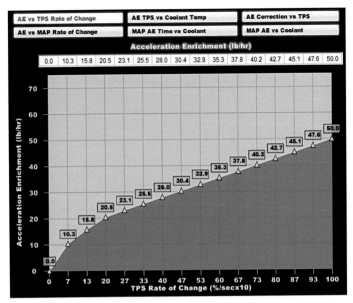

Fig. 7.2. This is where we started with the AE versus TPS rate of change.

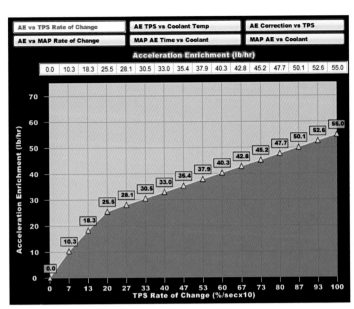

Fig. 7.3. After a few tweaks, this is where we ended up.

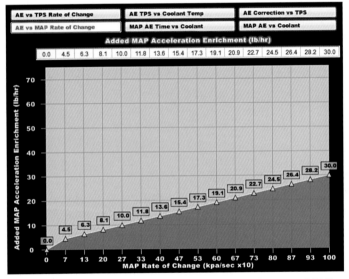

Fig. 7.4. This is where we started with the AE versus MAP rate of change.

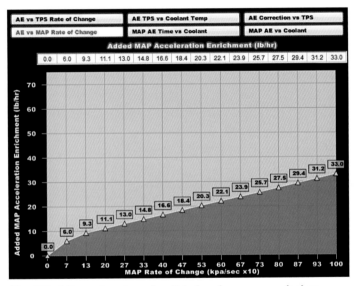

Fig. 7.5. After a few tweaks, this is where we ended up. Tuning the acceleration enrichment can take a little time to get it spot on.

acceleration enrichment versus TPS rate of change and AE versus MAP rate of change.

AE versus TPS Rate of Change: Using the white boxes at the top of the menu, I simply added to each of the values, except for the left two boxes. This is a starting point and it's easy to get back to where we started if needed.

AE versus MAP Rate of Change: Using the white boxes at the top of the menu, I simply added to each of the values, except for the left two boxes. Again, this is simply a starting point.

Right Bank Leaner than Left Bank

We drove the Olds a bit to verify this, and sure enough, the LM-2 showed 1.00 Lambda on the left

bank and 1.02 Lambda on the right bank when cruising at a steady speed; the right bank was 2 percent leaner than the left. We pulled over and I added 2 percent more fuel to each of the injectors of the right bank. Problem solved. We instantly had 1.00 Lambda left and right at idle.

With an EGT in each primary, you could really fine-tune each injector to

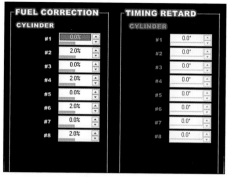

Fig. 7.6. Driving the vehicle and monitoring data via the Innovate LM-2 showed the passenger-side bank running 2 percent leaner than our desired 1.0 Lambda at cruise. I simply added 2 percent of fuel to each cylinder on the right bank and I did so without even leaving the vehicle.

achieve the ideal mixture in each cylinder. Oh, the possibilities here!

Drive It

When you make changes to the fuel metering aspects of the tune, you need to get some drive time to allow the ECU to remap the Learn Table to reflect the changes you've made. This is accomplished by driving the vehicle at various RPM and engine loads throughout the drivability area. The more you drive the vehicle, the more finely tuned the tune becomes.

Bill drove while I monitored the results of our efforts via the Holley software and the LM-2. Based on the live data available, Bill had me increase the acceleration enrichment a bit more. Afterward, he was happy with the results.

Some additional driving around town and we were convinced the drivability was about as ideal as we could have ever hoped from a vehicle with a 2,000-cfm throttle body and a 4,500-rpm converter. Our original tune required very little

adjustment to achieve this and the Holley software couldn't be easier to use. Grandma could drive this Olds around town in Drive without even realizing that she had more than 600 hp under her foot. In addition, the exhaust tone was as mild as it's ever been, giving no clue that this is a mid-10-second car.

Throttle response is instant. When you get aggressive with the pedal, the 455 responds without hesitation and the exhaust tone comes alive.

Bill and I found a deserted stretch of road to make a few WOT passes. Now, I had told Bill at the beginning of this project that his 950-cfm E85 was restrictive. I speculated that we would be easily able to prove this as the throttle body was more than double the size of the carburetor we removed. Let's see what our seat-of-the-pants dyno has to say.

WOT Pass 1 from 25 mph

This pass was aborted nearly immediately. When Bill floored the throttle, the Olds blew the tires off it. This had happened only maybe one time in the past that I can recall and not nearly to that extent. We elected to warm up the Mickey Thompsons a bit and try again.

WOT Pass 2 from 25 mph

We had nearly the same results. Pass aborted.

WOT Pass 3 from 25 mph, Roll into Throttle

Bill finessed into the throttle in first gear. Upon shifting into second gear, he was able to go WOT. Second and third gear happened so fast, it was as if it happened in slow motion. The exhaust tone was *so* much louder than we had ever heard from the 455.

Our collective jaws dropped and we looked at each other in amazement. I had never felt Bill's Olds pull this hard through second and third gears. I was supposed to be monitoring the A/F ratio on the LM-2 . . . Yeah, Okay. Fail.

Conclusions

It was immediately obvious that the 2,000-cfm throttle body had allowed the 455 to ingest all the air it could take and the ECU metered the fuel to achieve the A/F targets. Even though Bill had calibrated the carburetor to achieve the identical A/F ratio at WOT, the mass of air ingested by the Olds was greater with the larger throttle body.

The end result is that the 455 is now able to burn more fuel at WOT than before. The power comes from the fuel and Bill's Olds simply wasn't able to burn the same mass of it with the 950-cfm carburetor. It was also immediately obvious that we now had a traction problem that needed to be addressed. Welcome to my world, Bill! Time for some fresh tires.

Putting the Power of the ECU to Work

The ECU is the brains in the game and it controls all the parameters of the fuel injection. In this case, it also controls datalogging functions and input/outputs.

Datalogging

The internal datalogging capability of the Holley ECUs is a powerful tool. It allows you to datalog every parameter that you have a sensor monitoring. Bill made a few WOT datalogs in the following days. Man, do things look nice.

It goes without saying that WOT passes should only be done on a drag strip in a controlled environment. This is the best way to collect meaningful data, as traction problems are all but eliminated. Bill is quite fluent in tuning so he's able to readily interpret the data and use it for fine-tuning without fear of damaging his engine. If fine-tuning your engine isn't something you're comfortable with, datalogs can be shared (even by email) with an experienced tuner.

Depending on the system (or meter), you can program some units to datalog automatically. This is ideal

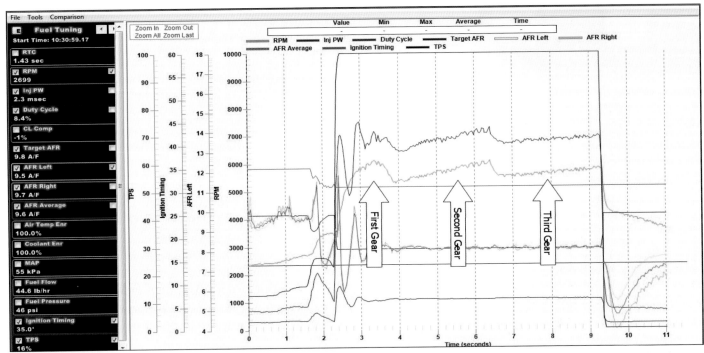

Fig. 7.7. The datalogger is an incredibly powerful tool. Here is a datalog from the ECU of the Olds. The left-hand column allows you to select the variables displayed and the vertical scales displayed, including TPS, Ignition Timing, etc. This datalog was acquired on a closed road from a 25-mph roll, which took approximately 7 seconds. The green line represents RPM, so gear changes are easy to spot, but I added the arrows to make it extra clear.

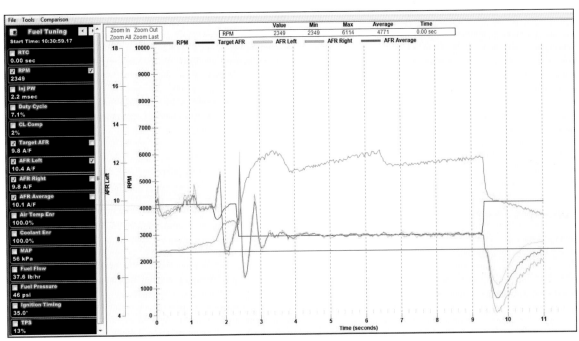

Fig. 7.8. I turned off all variables, except for RPM, Target AFR, AFR Left, AFR Right, and AFR Average so that you can have a close look at only these parameters. Look at how close the actual AFR is compared to the Target AFR.

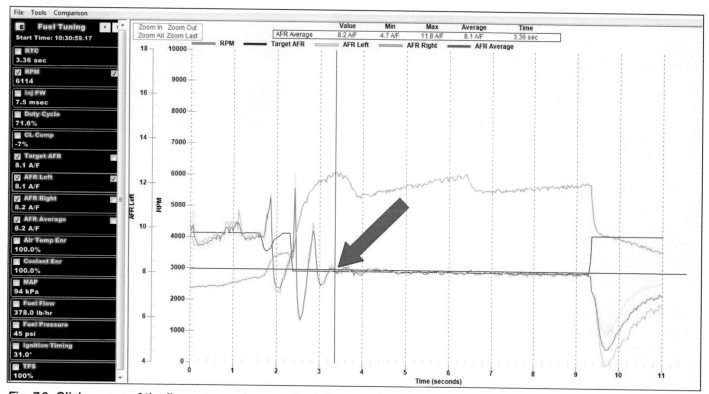

Fig. 7.9. Click on any of the lines at any place on the datalog and you can pull up the cross hatch (red arrow), which you can then move left or right via the arrow keys. This allows you to zoom in on any area of the datalog for a closer look. Notice the values in the left column are updated based on the location of the cross bar.

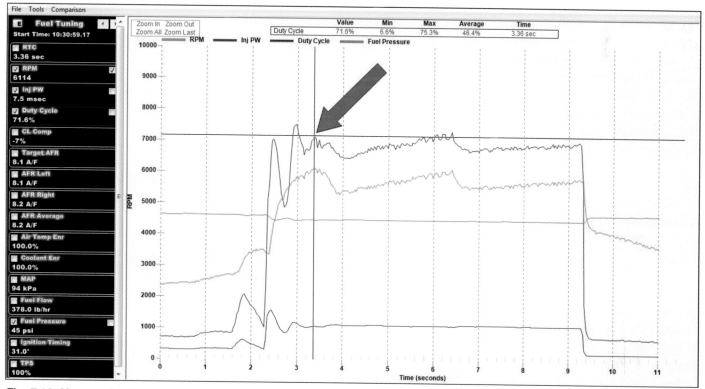

Fig. 7.10. You can look at nearly any value you want by selecting/de-selecting them in the left column. Look at how rock solid the fuel pressure is during this run.

for drag racing, so you can keep your mind on staging the car correctly and cutting a good light, not on whether you've remembered to activate the datalogger.

Inputs/Outputs

The Dominator ECU has seemingly endless connectivity. Let's make use of some of it. Specifically, let's do the following:

- Interface the roll control to activate a low-speed rev limiter
- Automate the operation of the electric fans
- Automate the operation of the second half of the fuel pump
- Interface the nitrous system

It's important to note that the Holley Dominator and HP ECU inputs and outputs are not specific to wires that pre-exist in the harness. This offers the utmost in flexibility. The idea here is to simply automate a bunch of existing circuits. Each is an incredibly simple interface, and similar to the ones I did on my own Olds in Chapter 4. Keep in mind that you need the Holley connector and pin kit (PN 558-408) to do so with the Dominator ECU.

Nitrous Configuration

After our local drag strip re-opens, Bill intends to use a *100 shot* of nitrous in an attempt to get his Olds into the 9s. This will come via a plate system under the throttle body. We elect to run a dry system and use the power of the Dominator ECU to enrich the mixture via the injectors as well as reduce timing automatically when using the nitrous. The additional fuel required should be well within the window of safe operating for the 83-pph injectors.

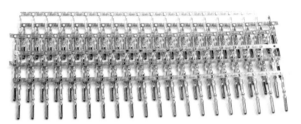

Fig. 7.11. The Holley connector and pin kit (PN 558-408) allows you to access all of the Dominator ECU's inputs and outputs. Obviously, the pins have to be terminated by the installer. (Photo Courtesy Holley Performance Products)

The Dominator ECU allows you the option of bringing the nitrous in progressively to avoid traction issues. Also, the Dominator ECU allows complete management for up to four stages of nitrous. We just need one.

Before we can begin setting up the inputs and outputs, we need to add a nitrous configuration file to our base tune. To do so, we simply add an Individual Configuration to the tune. Here's how:

1 Click the down arrow to the right of Toolbox; select Add Individual Config.

2 In the Files of Type box at the bottom of the window, click the down arrow at the right and select Holley EFI Nitrous Config (*.nitrous).

3 Click the Up One Level button (folder with green arrow pointing up) at the top of the window a few times until you get to the EFI folder.

4 Double click on the Individual Configuration Library folder.

5 Double click on the Nitrous folder.

6 Double click on the Base - Single Stage Dry.nitrous file.

7 Click Save.

We now have a nitrous configuration in the tune at which we can easily set up when we install the nitrous system. For now, let's proceed with programming the inputs and outputs.

Program Inputs/Outputs

Before connecting anything, we need to go into the ECU and program the appropriate inputs and outputs accordingly. This is easy. Before you do so, it's important to know how each of the systems we want to automate is triggered. In Bill's Olds, they are as follows:

- Electric Fans: fan relays are triggered via +12V from dash-mounted switch
- Fuel Pump: each half of the pump has a relay, which is triggered via +12V from a dash-mounted switch
- Roll Control: depressing the button sends +12V to the solenoid
- Nitrous: master arming switch switches +12V

1 Click on the System ICF icon on the toolbar at the top of the screen.

2 In the SYSTEM PARAMETERS box in the left column, click on Basic I/O. This brings up the outputs for the electric fans and fuel pumps. Set them as shown in Figure 7.12.

3 In the SYSTEM PARAMETERS box in the left column, click

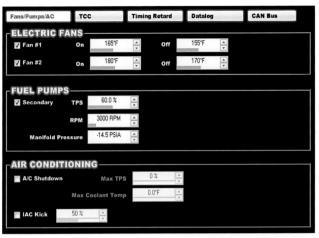

Fig. 7.12. I set up the ECU to activate each fan independently. I also set up the ECU to automatically engage the second half of the fuel pump, which is an incredibly useful feature. We set it to do so when the TPS reaches 60 percent. This way there is no way to forget to do this.

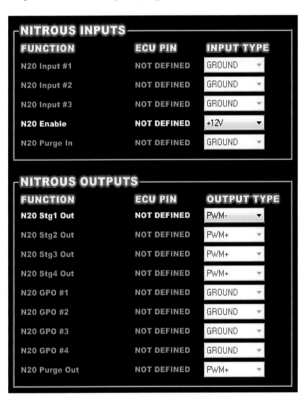

Fig. 7.14. Configure the inputs and outputs for the nitrous system. I set the arm input to be compatible with the +12V output of the switch panel in the vehicle.

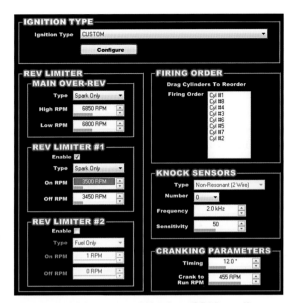

Fig. 7.13. Using one of the low-RPM rev limiters built into the ECU is an excellent way to prevent the tune from being affected when intentionally misfiring cylinders to limit RPM.

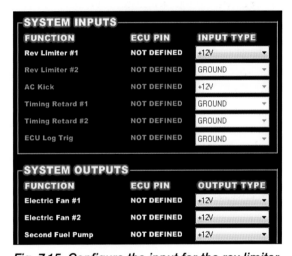

Fig. 7.15. Configure the input for the rev limiter. I set it to activate via the +12V output from the roll-control push button.

on Ignition Parameters. Enable REV LIMITER #1 as shown in Figure 7.13.

4 Click on the Nitrous ICF icon on the toolbar at the top of the screen.

5 Click on Inputs/Outputs. For a single stage, this should resemble Figure 7.14.

6 In the SYSTEM PARAMETERS box in the left column, click

on Inputs/Outputs. We set ours as shown in Figure 7.15.

7 Click on the PIN MAP icon on the toolbar at the top of the screen. This brings up the Pin Map for the ECU. You are looking at the View Inputs tab when this opens. The UNASSIGNED INPUTS show the inputs we've set in the previous steps as well as their polar-

ity (H = +12V, G = Ground). (See Figure 7.16.)

8 For this installation, we populate CONNECTOR J3 with the above inputs and outputs to simplify things. Now, we simply click and drag the Rev Limiter #1 and N20 Enable each to an input on CONNECTOR J3 that has the same Input Type (third column) as our programmed input as an option for the Pin (first column).

9 Click in the View Outputs tab at the top of the window. Repeat the process for the UNAS-SIGNED OUTPUTS, also to CONNECTOR J3. (See Figure 7.17 and 7.18.)

10 Click on the Done button to close the window.

11 Click on Save to save your changes.

Fig. 7.16. Once the inputs and outputs are configured, it's time to choose a location on the Pin Map so that you can interface them with the ECU. Both the Rev Limiter and Nitrous Enable are set to +12V (H) so we can drag and drop them (with the mouse) to any pin that shows H as an option.

Fig. 7.17. Dragged and dropped.

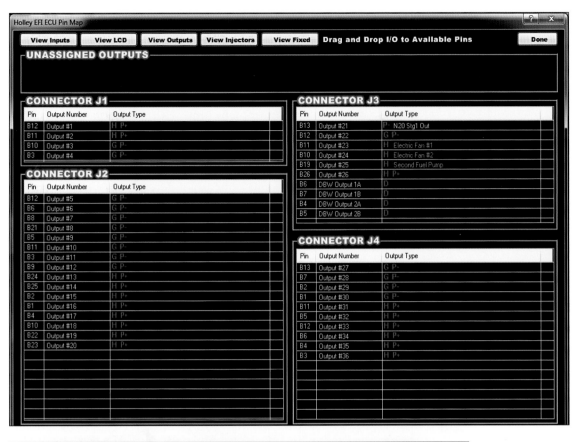

Fig. 7.18. I repeated the process and the results are illustrated in Figures 7.16 and 7.17 for the outputs we've configured. I elected to put all of the inputs and outputs on the J3B connector. This allows me to use that one connector for everything.

Fig. 7.19. Bill programmed the HEFI Gauge Panel to provide all the data he could ever need at a glance. This is easily accomplished because the software allows you to select what each gauge displays as well as define the range of each gauge. In addition, you can select any four screens of the Data Monitor to be displayed across the bottom. This is a really cool feature of the Holley V2 software.

Electrical Interface Changes

Now, we need to make the actual electrical interfaces to the existing systems in Bill's Olds.

At this stage, we need to interface the roll control to activate a low-speed rev limiter. Just as before, this interface activates a low-speed rev limiter and puts the ECU into open loop as long as the roll-control button is held down.

Next we need to automate the operation of the electric fans. Bill's fan circuit is more traditional than the one in my Olds. I set the ECU to turn on one fan at 160 degrees and the second fan at 180. Because the circuit is pre-existing, you can see the before and after in Figure 7.22 and Figure 7.23.

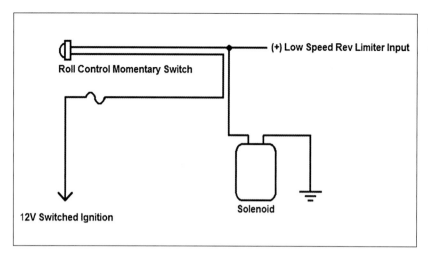

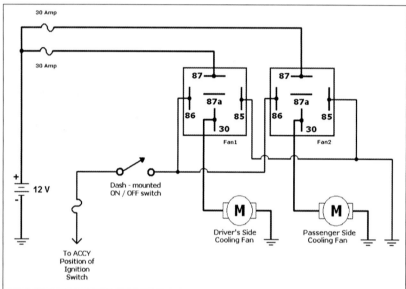

Fig. 7.20. This roll-control interface to the low-speed rev limiter is the simplest of the bunch.

It's time to automate the operation of the second half of the fuel pump. Anytime you run a fuel pump with a variable output, it's a good idea to install a manual override to run the fuel pump at its maximum output when going WOT. That being said, any manual override is only as good as the operator's memory. Do you really want to chance forgetting this?

This interface allows the ECU to activate the second half of the fuel pump automatically. This allows you to focus more on operating the vehicle and less on flipping switches. Refer to Figure 6.21 on page 104 for the original way that we set this up.

Interface the Nitrous System

Setting up this interface requires a master Arming Switch; the Holley 554-111 Nitrous Solenoid Driver is a simple interface. Bill has an additional switch in his switch panel for this, so we make use of it. For now, we install the driver, but not the nitrous kit as Bill needs to park a few more cars to afford that.

Building a Vehicle-Specific EFI Harness

Just before completing this book, I was called to assist my buddy Frank Beck with an all-aluminum 540-ci big-block Chevy he was building for one of his best customers. Frank liked the results we obtained with the Holley Dominator system and wanted to use a similar setup for this project. This 540-ci package will have a single shot of nitrous oxide, managed

Fig. 7.21. This is the existing fan circuit in Bill's Olds. We retain it and simply interface the ECU to it.

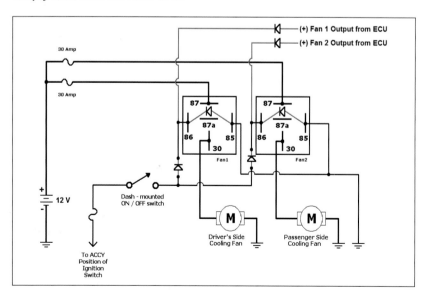

Fig. 7.22. Interfacing the ECU to the existing circuit isn't all that difficult. Note that I've added diodes across the coils of the relays and inline on the outputs from the ECU. Both are required to prevent possible damage to the outputs of the ECU. The remaining pair of diodes are required to allow the ECU to operate each fan independently but still permit the dash-mounted switch to operate both fans simultaneously.

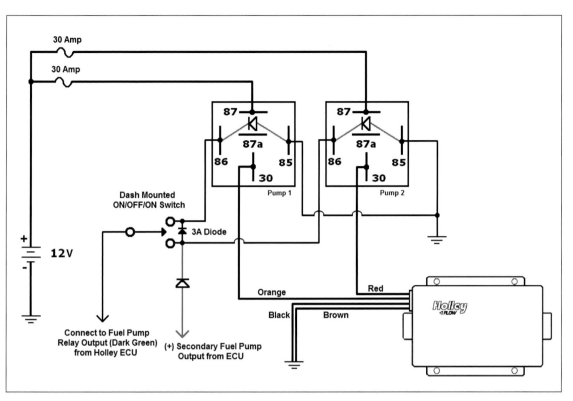

Fig. 7.23. Interfacing the ECU to the existing fuel pump circuit is similar to the electric fan interface. Refer to Figure 6.21 for the original circuit.

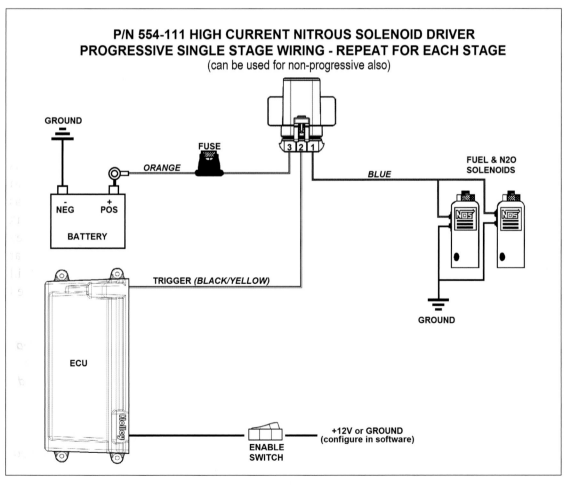

Fig. 7.24. The Holley Nitrous Solenoid Driver is simply a solid-state relay that can be driven with PWM. This requires a single connection to the ECU. An enable switch is required as well. This tells the ECU that the nitrous system is in use based on the user-defined parameters in the software. (Illustration Courtesy Holley Performance Products)

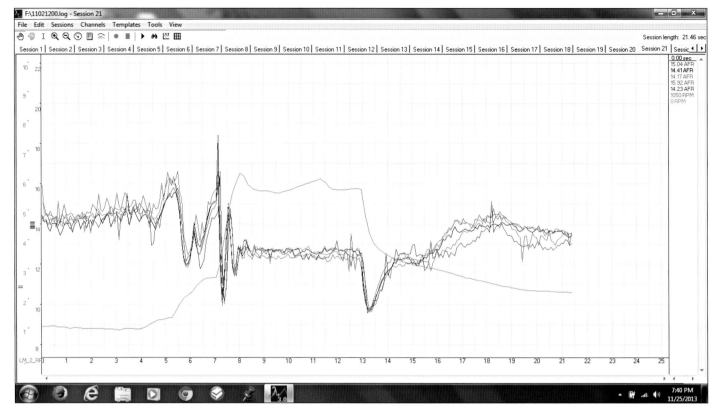

Fig. 7.25. The datalogger function of the Innovate LM-2 is an incredibly powerful tool. This is a datalog taken from the Olds featured in Chapter 6 and Chapter 7. WOT takes place beginning at about 7 seconds and lasts about 6 seconds, as illustrated by the orange line, which represents RPM.

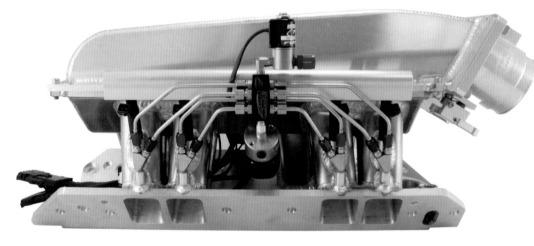

Fig. 7.26. This is one sweet induction setup. You're looking at a custom Hogan's sheet-metal manifold with dual Wilson Manifolds throttle bodies and a Nitrous Proflow fogger setup. (Photo Courtesy David Segundo/ Wilson Manifolds)

progressively, and make more than 1,000 hp.

Frank ordered a custom-built Hogan's intake manifold with dual throttle bodies to top off this engine (you saw a glimpse of it in Chapter 3). It's outfitted with a Nitrous Proflow wet fogger system and the overall packaging is super clean.

Frank also ordered a system similar to what we used in Bill's Olds. Frank added a Holley 8-cylinder DIS (waste fire) ignition system (PN 556-101) and elected to purchase an un-terminated harness assembly (shown on page 109) as the vehicle builder specified that Frank provide a custom harness assembly that fit the

vehicle perfectly.

That's where I came in. I was hired to shorten, terminate, and loom the harness. This was a serious job, taking numerous days to complete. In addition, a job like this requires access to several expensive crimping tools, each specific to a certain family of connector.

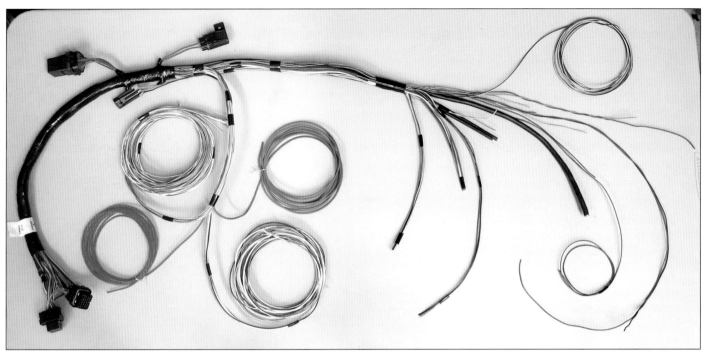

Fig. 7.27. This may not look like much work, but Frank and I spent four to five hours sorting and grouping the wires so that I could shorten them accordingly. A harness like this consists of mostly 22 and 20 AWG wires, so telling the white/blue from the blue/white requires that you refer to the main diagram and use a DMM to verify continuity from pin to wire before cutting.

Frank does all tuning in-house, so once the harness was shortened and terminated, I delivered it to him un-loomed and without the nitrous relays so that he could get to work making naturally aspirated pulls on the engine dyno. As I mentioned earlier, Frank elected to do a bunch of the tuning in open loop, using an Innovate LM-2 and his dyno to monitor the A/F ratio.

After Frank was happy with the power and torque numbers the engine made naturally aspirated and he was happy with the tune in general, I got the harness back to set up the nitrous solenoid drivers and loom it. As the Nitrous Proflow solenoids require approximately 25 amps of current on each side of the manifold, it was necessary to use a pair of

Fig. 7.28. The dual throttle bodies provide all the airflow the 540 requires and gives this manifold a menacing look. (Photo Courtesy David Segundo/Wilson Manifolds)

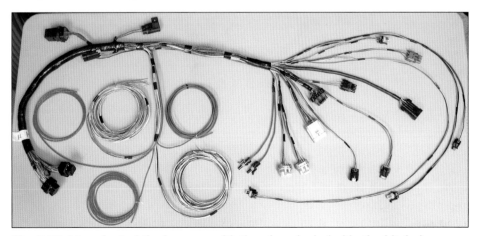

Fig. 7.29. I terminated the harness with the plugs included in the kit. I also added 14-gauge power leads (terminated with single-position Weatherpack plugs in the center) for the DIS coil packs.

Waste Fire Ignition Systems

A waste fire ignition system utilizes fewer coils than the engine has cylinders. Each coil has two towers and each is fired twice in a single firing order. Each time the coil is fired, both towers are fired. One of the towers fires on one cylinder's compression stroke (as any normal ignition system would), and the other tower is fired simultaneously on another cylinder's exhaust stroke. This provides excellent performance and can reduce emissions.

Connecting such a system can be tricky. Holley includes a simple chart with their systems to be used to determine which cylinders are fired by which coils, as well as how to connect the coils properly to the ECU.

If only my job were that easy. The 540-ci big-block Chevy featured here was built with a non-standard firing order. In that case, one must enter the correct firing order in the yellow boxes at the top of the page to derive the correct orientation and wiring of the coils. Once I wrapped my head around this, it was straightforward and made perfect sense.

Anytime you set up such a system, you really should ensure that cylinders are firing in the order you desire before attempting to start the engine. That is simple enough to do with a timing light and the injector harness disconnected, following the instructions included with the system. After verifying this with the 540, the engine started on the first try. ■

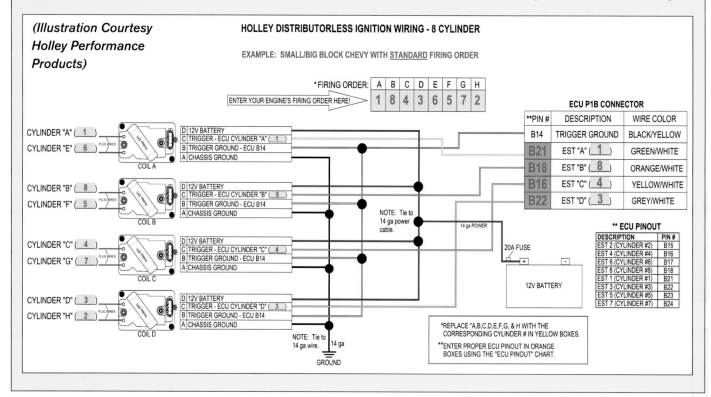

(Illustration Courtesy Holley Performance Products)

the Holley 554-111 nitrous solenoid drivers to drive them. Because these drivers require minimal current to operate, it is perfectly acceptable to drive them both from the same output of the ECU.

Frank added a Nitrous ICF file to his base tune, set it up for one progressive wet stage, and in short order he was off to the races making nitrous pulls.

So, what kind of power did this 540 make? Insane power. Naturally aspirated, it produced 782 hp at 6,400 rpm and 707 ft-lbs of torque at 5,000 rpm on 91-octane pump gas. With one stage of nitrous, it made 980 hp at 6,200 rpm and 948 ft-lbs of torque at 4,700 rpm with 91-octane pump gas and a 175-hp shot of nitrous.

Like Bill, Frank is very happy with the tuning flexibility and ease the Holley software offered. I'm amazed at how quickly Frank was able to achieve the results he was after. I sat in on several tuning sessions with Frank. When he needed to make changes, we could do so quickly and easily via the software. We configured the datalogger to

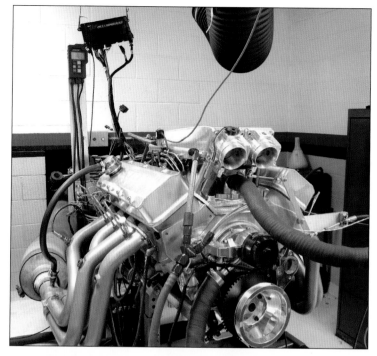

Fig. 7.30. Frank suspended the ECU behind and over the engine to keep it out of harm's way during the dyno sessions. Holley includes a lengthy USB cable with the ECU, but it's not long enough to connect to a laptop on the dyno console.

Fig. 7.31. A single IAC proved too restrictive. I added a second harness (in parallel with the main IAC harness) to allow Frank to plug in a second IAC.

Fig. 7.32. Frank fabricated mounts for the DIS coils on the rear of each cylinder head. He built these on the mill from 3/8-inch-thick aluminum and mounted them directly to the cylinder heads. This keeps them out of the way and allows the valve covers to be easily removed to run the valves, etc.

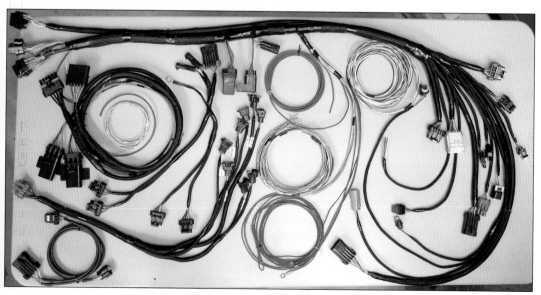

Fig. 7.33. Looming such a harness (and all sub-harnesses) in split-braided tubing is incredibly time consuming. This took the better part of a full day. Notice the dual Holley nitrous solenoid drivers just below the main ECU connectors on the left. I set up the nitrous harness with the mating Weatherpack connectors supplied with the Nitrous Proflow system, which was pre-wired on the manifold.

automatically create logs once TPS exceeded 90 percent, so Frank was able to easily and readily access this data after any power pull.

Heck, I've been sold on EFI conversions ever since I converted my Olds. After completing the projects in this book, I simply can't fathom hot rodding any other way.

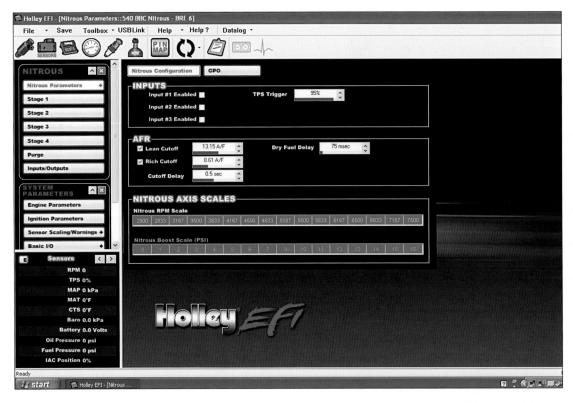

Fig. 7.34. NITROUS CONFIGURATION: Here you can set the specifics on how you'd like to govern the operation of the nitrous. Frank set the nitrous to trigger only after TPS reached 95 percent. In addition, he set the ECU to disable to the nitrous if the A/F ratio is leaner than 13.15:1 or richer than 8.61:1.

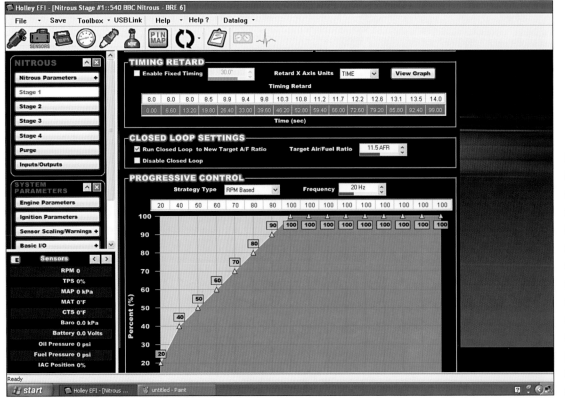

Fig. 7.35. STAGE 1: Frank set the ECU to operate in closed loop to achieve a target Air/Fuel ratio of 11.5:1 when the nitrous is activated. In addition, he set the nitrous to come in progressively based on the table at the bottom. Not visible is the RPM scale along the bottom of the table.

EPILOGUE

Wow, we've covered a lot of ground in a single book. I hope that you agree that converting from a carb to EFI has much to offer. Whether you're someone who prefers to drive it and enjoy it, like Keith, or you're a person who prefers to dial in the tune to the nth degree, like Bill, there is a system to meet your exact needs.

This may be the single most exciting upgrade you can make to your vehicle. If you follow the methods I've outlined, you'll spend your time enjoying your new EFI system and not trying to figure out why it doesn't work correctly.

I take my hat off to the designers, engineers, and manufacturers of these systems. They've given enthusiasts a huge selection of EFI systems they could have only dreamed of 10 years ago, and they're affordable at that.

You simply can't afford to not consider this upgrade!

SOURCE GUIDE

Aeromotive
7805 Barton St.
Lenexa, KS 66214
913-647-7300
aeromotiveinc.com

Auto Meter
413 West Elm St.
Sycamore, IL 60178
866-248-6356
autometer.com

Automotive Diagnostic
 Specialties
6835 W. Chandler Blvd.
Chandler, AZ 85226
480-961-8704
adsautorepair.com

Beck Racing Engines
2639 N. 33rd Ave.
Phoenix, AZ 85009
602-477-1700
beckracingengines.com

CE Auto Electric Supply
Chandler, AZ 85248
602-999-0942
ceautoelectricsupply.com

Edelbrock
2700 California St.
Torrence, CA 90503
310-781-2222
edelbrock.com

Fluke
6920 Seaway Blvd.
Everett, WA 98203
425-347-6100
fluke.com

Fuel Air Spark Technology
3400 Democrat Rd.
Memphis, TN 38118
877-334-8355
fuelairspark.com

Fuelab
826-A Morton Ct.
Litchfield, IL 32056
217-324-3737
fuelab.com

Holley
1801 Russellville Rd.
Bowling Green, KY 42101
270-782-2900
holley.com

Imagine Injection
5830 W. Thunderbird Rd.
Glendale, AZ 85306
602-377-4093
imagineinjection.com

MagnaFuel
615 Wooten Rd., Ste. 120
Colorado Springs, CO 80915
800-321-7761
magnafuel.com

Mechman
7501 Strawberry Plains Pike
Knoxville, TN 37924
888-632-4626
mechman.com

Mitchell1
14145 Danielson St.
Poway, CA 92064
888-724-6742
mitchell1.com

MSD Performance
1490 Henry Brennan Dr.
El Paso, TX 79936
915-857-5200
msdignition.com

Painless Performance Products
2501 Ludelle St.
Fort Worth, TX 76105
817-244-6212
painlessperformance.com

Precision Research
506 E Juanita Ave., #9
Mesa, AZ 85204
480-926-2127

Ron Davis Racing Products
7334 N. 108th Ave.
Glendale, AZ 85307
rondavisradiators.com

Ron Fassl and Sons
 Automotive
7117 E. Angus Dr.
Scottsdale, AZ 85251
480-945-0494

XS Power Batteries
2847 John Deere Dr., Ste. 102
Knoxville, TN 37917
888-497-7693
xspowerbatteries.com